Frommer's®

Ireland

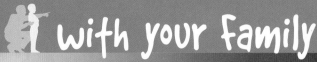 with your Family

From vibrant towns to picnic perfect countryside

by Terry Marsh

JOHN WILEY & SONS LTD

ISBN: 978-0-470-51878-6

UK Publisher: Sally Smith
Executive Project Editor: Daniel Mersey (Frommer's UK)
Commissioning Editor: Mark Henshall (Frommer's UK)
Development Editor: Kate Calvert
Content Editor: Hannah Clement (Frommer's UK)
Cartographer: Tim Lohnes
Photo Research: Jill Emeny (Frommer's UK)
Typeset by Wiley Indianapolis Composition Services
Printed and bound in China by SNP LeeFung Printers Ltd.

5   4   3   2   1

Contents

About the author

Terry Marsh is an award-winning freelance travel writer and photographer, and, since starting to write professionally in 1980, author of 60 plus books. His areas of interest include the UK, Ireland, France, Denmark, Madeira, the Azores and Australia. He is a writer on many topics, including the countryside, walking, independent and family travel, food and drink. He holds a Master of Arts degree in Lake District Studies, and is currently undertaking research leading to a PhD in Historical Geography.

Additional material and research supplied by Dennis Kelsall.

Dedication

To Eileen Cronin for her generous and never to be forgotten hospitality to us both.

An Additional Note

Please be advised that travel information is subject to change at any time and this is especially true of prices. We therefore suggest that you write or call ahead for confirmation when making your travel plans. The authors, editors and publisher cannot be held responsible for experiences of readers while travelling. Your safety is important to us however, so we encourage you to stay alert and be aware of your surroundings.

Star Ratings, Icons & Abbreviations

Hotels, restaurants and attraction listings in this guide have been ranked for quality, value, service, amenities and special features using a star-rating system. Hotels, restaurants, attractions, shopping and nightlife are rated on a scale of zero stars (recommended) to three (exceptional). In addition to the star rating system, we also use 5 feature icons that point you to the great deals, in-the-know advice and unique experiences. Throughout the book, look for:

FIND   Special finds – those places only insiders know about

MOMENT   Special moments – those experiences that memories are made of

VALUE   Great values – where to get the best deals

OVERRATED   Places or experiences not worth your time or money

GREEN   Attractions employing responsible tourism policies

The following abbreviations are used for credit cards:

AE   American Express
MC   Mastercard
V   Visa

A Note on Prices

Frommer's provides exact prices in each destination's local currency. As this book went to press, the rate of exchange was €1 = £0.72. Rates of exchange are constantly in flux; for up-to-the-minute information, consult a currency-conversion website such as *www.oanda.com/convert/ classic.* In the Family-friendly Accommodation section of this book we have used a price category system.

An Invitation to the Reader

In researching this book, we discovered my wonderful places – hotels, restaurants, shops and more. We're sure you'll find others. Please tell us about them, so we can share the information with your fellow travellers in upcoming editions. If you were disappointed with a recommendation, we'd love to know that too. Please write to;

Frommer's Ireland with your Family, 1st Edition
John Wiley & Sons, Ltd
The Atrium
Southern Gate
Chichester
West Sussex, PO19 8SQ

Photo Credits

1 Family Highlights of Ireland

We both first got to know Ireland in the 1970s, when Terry was racing up and down mountains to raise money for charity. Since then we've slowed down, and begun to appreciate this fabulous country at the rather more leisurely pace of 2gph (two Guinness per hour).

Despite our youthful speed, the country, the landscapes and the warmth and sincerity of the people simply left us mesmerised, in spite of 'The Troubles'. We stopped telling Irish jokes. How can you poke fun at a nation that has great food, legends and folklore galore, and some of the finest scenery and most vibrant towns and villages anywhere in Europe? And, moreover, is a country that has battled on through some of the most horrendous times of modern history, and come out the other side, as keen, energetic and enthusiastic as ever.

Later, we returned separately to explore with children in tow. We quickly discovered that families in Ireland are drawn to the edges, that is the coast – and what a coast; high quality, Blue Flag sandy beaches, often sandwiched neatly into a sheltered niche between towering cliffs and dramatic headlands, catering perfectly to the bucket-and-spade brigade.

Inland, the powerful landscape will either excite children or leave them dumbstruck. There are rough mountains, clichéd boglands, the bizarre and wonderful limestone scenery of The Burren in Co Clare, and the internationally renowned Giant's Causeway in Co Antrim.

To ensure better coverage, to compile this guide Terry Marsh researched the introductory chapters and those for Belfast, Northern Ireland, the North-west and West, while Dennis Kelsall did the rest.

We found that for our families Ireland was about enjoying the outdoors and adventure sports – walking, cycling, horse riding, surfing, sailing, cruising – but it was also about heritage, culture and folklore, with much of the country's cultural and social heritage explained in outstanding museums. We found that the reputations of the big museums such as the National Museums of Ireland in Dublin and Castlebar, or the Ulster Folk and Transport Museum in Co Down, are well deserved, but we were perhaps more touched by much smaller ones of local significance, such as the Doagh Island Famine Village in Co Donegal.

But Ireland is not just about official sights. You can learn far more than you might imagine from a few nights spent relaxing in a typical Irish pub. We discovered that children are welcome in many pubs, and that they appreciate as much as parents the impromptu entertainment that often springs up as the evening wears on.

This attitude to children is a key facet of Irish life: children are neither simply tolerated nor matter-of-factly accommodated; they are part of the extended Irish family, and in Ireland, a great deal revolves around the family. So, catering for youngsters is second nature.

You'll need a car to explore Ireland fully; in fact, there's probably far too much to compress into a single visit, unless it's a very long one, so return visits are ideal. But, with a car, you can make best use of your time, and explore places that public transport doesn't reach all that regularly.

Politically, there are two Irelands, the Republic and Northern Ireland. The distinction is one that this guide largely ignores; to be honest the only major difference you will notice as a visitor is a change of currency. Often the only way you can spot the border between the Republic and Northern Ireland is by the plethora of currency exchange outlets that straggle the invisible divide. Of course, there are other differences, but few that impact on the visitor, the tourist, or the family in search of Ireland. Go now, and you'll find a welcome to warm your heart.

FAMILY-FRIENDLY PROMISE

The Discover Ireland website (*www.discoverireland.ie*) lists a host of tourism providers. All those listed on the website have signed up to a family-friendly charter. They welcome families with children and will do all they can to make your time with them enjoyable and memorable.

Look out for this **Family Friendly** logo throughout your stay. Wherever it's displayed, there will be a warm welcome and friendly service for you and your family.

BEST FAMILY EXPERIENCES

Best Family Events Almost every town and village in Ireland has its own 'organised' annual festival at some time during the year, though you can gatecrash mini-festivals almost anywhere, any time. From the Discover Ireland website you can get up-to-date information about the main events, some wacky options ranging from well-organised festivals that specifically target children – such as the **Belfast Children's Festival** (see p. 223), where all ages can take part in plays or mess about with paints, water and all manner of sticky substances – to other (seemingly) disorganised fun and merriment such as **Puck Fair** in Killorglin, Co Kerry, one of Ireland's oldest fairs (see p. 146), featuring parades, fireworks, dancing displays, street entertainment, children's competitions and concerts, and ending with the coronation of King Puck, a mountain goat.

One festival gaining an enviable reputation is that at Clonmany in Co Donegal. Clonmany parish is renowned for its lovely beaches and glens, but the annual **Clonmany Family Festival** (see p. 196) promises music, high jinks, fun and games with some of the top Irish artists. It also features a variety of supporting events, including an agricultural show, singing competition, car treasure hunt, and raft race, plus disco and dances, ceilidh dancing, tug-o-war, children's sports, and car boot sales. Delightful mayhem, really.

Best Natural Attractions

For many years the finest natural attractions of Ireland were the **Giant's Causeway** in Co Antrim, and the **Cliffs of Moher**, in Co Clare. This still remains true, but both these places suffer from over attention, and wonderful as they are, come across as a bit of a disappointment. But there are plenty of alternatives. To see mountains at their best drop in for coffee at **Cronin's Yard** (see p. 149), and maybe take a short walk up the Hag's Glen in the shadow of Ireland's highest mountain, **Carruantoohill**. Equally enthralling are the Mourne Mountains of Northern Ireland both in the beguiling display of craggy summits and the picnic-perfect confines of the **Silent Valley** (see p. 231).

Best Wildlife Experience

Both Dublin and Belfast have excellent zoos, but **Dingle Oceanworld** in Co Kerry (see p. 150) lets children meet creatures from all over the world face-to-face and enjoy a journey through the magical world of underwater wildlife...without getting wet. At the **Irish Raptor Research Centre (Eagles Flying)** in Ballymote, Co Sligo (see p. 205), there's a real chance of getting up close to owls, falcons and eagles. And we mustn't forgot **Fungie, the Dingle Dolphin**. Ever since he took up residence in Dingle Bay in 1983, Fungie has been delighting

Giant's Causeway, Co Antrim

Fungie, The Dingle Dolphin

visitors of all ages. Trips to see Fungie operate all year and give parents a win-win scenario; if Fungie doesn't show, you're not charged – so you get the boat trip for free (see p. 150).

Best Prehistoric Experience

Pitch it right to the children, and 'Taking a walk through a grave-yard' takes on a Harry Potterish aura, and Ireland offers you plenty of chances to do just that. Brú na Bóinne in Co Meath (see p. 75) is the most intriguing site. Older than Egypt's pyramids and Stonehenge, the Boyne burial complex is one of the most important prehistoric sites in Europe with more than 40 separate monuments. At its heart is the stunning Newgrange tomb, built more than 5,000 years ago. Just as fascinating, or puzzling, is Poulnabrone Portal Tomb (see p. 179), in a field beside the Corofin-Ballyvaughan road, and one of Ireland's most photographed dolmens, dating from the Late Stone Age (4th millennium BC).

Best Beach Ireland's beaches are among the best in Europe and the Discover Ireland website lists 76 of them, 68 of which have Blue Flag status (see p. 33). Among the finest, Inch Strand, the location for the film *Ryan's Daughter*, offers four kilometres of sand for bathing, surfing, sea angling, burying dad and building castles. But although the Blue Flag guarantees a certain standard, there are many other excellent beaches – Tullagh Strand near Clonmany comes to mind – where children can have simple fun all day long, and at times you can have the beach entirely to yourselves.

Tullagh Strand near Clonmany

Best Island Ireland has a lot of islands and there really isn't a 'best' one as they all have a magical quality. But if we had to choose one it would be **Achill Island** in Co Mayo (see p. 174). It has been settled by humans since the time of its megalithic tombs and promontory forts dating back 5,000 years. There's a 15th-century fortified tower house, **Kildamhnait Castle**, the 19th-century **Achill Mission** and the deserted villages at Slievemore and Ailt.

The Achill landscape is also a major draw with superb Blue Flag beaches, some of Europe's highest cliffs, and large tracts of blanket bog sweeping down to the shore. The 40km Achill Drive takes in the best of this scenery, while walking and cycling along the quiet lanes and trails is a wonderful way to discover the island's interior. It's a place for lingering, beach combing and mooching about.

Best Boat Trip There's a lot to be said for the boat trip around Dingle Bay in search of Fungie the dolphin (see p. 150), but equally delightful is the tour of Donegal Bay on the **Waterbus** (see p. 201), which offers a good chance of seeing seals and birdlife along with the historic sites around the bay.

Best Castle In a country liberally bestowed with castles, there are plenty to choose from. No castle is really complete without a ghost or two, but at **Malahide**, Co Dublin, you get your money's worth with five (see p. 60). A bit less scary, the cellars of **Belfast Castle** (see p. 225) have been transformed to take you back in time into Victorian narrow, paved streets, shop fronts, gaslights etc. In addition, it's part of the **Cave Hill Country Park** (see p. 225) complex where children can romp about all day, is close to Belfast Zoo, and offers plenty of places on site for snacks and light meals.

Best Museum We couldn't agree on this. On the one hand the National Museum of Ireland (see p. 54) is 'the' museum to see, so huge it's spread across three sites in Dublin with a fourth at Castlebar in Co Mayo. This is the archetypical museum, displaying a vast and eclectic mix of items from all over the world. But the Ulster Folk and Transport Museum at Holywood in Co Down (see p. 231) is more relevant to Ireland, and isn't quite so impersonal. Both venues have interactive attractions to keep children amused for hours; in fact, visit both and you'll be well and truly museumed-out at the end of it.

BEST ACCOMMODATION

Most Family-friendly Option

Tucked away in the north of Co Donegal, the Shandon Hotel at Sheephaven Bay (see p. 209) is an inspiration. Catering for families is the raison d'être of the hotel, and here they do it with panache and attention to detail. Sizeable family rooms with independent children's bedrooms, fridges, freezers, washing machines and microwave ovens help parents along. The leisure centre and independent adventure playhouse supervised by trained childminders give children a lot to do while allowing parents the time to relax and indulge in a little pampering in the child-free zone of the Spa and Wellness Centre. Outdoors there's a grass tennis court and a floodlit all-weather court, plus 9-hole pitch and putt course. The Blue Flag Marble Hill Strand nearby offers all the fun of one of Ireland's best beaches.

Best City Centre Hotel Luxury hotels don't come any more family-friendly than The Clarence in Dublin (see p. 62). Overlooking the River Liffey on the edge of the Temple Bar area of town, older children will be wowed by the fact that it's owned by Bono and The Edge of the Irish rock group U2. Embodying the best of Irish hospitality, The Clarence offers elegant comfort and attention to detail throughout. They go out of their way to make younger guests welcome, with 'Clarence Kids Cocktails', special gifts, Playstation and family movies.

Best Coastal Hotel Not just comfortable, most rooms at the Baltimore Harbour Hotel in West Cork (see p. 161) offer a stunning sea view. During the summer holidays Sammy the Seal Children's Club offers supervised games, swimming competitions, painting, outdoor games, videos and Playstation, and if it rains you can head indoors for the swimming pool, the fully equipped fitness centre, or indulge in a little relaxation and beauty therapy.

The Clarence Hotel, Dublin

Best 'Castle' Hotel With its romantic Victorian castle setting, **Cabra Castle Hotel** in Kingscourt, Co Cavan (see p. 131) offers elegantly furnished rooms and public areas that hark back to an earlier age, while the sun terrace looks out over extensive grounds with a tennis court and golf course. Early dinners for children are a big plus, and can be taken in the more informal setting of the bar, so parents can enjoy a later and more relaxing meal in the restaurant.

Most Enterprising Hotel The 4-star **Station House Hotel** in Clifden, Co Galway (see p. 185) is much more than a hotel; its courtyard houses shops, restaurants, self-catering apartments and full leisure facilities including an 18m indoor heated swimming pool, children's playroom and Jacuzzi. A particularly nice touch is that when adults check in to the hotel, the staff also ask the children for their names; it's just a small thing, but makes all the family feel welcome.

During summer months, the hotel runs a Railway Children's Club with games, splash time in the pool, children's dinner in the restaurant, children's videos and competitions. For under-4s, there is a supervised playroom session with games, stories, toys and organised mayhem. During winter, the courtyard of the hotel is turned into an ice skating rink.

Best Guesthouse **Rusheen Lodge** at Ballyvaughan in Co Clare (see p. 183) is an elegant 4-star guesthouse in one of the most beautiful parts of the west of Ireland. A choice of rooms and suites makes it perfectly suited to families exploring The Burren, and a comfortable guest lounge makes a perfect place for parents to relax away from sleeping children in the elegant bedrooms.

BEST EATING OPTIONS

The two main cities, Dublin and Belfast, have a growing reputation for excellence in food, with four Michelin-starred restaurants between them, and many more pressing for similar status. But there are plenty of other restaurants as well that don't seek Michelin glory, and among these you find the essence of Irish cuisine, making good use of local produce, and dishing it up with enthusiasm, usually in copious quantities.

On the increase are the number of cafés, brasseries, bistros and restaurants that dedicate themselves to catering for family groups, even in some places offering completely separate 'Family Eating Alcoves'.

Most Child-friendly Restaurants Facing the castle, in the former stables and coach house above the **Design Centre** in Kilkenny (see p. 112), is the centre's excellent restaurant. It's a great place to bring youngsters; not only are the surroundings and food first class, but the staff go out of their way to remove the stress of eating out with a family. There are colouring books and crayons to keep children amused and plenty of space round the tables too, a big help when you're struggling with a baby buggy.

The same 'Give plenty of space' approach applies in **Pinky Moons Diner** (see p. 239) in Larne, Co Antrim and children will be bowled over by the 1950s-style décor with posters featuring John Wayne, James Dean, Johnny Cash and Elvis, the family cubicles, and the 'original' jukebox.

Best Seafood With a children's menu featuring lobster chops, crab cakes, chargrilled sirloin and tagliatelle carbonara, **Ouzo's**

Traditonal Irish Stew

Irish Cuisine

Irish cuisine falls into two categories – traditional, mainly simple dishes served in pubs and simpler eating-places, and more modern fare, served in restaurants and hotels.

Traditional dishes include colcannon, made of potato and wild garlic (the earliest form), plus cabbage or curly kale. Champ is served almost everywhere and consists of mashed potato into which chopped spring onions are mixed.

Other simple Irish dishes are Irish stew, and bacon and cabbage (boiled together in water). Boxty is a type of potato pancake and in Dublin check out coddle, which consists of layers of boiled pork sausage and streaky bacon with sliced potatoes and onions cooked in the stock.

The Full Irish Breakfast is not for the faint-hearted, or those on a diet. This is a fried meal generally including bacon, egg, sausage, black and white pudding, fried tomato and may also include fried potato slices.

Seafood has always been eaten in Ireland but shellfish dishes have increased in popularity in recent times, even if much of the catch finds its way to other countries in Europe. You get superb oysters here and numerous 'Oyster Festivals' are held annually around the coast, notably in Galway in September, the oysters often being served with Guinness.

Traditional Irish breads include soda bread, wheaten bread, soda farls, and blaa, a doughy white bread roll and delicacy that is one of Waterford's best-kept secrets.

in Ranelagh, Dublin (see p. 66) ensures the freshest possible seafood by catching it from their own boats out in Dingle Bay in Co Kerry and racing the catch across the country to be served the same day.

Best Traditional Irish Cuisine

You can argue all day about this, but **Coach Lane @ Donaghy's** (see p. 213) is what the parents we met in Sligo Town were all raving about. The emphasis is on the food, and children get half-sized portions of the adult menu rather than a children's menu of junk food. They even have a private room to accommodate family groups of up to eight, and dining directly above a traditional Irish pub in a remarkably Irish town, allows the flavour of Ireland to hit all your senses.

Best Breakfast The best breakfast we found was served in **Buttermilk Lodge** in Clifden, Co Galway, which also accommodates families with children aged over five. You can start the day with the traditional Full Irish, or opt for smoked salmon, pancakes and changing daily specials, including smoked salmon filled with cream cheese or waffles and fruit.

2 Planning a Trip to Ireland

IRELAND

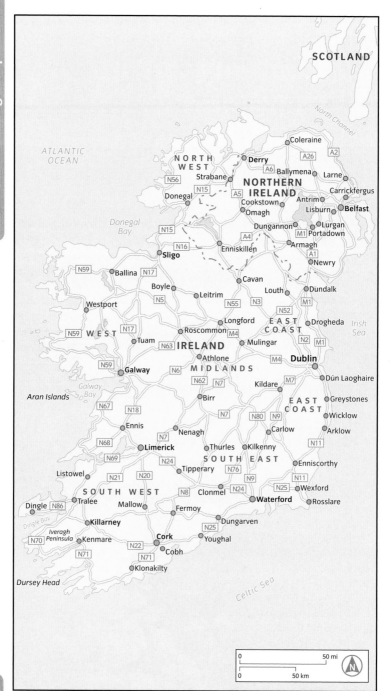

There's a skill to organising a family holiday, and that skill involves one very important fundamental: *involve everyone in the decision-making process.* Avoid 'We're going to Ireland for a holiday', and turn it into something special by marshalling all the information you can about where you are going, and by having family planning meetings.

Talk about what you'd *all* like to see and do; consider everyone's needs and wishes – and do your research. That way you'll avoid spending time sitting on a beach (not that anything is wrong with that), only to discover when it's too late that there's a children's festival going on in the next village.

What will work best depends very much on the interests and characters of your children. This guide offers some pointers on minimum and sometimes maximum suitable ages for each attraction, but these are approximations only and as a parent you'll be able to make the best judgement about what is likely to suit.

To allow flexibility, it's important to build in 'white time', time not specifically allocated for anything – serendipity can be wonderful, but not if you don't have the time to make the most of it.

There are two parts to Ireland but the political, sectarian and ideological divides on the single island have no place in a holiday plan. You won't enjoy Northern Ireland any less than the Republic just because it has been the cauldron of trouble for so many decades. The only difference you are likely to note is that the two countries deal in different currencies and have different speed limits on the roads; in fact, these days the only way you can tell that you have passed from one part to the other at what used to be a border is the plethora of currency exchanges.

VISITOR INFORMATION

The best place to start doing your research is the Internet. There are numerous tiers of Internet sites in Ireland, starting with the national site *www.discoverireland.com*. Below that there are regional Internet sites, and then masses of sites dealing with specific themes and topics, such as the following:

Republic of Ireland

The Heritage Service – *www.heritageireland.ie*
Heritage Towns of Ireland – *www.heritagetowns.com*
Houses, Castles and Gardens of Ireland – *www.gardensireland.com*
Heritage Island – *www.heritageisland.com*

Northern Ireland

The National Trust – *www.nationaltrust.org.uk*

Museums and Galleries of Northern Ireland – *www.magni. org.uk*

Northern Ireland Museums Council – *www.nimc.co.uk*

If you're looking for information on themes, for example cycling, watersports, activities, or even the weather, begin with the **Discover Ireland website**, which has many branches and trails to follow.

You can order brochures online, once you have developed an outline idea of where you would like to go.

In spite of the wealth of information, there are no family specific websites covering Ireland. That's because in Ireland, children are involved in just about everything, as a matter of course.

Of course, it does no harm to enquire – the local tourist information offices are the best places – if there is some special attraction nearby that would particularly appeal to children, or an especially clued-in children's eatery, or family friendly accommodation. But, with a few exceptions such as smarter restaurants, children are welcome everywhere.

In the UK

Irish Tourist Board, 103 Wigmore Street, London, W1U 1QS. (📞 *0207 518 0800. www. discoverireland.com*).

In Ireland

Fáilte Ireland, 88–95 Amiens Street, Dublin 1 (📞 *1 800 242473. www.discoverireland.ie*).

In Northern Ireland

Northern Ireland Tourist Board, St Anne's Court, 59 North Street, Belfast, BT1 1NB. (📞 *028 9023 1221. www. discoverireland.com*).

In the United States

Irish Tourist Board, 345 Park Ave., New York, NY 10154 (📞 *800/223-6470* in the U.S., or 📞 *212/418-0800. www. discoverireland.com*).

In Canada

Irish Tourist Board, 2 Bloor St. W., Suite 1501, Toronto, ON M4W 3E2 (📞 *800/223-6470* or 📞 *16/925-6368. www.discover ireland.com*).

Some General Information

Ireland is 486km (302 miles) long and 275km (174 miles) wide from east to west. The entire island is divided into four historic provinces – Ulster, Munster, Leinster and Connacht – and 32 counties, of which 26 are in the Republic of Ireland and six in Northern Ireland. The Republic is a parliamentary democracy headed by the President of Ireland, while Northern Ireland has its own national, regional and local government, and is part of the United Kingdom.

Children will feel at home here: more than 50% of the population of 5.7 million people is aged under 30. More than

4 million people live in the Republic of Ireland, and 1.7 million in Northern Ireland.

Entry Requirements & Taking Pets

Passports & Visas

UK citizens do not require a passport or visa to enter Ireland, but most carriers by air or sea ask for some form of photographic identity, usually a passport or driving licence. If you have both, it's advisable to take both with you.

Non UK nationals must have a valid passport or national ID card. EU nationals and travellers from the US, Canada, Australia, New Zealand and South Africa need only show a passport. Visitors of all other nationalities should contact their local Irish Embassy/Consulate prior to travelling to the Republic of Ireland, and visitors to Northern Ireland should contact their local British Embassy, High Commission or Consular Office.

Taking Your Pet

There are no restrictions on animals being brought into Ireland from Britain, although there are special regulations applying to certain breeds of dog. Pets entering the UK from the EU can travel into Ireland without quarantine, provided that they satisfy the requirements of the UK Pet

Travel Scheme (call ☎ *0870 241 1710* or visit *www.defra.gov.uk* for the latest information).

For more information about the regulations in Ireland contact the Department of Agriculture and Rural Development for Northern Ireland (☎ *028 905 24715*, *www.dardni.gov.uk*), or the Department of Agriculture in the Republic (☎ *+353 (0)1 607 2000*, *www.agriculture.gov.ie*).

Less-abled Visitors, the Elderly & Students

Visitors with a Disability

Increasingly, Ireland is catering for visitors with disabilities, and many public places and visitor attractions are accessible to wheelchair users. An increasing number of hotels and restaurants are well equipped to accommodate less-abled guests.

A useful contact in Northern Ireland is the Disability Action Line (☎ *028 9029 7880*, *www. disabilityaction.org*); in the Republic there is the National Disability Authority (☎ *01608 1608 0400*, *www.nda.ie*).

The Elderly Across Ireland, men and women over the age of 65 are recognised as 'Senior Citizens' and enjoy a range of discounts and privileges.

Students Ireland is very student friendly, and many attractions offer reduced rates for students on presentation of a valid student ID card.

Money

Northern Ireland

In Northern Ireland the currency is the same as in Britain, pounds and pence, but the Northern Irish notes and coins are not legal tender in the UK.

The Republic of Ireland

In common with other countries in the EU, the Republic of Ireland uses the euro as its currency. There are 100 cents in one euro, with notes for €5–500 (although many establishments are reluctant to accept €500 notes). Coins range from one cent to €2, although most prices rarely require the use of one cent pieces.

For current exchange rates, see *www.xe.com*.

Credit & Debit Cards

Most Irish shops, restaurants and hotels take credit or debit cards, with Visa and Mastercard being the most widely accepted. American Express and Diners Club cards tend to be accepted in the more expensive hotels and restaurants. There are few places that are unlikely to accept credit or debit cards, and these tend to be small B&Bs or rural pubs.

Before leaving home let your credit card company know that you are going to be using it abroad; some companies will decline cards that suddenly turn up unexpectedly in a foreign country. Also, be sure that you have details of the telephone numbers you need to ring in the event of lost or stolen cards.

Cash Points

Travellers cheques are virtually collectors' items these days, having been effectively replaced by 24-hour cash point machines (ATMs) outside all banks, in supermarkets, even in some hotel foyers. Withdrawing cash is seldom a problem, although you may have to travel some distance, for example, through the wilds of Donegal, to find a machine.

Many banks charge commission for withdrawing cash abroad, although one or two British banks and building societies make a point of not charging. If you are going to be charged it is better to withdraw the maximum amount each time rather than make more frequent small-amount withdrawals. Of course, you do then need to ensure that your cash is kept in a safe place.

When To Go & What To Pack

Information about Irish weather is available from *www.discover ireland.com/weather*, but it's not very different from the rest of the British Isles. (See also 'Climate', on p. 34). The West Coast, of course, is the first to see bad weather from the prevailing southwesterly direction, and has a ragged, weather-beaten

Public Holidays 2008

	Republic of Ireland	Northern Ireland
New Year's Day	1st January	1st January
St Patrick's Day	17th March	17th March
Good Friday	21st March	21st March
Easter Monday		24th March
May Bank Holiday	5th May	5th May
May Bank Holiday		26th May
June Bank Holiday	2nd June	
July Holiday		14th July
August Bank Holiday	4th August	25th August
October Bank Holiday	27th October	
Christmas Day	25th December	25th December
Boxing Day	26th December	26th December

coastline to prove it. Elsewhere as in Britain you should plan for anything and everything. Even during the summer months you will need light sweaters and a lightweight waterproof jacket as well as swimwear, sunhats with brims and high factor sun block.

If you plan to eat in some of the more upmarket restaurants, in Dublin or Belfast for example, smart clothes are the order of the day. They don't quite require ties for men but it would be wise to take one. Most hotel restaurants, even in the 4-star hotels, are happy with smart casual dress.

July and August are when most of Ireland is on holiday, so attractions can get crowded. To avoid that period, May, June, September and October are good times to visit – say Easter, or May and October half-terms. However, note that many attractions are not open fully until late June or early July and lifeguards don't patrol the beaches outside the main tourist season – although that does mean that

there's a good chance you'll have many of the places to yourselves.

Ireland is a fairly temperate place: January and February bring frosts but seldom snow, and July and August are very warm, but rarely hot. The Irish consider any temperature over 20°C (68°F) to be 'roasting', and below 1°C (34°F) as bone-chilling. For a complete online guide to Irish weather, consult *www.ireland.com/weather*.

Health, Insurance & Safety

Medical

There are no real health risks while travelling in Ireland and vaccines are not compulsory or necessary unless travelling from an infected country.

British visitors to Northern Ireland need no documentation, and will receive treatment as they would in Britain. UK visitors to the Republic of Ireland are covered under an agreement with the Department of Health, although some form of identification, or a **European Health Insurance Card** (EHIC) is necessary – the E111 form is no longer valid. Visitors from all other EU countries should also obtain an EHIC prior to departure, details at *www.ehic.org.uk* or ☎ *0845 606 2030*. You can get a form from main post offices.

It will still be necessary to pay for treatment; the doctor will give you a form you can use to reclaim most of the money. But the EHIC only covers necessary medical treatment, not repatriation costs, lost money, etc., and is not a replacement for travel insurance.

Visitors from non-EU countries are strongly advised to obtain private medical insurance.

If any of the family is taking prescribed medicines, keep copies of the prescription in case you run out, and also a note of the generic name of your drugs, in case local pharmacies are not familiar with a particular brand name.

Outside the UK

As a rule, no health documents or vaccinations are required to enter Ireland from the United States, Canada or most other countries. If, however, you have visited areas in the previous 14 days where a contagious disease is prevalent, proof of immunisation may be required.

Healthcare in Ireland is comparable to that in the US, and it is a similar system in which private doctors and hospitals provide care and patients purchase healthcare insurance.

Contact the **International Association for Medical Assistance to Travelers (IAMAT)** (☎ *716/754-4883*, or ☎ *416/652-0137* in Canada; *www.iamat.org*) for tips on travel and health concerns in Ireland, and for lists of English-speaking doctors. The United States **Centers for Disease Control and Prevention** (☎ *800/311-3435*; *www.cdc.gov*) provides up-to-date information on health hazards by region or country and offers tips on food safety. The website *www.tripprep.com*, sponsored by a consortium of travel medicine practitioners, may also offer helpful advice on travelling abroad. You can find listings of reliable clinics overseas at the **International Society of Travel Medicine** (*www.istm.org*).

Medical Insurance

For travel overseas, most US health plans (including Medicare and Medicaid) do not provide coverage, and the ones that do often require you to pay for services upfront and reimburse you only after you return home. As a safety net, you may want to buy travel medical insurance, particularly if you're travelling to a remote or high-risk area where emergency evacuation might be necessary. If you require additional medical insurance, try **MEDEX Assistance** (☎ *410/453-6300*; *www.medexassist.com*) or **Travel Assistance International** (☎ *800/821-2828*; *www.travel assistance.com*; for general information on services, call the company's Worldwide Assistance Services, Inc., at ☎ *800/777-8710*).

Travel Insurance

Travel insurance is available from multiple sources but may not cover the actual problem you encounter. For example, in 2003 my ferry out of Dublin Port was cancelled because of bad weather. The captain, having managed to berth only at the third attempt, and many hours late, announced he was not taking his boat back to Holyhead. The insurance company couldn't tell me whether I could claim for the nearest hotel – a four-star – so that I could leave as soon as the weather improved, or had to look for somewhere cheaper but farther away. They said I would have to submit a claim to find out.

If you're buying a family policy, check how many children are covered and whether family members are covered if they travel separately (say one parent has to arrive late or leave early because of work). Also ask about cover during pregnancy and sports cover, including riding and surfing.

Look carefully at medical cover – if one child gets chickenpox and has to stay with a parent can the other children stay too? If they get really sick is there a proper repatriation service?

Is there trip cancellation cover and a refund if you have to

return home early – a possibility with children. And what is offered for delays and delayed/lost baggage?

Finally, does your travel insurance cover you if your tour operator goes into liquidation, or is otherwise unable to fulfil the terms of your travel contract with them?

US Travellers

Expect to pay between 5% and 8% of the holiday itself for travel insurance. You can get estimates from various providers through *www.InsureMyTrip.com.* Enter your trip cost and dates, your age, and other information, for prices from more than a dozen companies.

Trip Cancellation Insurance

Trip-cancellation insurance will help retrieve your money if you have to back out of a trip or depart early, or if your travel supplier goes bankrupt. Permissible reasons for trip cancellation can range from sickness to natural disasters to the State Department declaring a destination unsafe for travel.

For more information, contact one of the following recommended insurers: **Access America** (☎ *866/807-3982*; *www.accessamerica.com*); **Travel Guard International** (☎ *800/826-4919*; *www.travelguard.com*); **Travel Insured International** (☎ *800/243-3174*; *www.travelinsured.com*); and **Travelex Insurance Services** (☎ *888/457-4602*; *www.travelex-insurance.com*).

Safety

Ireland, and Northern Ireland in particular, has seen an inordinate amount of unrest and violence for many years. All the signs are that this troubled time is history, but it was rarely the case that even at its height any of the troubles affected tourists.

Today, travelling in Ireland is no more – and no less – risky than travelling anywhere in the British Isles. Wherever you are it remains prudent to take simple precautions to safeguard against petty thieves and pickpockets. If you are in a crowded place, do not let children out of your sight; their safety is more important than the price of some souvenir.

Although the general level of personal safety is high, should you be unfortunate enough to be a victim of crime, contact the following:

Republic of Ireland

Irish Tourist Assistance Service, Black 1, Garda HQ, Harcourt Square, Dublin 2 ℓ *01478 5295*, *www.itas.ie*.

Northern Ireland

Contact local police station ℓ *028 9065 0222*, *www.psni.police.uk*.

US Travellers

If you have any questions or concerns, contact the **U.S. State Department** to obtain the latest safety recommendations (ℓ *202/ 647-5225*, *http://travel.state.gov*).

THE 21ST-CENTURY TRAVELLER

Mobile Phones

Dual-band mobile phones will automatically switch to the appropriate Republic network when you arrive in Ireland – in Northern Ireland you are still connected to your UK network, and this will operate within a few miles of the border, though how far is variable. You can call Irish numbers directly, but calling numbers in the UK is also variable; sometimes you simply dial the UK number, and it all works fine. At other times, and especially if you are calling another mobile phone in your party, you need to prefix +44, and drop the first zero from the number.

Make sure with your provider that your phone is set for international roaming. Accessing voice mails is also something you might want to clarify with your provider as systems vary. Quite often, when you arrive in Ireland, you will get a text message explaining how to pick up voice mails, but this is not always the case.

Call charges also differ, and steps are being taken at a UK national level to get call charges significantly reduced. But, as things stand, call charges back to the UK will be higher than in the UK, *and* you pay to receive calls, too.

If you make regular trips to Ireland, it may be worth buying a pay-as-you-go mobile phone or sim card locally.

US Travellers

If your mobile phone is on a GSM system (Global System for Mobiles), and you have a world-capable multiband phone such as many Sony Ericsson, Motorola, or Samsung models, you can make and receive calls across civilised areas around much of the globe. Just call your wireless operator and ask for 'international roaming' to be activated on your account.

For many people, **renting** a phone is a good idea.

Although you can rent a phone from any number of overseas sites, including kiosks at airports and at car-rental agencies, we suggest renting the phone before you leave home. North Americans can rent one before leaving home from **InTouch USA** (☎ *800/872-7626*; *www.intouchglobal.com*) or **RoadPost** (☎ *888/290-1606* or ☎ *905/272-5665*; *www.roadpost. com*). InTouch will also, for free, advise you on whether your existing phone will work overseas; simply call ☎ *703/222-7161* between 9am and 4pm EST, or go to *http://intouchglobal.com/ travel.htm*.

There's a Vodafone shop in Dublin airport where you can purchase an Irish sim card for your own phone – this allows you to pay in-country rather than international rates for calls you receive while you're there. They also rent and sell mobile phones.

Buying a phone can be economically attractive, as many nations have cheap prepaid phone systems. Once you arrive at your destination, stop by a local mobile phone shop and get the cheapest package; you'll probably pay less than $100 for a phone and a starter calling card. Local calls may be as low as 10 cents per minute, and in many countries incoming calls are free.

Other Phones

For information about area and international dialling codes and public phones, see p. 38.

The Internet

Most hotels in Ireland provide some form of Internet service for guests. At the most basic, it's a pay system in the hotel foyer; but increasingly hotels are providing free **WiFi (wireless) Internet services** or high-speed room connections. Of course, to use the in-room facilities you need to take your own laptop with you, and an Ethernet data cable (although the hotels can usually supply these). Or you can use dial-up from your room by using the telephone, but be warned, you will pay the hotel's (usually) high rate for phone calls.

To connect using WiFi, you need a wireless card in your laptop. To use high-speed connections, you should be okay to do much the same as at home, provided your system is configured correctly.

If you know your POP3 log-in details (your service provider

can tell you these), you may find that *www.mail2web.com* is a good way of connecting to your emails, one that allows you to delete the spam before dealing with the legitimate emails. If you have to use dial-up, you need a local phone number to connect to; these are not always obvious. But *www.net2roam.com* provides a worldwide network of local numbers to call. You pay to buy credit from them, but can do this online, and you are only dialling a local number rather than calling your server's number back home at international rates.

Of course, many systems already allow you to connect to your emails, e.g. Yahoo, Hotmail, etc., but you could consider using Google Mail (*www.googlemail.com*) for your emails, especially if your server has a system that enables you to divert your emails to your new Gmail address.

Internet cafés can be found in large towns and cities throughout Ireland, and many libraries also have Internet facilities.

ESSENTIALS

Getting There

By Air Low-cost airlines have made flying to Ireland a doddle. But the situation is constantly changing. At the time of writing, you can fly from 26 airports in England, Wales and Scotland, plus the Isle of Man and the Channel Islands, to 101 destinations in the Republic

of Ireland, and 3 in Northern Ireland.

British airports with flights to Ireland:

England

Birmingham

Blackpool

Bournemouth

Bristol

Doncaster

Durham

East Midlands

Exeter

Gatwick

Heathrow

Leeds/Bradford

Liverpool

London City

Luton

Manchester

Newcastle

Newquay

Norwich

Southampton

Stansted

Wales

Cardiff

Scotland

Aberdeen

Edinburgh

Glasgow

Inverness

Prestwick

From the United States & Canada

The Irish national carrier, **Aer Lingus** (☎ *800/474-7424* in the U.S., or ☎ *0818/365-000* in Ireland. *www.aerlingus.ie*) provides transatlantic flights to Ireland with scheduled, nonstop flights from New York (JFK), Boston, Chicago, Los Angeles, and Baltimore to Dublin, Shannon, and Belfast international airports.

American Airlines (☎ *800/433-7300. www.aa.com*) flies directly from New York (JFK), Boston and Chicago to Dublin and Shannon. **Delta Airlines** (☎ *800/241-4141. www.delta.com*) flies directly from Atlanta and New York (JFK) to Dublin and Shannon. **Continental Airlines** (☎ *800/231-0856. www.continental.com*) offers nonstop service to Dublin, Shannon, and Belfast from Newark.

Airline UK Contact Details		
Aer Arann	☎ *0800 587 2324*	*www.aerarann.com*
Aer Lingus	☎ *0870 876 5000*	*www.aerlingus.com*
Air Berlin	☎ *0870 738 8880*	*www.airberlin.com*
Air France	☎ *0870 142 4343*	*www.airfrance.co.uk*
Air Southwest	☎ *0870 241 8202*	*www.airsouthwest.com*
Bmi	☎ *0870 60 70555*	*www.flybmi.com*
Bmibaby	☎ *0871 224 0224*	*www.bmibaby.com*
British Airways	☎ *0870 850 9850*	*www.ba.com*
British Northwest Airways	☎ *01253 349 073*	*www.flybnwa.co.uk*
EasyJet	☎ *0905 821 0905*	*www.easyJet.com*
Euromanx Airlines	☎ *0870 787 7879*	*www.euromanx.com*
Flybe	☎ *0871 700 0123*	*www.flybe.com*
Jet2.com	☎ *0871 226 1737*	*www.jet2.com*
Luxair	☎ 0800 389 9443	*www.luxair.lu*
Manx2	☎ *0870 242 2226*	*www.manx2.com*
Ryanair	☎ *0871 246 0000*	*www.ryanair.com*

Sea Routes		
Depart	Arrive	Carrier
Cairnryan	Larne	P&O Irish Sea
Fishguard	Rosslare	StenaLine
Fleetwood	Larne	StenaLine
Holyhead	Dublin Port	Irish Ferries
		StenaLine
Holyhead	Dun Laoghaire	StenaLine
Isle of Man	Belfast	Steam Packet Company
Isle of Man	Dublin	Steam Packet Company
Liverpool	Dublin	P&O Irish Sea
Liverpool (Birkenhead)	Dublin	Norfolkline
Liverpool (Birkenhead)	Belfast	Norfolkline
Pembroke	Rosslare	Irish Ferries
Stranraer	Belfast	StenaLine
Swansea	Cork	Swansea Cork Ferries
Troon	Larne	P&O Irish Sea

From Canada, **Air Canada** (☎ *888/247-2262* in the U.S. and Canada, or ☎ *0180/070-0900* in Ireland) runs frequent direct flights to Shannon and Dublin from major Canadian cities.

It's possible to save money by booking your air tickets through a consolidator (also known as a bucket shop) who works with the airlines to sell off their unsold air tickets at a cut price. But note that the savings generally range from minuscule in the high season to substantial in the off season. **UK Air** (☎ *888/577-2900; www.ukair.com*) sells tickets to Britain, Ireland, and the rest of Europe on regular Delta, British Airways, and Continental flights.

The London–Dublin and London–Shannon routes are two of the busiest flight paths in Europe, and competition is stiff – which means that you can often get a fantastic deal; see the UK airline operators above.

By Ferry Ireland has six main ferry ports: Belfast, Cork, Dublin Port, Dun Laoghaire, Larne and Rosslare.

Even if travelling with a number of children, it's worth enquiring once on board about the cost of upgrading to **Club Class.** The cost per head is around €15 (£10), and this entitles you to use of a spacious lounge, secured once the ship is under way, with complimentary refreshments including tea, coffee, soft drinks and food.

By Bus Bus Éireann/Eurolines offers great value daily coach services from a wide range of UK and European destinations. Bus Éireann is part of Europe's express coach network operating in 25 countries in Europe under

Ferry Operators UK Contact Details

Irish Ferries	📞 08705 17 17 17	www.irishferries.com
Steam Packet Company	📞 08705 523 523	www.steam-packet.com
Norfolkline	📞 0870 600 4321	www.norfolkline.com
P&O Irish Sea	📞 0870 24 24 777	www.poirishsea.com
Stena Line	📞 08705 70 70 70	www.stenaline.co.uk
Swansea Cork Ferries	📞 01792 456 116	www.swanseacork ferries.com

the 'Eurolines' brand. The Eurolines service offers a comprehensive network of connections from all parts of Ireland to more than 1,500 locations in Britain with onward connections from London to over 400 major European destinations.

Eurolines services to and from Ireland offer you a number of options: travel on Eurolines coach services connecting with day or night sailings from Dublin Ferryport (operated by StenaLine and Irish Ferries) or Dun Laoghaire (operated by Stena Line). Alternatively you may travel on the night sailing from Rosslare Harbour (operated by Stena Line).

Your fare includes travel on **Bus Eireann's Expressway** coach and local bus services to and from the Bus Eireann/Eurolines departure point nearest to you (where services suit). Connections are available from almost every part of Ireland. All Eurolines services are operated with luxury coaches equipped with on-board toilets, reclining seats and panoramic viewing windows.

Travel information and reservations may be obtained at

Eurolines or any National Express travel agent. For advice, ticket amendments, refunds and cancellations, call 📞 *08705 808080* between 8am and 8pm. Travel information on Eurolines services may also be obtained from Eurolines offices in most European countries or at *www. eurolines.com*.

Getting Around

By Car Having a car of your own, or a rental car, is by far the most efficient way of getting around Ireland, and gives you a flexibility you do not have with public transport. Your own car is also familiar to the driver – an important consideration on some of Ireland's narrow and twisting roads – and makes it easy to pack the multiple items that different family members want or need to bring along. All the ferry operators are utterly efficient at getting you and your car across to Ireland in safety and comfort.

For information on '**Driving in Ireland**', see p. 35, and for information on '**Car Rental**', see p. 33.

Road Rules in a Nutshell

1 Drive on the left side of the road.

2 Road signs are in kilometres in the Republic and in miles in Northern Ireland.

3 On motorways, the left lane is the travelling lane. The right lane is for passing (though many drivers just use it as the 'fast lane').

4 Everyone must wear a seat belt by law. Children must be in age-appropriate child seats.

5 Children aged under 12 are not allowed to sit in the front seat.

6 When entering a roundabout, give way to traffic coming from the right.

7 The speed limits are 50kph (31mph) in built-up areas; 80kph (50mph) on regional and local roads, sometimes referred to as non-national roads; 100kph (62mph) on national roads, including dual carriageways and 120kph (75mph) on motorways.

US Travellers

In high season, weekly rental rates on a manual-transmission compact vehicle begin at around $245 (and that's if you've shopped around) and ascend steeply – but it's at the fuel pump that you're likely to go into shock. Irish gas prices can be triple what you pay in the United States. And although Ireland is a tiny country by comparison, and distances between places are relatively short, the roads in the countryside can be so narrow and winding that getting from A to B rarely takes as little time as it looks.

Another potential pitfall is that rental cars in Ireland are almost always equipped with standard transmissions – you can rent an automatic, but it will cost substantially more (about $200 per week). Driving on the left side of the road and shifting gears with your left hand can take some getting used to. Also consider that another fact of life in Ireland is cramped roads. Even the major Irish motorways are surprisingly narrow, with lanes made for the tiniest cars – just the kind you'll wish you had rented once you're underway. Off the motorways, it's rare to find a road with a hard shoulder – leaving precious little manoeuvring space when a bus or truck is coming from the opposite direction. So think small when you pick out your rental car. The choice is yours: room in the car or room on the road.

Unless your stay in Ireland extends beyond six months, your own valid U.S. or Canadian driver's licence (provided you've had it for at least six months) is all you need to drive in Ireland. Rules and restrictions for car rental vary slightly and correspond roughly to those in the United States, with two important distinctions. Most rental-car agencies in the Republic won't rent to you (1) if you're under 23 or over 74 (there's no upper age limit in Northern Ireland) or (2) if your licence has been valid for less than a year.

Note: Double check your credit card's policy on picking up the insurance on rental cars. Almost none of the American-issued cards – including gold cards – cover the collision damage waiver (CDW) on car rentals in Ireland anymore.

By Train Ireland's railways are centred on Dublin and Belfast, and there are comparatively few local lines other than the suburban networks around the two capitals. So although the network looks impressive there are massive swathes of Ireland that don't have a rail service, and, unless you are going to specific en-route or end-of-line destinations, getting around by train has severe limitations.

Rail Operators Enterprise Trains: Northern Ireland (*028 9066 6630* Republic of Ireland (*01 703 4070, www.translink. co.uk* or *www.irishrail.ie*.

Irish Rail (Iarnród Éireann), Travel Centre, 35 Lower Abbey Street, Dublin D1 (*01 836 6222, www.irishrail.ie*.

Northern Ireland Railways, Central Station, Belfast (*028 9066 6630, www.translink.co.uk*.

INSIDER TIP ›
Check for specially discounted fares when travelling by public transport, like the Freedom of Northern Ireland/Emerald Card/Irish Rover tickets, which offer unlimited bus/train travel for 3, 5, 8 or 15 days.

Eurailpass Of the dozens of different Eurailpasses available, some are valid for unlimited rail travel in 17 European countries – but none include Britain or Northern Ireland. Other passes let you save money by selecting fewer countries. In the Irish Republic, the Eurailpass is good for travel on trains, Expressway coaches, and the Irish Continental Lines ferries between France and Ireland. For passes that let you travel throughout continental Europe and the Republic of Ireland, first-class passes begin at $605 for 15 consecutive days of travel; youth passes (passengers must be under 26 years old) begin at $394 for 15 consecutive days of travel in second class. The pass must be purchased 21 days before departure for Europe by a non-European Union resident. For further details or for purchase, call **Rail Pass Express** (*800/722-7151*; *www.eurail. com*). It's also available from **STA Travel** (*800/781-4040*; *www.sta.com*) and other travel agents. You can also find more information online at *www. eurail.com*.

BritRail Pass + Ireland Includes all rail travel throughout the United Kingdom and Ireland, including a round-trip ferry crossing on Stena Line. A pass good for any 5 days of unlimited travel within a 30-day period costs $590 first class, $427 second class; 10 days of unlimited travel within a 30-day period costs $973 first class, $680 second class. It must be purchased before departure for Ireland or the United Kingdom. Available from **BritRail** (☎ 866/BRITRAIL; *www.britrail.net*).

By Bus In the Republic, **Bus Éireann**, and **Ulsterbus** in Northern Ireland are the two interconnecting bus companies that, between them, effectively cover Ireland. All bus and rail services in Northern Ireland are controlled by Translink. Many towns have their own localised transport – Dublin Bus and Citybus in Belfast. In addition, there are many small county-based companies. As a result, there are few places in rural Ireland that cannot be reached by bus. However, these services

are primarily there for locals, not tourists; they are infrequent, and inordinately slow, even if they are a fascinating way to explore. Information about these local services is available at tourist information centres.

Bus Éireann have routes to every part of the Republic, mainly spreading out from Dublin. They offer fare reductions for under-16s as well as student discounts. Contact them at Bus Éireann, The Travel Centre, Central Bus Station, Store Street, Dublin 1 ☎ *01 836 6111*; *www. buseireann.ie*.

Ulsterbus/Translink runs buses in Northern Ireland, except Belfast City, and offers a Freedom of Northern Ireland unlimited travel ticket. Contact them at Ulsterbus/Translink, Europa Bus Centre, Great Victoria Street, Belfast ☎ *028 9066 6630*; *www.ulsterbus.co.uk* or *www.translink.co.uk*.

By Air Although the delight of travelling in Ireland is taking it at a steady pace, it is possible to take quite a few internal flights:

From	To	Airline
Belfast City	Cork	Aer Arann
Cork	Galway	Aer Arann
Dublin	City of Derry	Logan Air
Dublin	Cork	Aer Arann, Ryanair
Dublin	Donegal	Aer Arann
Dublin	Kerry	Aer Arann
Dublin	Galway	Aer Arann
Dublin	Shannon	Aer Arann
Dublin	Sligo	Aer Arann
Dublin	Knock	Logan Air

Regional Flights from the UK are Operated by		
Airline	**Telephone**	**Website**
Aer Arann	0800 587 2324	**www.aerarann.com**
Aer Lingus	0870 876 5000	**www.aerlingus.com**
British Airways (operated by Logan Air)	08708 509 850	**www.ba.com**
Ryanair	0871 246 0000	**www.ryanair.com**

By Bike If you want to tour by bike there are hire companies that allow you to pick up and collect at different points for one-way trips. Raleigh Rent-a-Bike (*www.raleigh.ie*) has rental centres at a number of towns throughout Ireland, or there's Irish Cycle Hire, Enterprise Centre, Ardee, Co Louth, who have a network of depots across the country (*041 685 3772. www.irishcyclehire.com*). They have children's bikes, child seats, children's trainers, tag along, bags and panniers, and car-racks, all available for hire by the day or week. They also offer self-guided package holidays, moving your luggage from one place to another leaving you free to enjoy the day's ride unencumbered. A touring bike is €70 per week or €15 per day, and a child's bike is €50 per week.

GETTING THE CHILDREN INTERESTED

Travelling as a family ought to be fun, and generate excitement and memories that can be savoured, and probably laughed about, for years to come.

One good way to get your children interested in the destination is to give them books of Irish tales to read in the lead up to the holiday. Here are a few recommendations (all available from **www.amazon.co.uk** and good booksellers):

Tales from Old Ireland by Malachy Doyle and Niamh Sharkey. Marvellous retelling of best-loved Irish folk tales.

Too Many Leprechauns by Stephen Krensky and Dan Andreasen. Charming tale of how that pot o' gold got to the end of the rainbow.

Fergus and the Night-Demon by Jim Murphy and John Manders. Humorous, quick-witted story of Fergus O'Mara, a lazy lad who skips out on his chores.

Lara and the Gray Mare; *Lara and the Moon-Colored Filly*; *Lara at Athenry Castle*; *Lara and the Silent Place* by Kathleen Duey. Intriguing adventures of Lara and Dannsair, a rare silvery white horse, set in 14th century Ireland

The Last Wolf of Ireland by Elona Malterre. Based on real events in 1786.

Celtic Animals Coloring Book by Mallory Pearce. As you travel

It's not necessary to speak Irish (*Gaelic* – pronounced Gay-lic, not Gah-lic) any-where in Ireland. There are extensive areas where Irish is the first language of the people – the Gaeltacht – but just about everyone speaks English through-out the country.

around Ireland, you'll see distinctive Celtic motifs everywhere you look.

Information about travel in Ireland is well covered on the Internet – see p. 13 for some relevant websites – but there are others that deal in whole or in part with family aspects. Sadly, some of these websites are here today, gone tomorrow, and most are not kept keenly up to date. So, before relying on information contained on websites, do check how current it is.

www.tinytotsaway.com: with increasingly tight luggage restrictions, increasing costs of excess baggage and no luggage allowance at all for children under the age of 2 years, you need something to lighten the load. The people behind this website do just that: you go online, order all the things you would normally pack to take away, from nappies to baby's favourite food, and they buy it all and ship it to your hotel/destination, to be there as you arrive.

www.babygoes2.com: contains pages of information that will help parents travelling with small children, including recommendations on hotels with child care facilities.

www.travellingwithchildren.co. uk: comprehensive online sales

site offering a wide range of products and handy tips for travelling parents, and catering for children from newborn to 14 years.

You will find useful information about the problems of travelling with children debated on *www.deabirkett.com* – check out the 'Travelling with Kids Forum'.

To keep sticky hands clean, always carry a bottle of hand sterilising gel, these days available in most high street chemists. No need for a towel, you're always able to clean hands before eating, and it's kinda fun and squidgy between the fingers.

ACCOMMODATION & EATING OUT

Accommodation

Wherever you go in Ireland you will find accommodation of all standards and, most importantly, a welcome for every member of the family unsurpassed in the British Isles. In many hotels, children sharing their parents' room receive discounts ranging from 50–100%; the age varies, but in some places is as high as 16 years.

There is the customary range of styles, from 4- and 5-star

hotels – which are very family-friendly – to charming guest-houses and B&Bs that display considerable enterprise and enthusiasm. Most can cater for disabled guests to some degree.

Even the most expensive hotels offer excellent value for money compared with comparable hotels in Britain. Many hotels have special offers or 'last minute' deals through their websites, many of them two- or three-night inclusive packages, with thousands of offers on *www. discoverireland.com/offers*. Even if nothing is specified it is always worth asking for the best rate available.

All the hotels and guesthouses recommended in this guide have been visited personally by one or other of the authors, and we can vouch for their quality at every level. But they are only a representative sample.

Guesthouses and B&Bs are classified by a star system ranging from one to four or five stars. You can choose from elegant country homes to luxury castles, village pubs, farm accommodation (including a chance to milk the cows), manor houses and budget hotels. Many of the upmarket hotels offer, on top of everything you would traditionally expect, excellent food, cookery courses, entertainment, and leisure and sporting facilities, including golf. Some of the pubs, especially in the more remote parts of Ireland (as well as the cities) are renowned for impromptu music and dancing.

For the budget traveller, Ireland's network of hostels offers great independence. But facilities do vary, so check in advance. There are also more than 200 camping and caravanning sites, most near outstanding scenery.

Information about accommodation is available from the following organisations:

Hotels & Guest Houses

The Irish Hotels Federation *(+353) 01 497 6459*; *www. irelandhotels.com*

Northern Ireland Hotels Federation *028 9035 1110*; *www.nihf.co.uk*

Manor House Hotels and Irish Country Hotels *(+353) 01 295 8900*; *www.cmvhotels.com*

Ireland's Blue Book, *(+353) 01 676 9914*; *www.irelandsblue book.com*

Bed & Breakfasts

Town and Country Homes Association *071 982 2222*; *www.townandcountry.ie*

The Friendly Homes of Ireland *(+353) 01 660 7975*; *www. tourismresources.ie/fh*

Bed and Breakfast Association of Northern Ireland *028 9145 8820*

Farmhouses

Irish Farmhouse Holidays *(+353) 061 400 700*; *www. irishfarmholidays.com*

Having found suitable accommodation on the various websites, make contact and check what is provided for children, from babysitting or baby listening services, to games and leisure activities. Make contact by email if possible, so that you have something in writing in the event of a discrepancy at check in. And when you arrive at your hotel, be sure to confirm the agreed rate at the start of your stay.

Northern Ireland Farm and Country Holidays Association

☎ *028 8284 1325*; *www.nifcha.com*

Country Houses

The Hidden Ireland Guide

☎ *(+353) 01 662 7166*; *www.hiddenireland.com*

Hostels

An Óige (Irish Youth Hostel Association) ☎ *(+353) 01 830 4555*; *www.irelandyha.org*

Independent Holiday Hostels

☎ *(+353) 01 836 4700*; *www.hostels-ireland.com*

Celtic Budget Accommodation ☎ *(+353) 01 855 0019*; *www.celtic-accommodation.ie*

Hostelling International Northern Ireland ☎ *028 9032 4733*; *www.hini.org.uk*

The website *www.discoverireland.com* has a comprehensive list of every registered accommodation unit across the whole of Ireland including hotels, guest houses, B&Bs, self catering, camping and caravanning.

Eating Out

Wherever you stay, eating out in Ireland is a superb experience and ranges from fun-filled eateries that specifically target children to some very upmarket restaurants, notably in Dublin and Belfast, but increasingly elsewhere.

There are the usual fast food places like McDonald's, Burger King and Pizza Hut, but you're sure to get a whole lot more atmosphere in a rural pub/restaurant, often with a separate dining room. Most welcome children until 9pm, or generally to 6pm in Northern Ireland.

Many of the attractions that appeal to children also have some form of dining facility attached. Usually this is a family-friendly tearoom or coffee shop though sometimes there's only the pub. (Be aware that if you're visiting very remote places, you may need to take your own refreshments.)

Many eating-places have children's menus, usually very conventional, and child portions are often available from the main menu. At the smarter restaurants however children should not be allowed the freedom to roam permitted elsewhere.

Almost all cafés and restaurants provide high chairs for babies, and have baby-changing facilities. An increasing number offer diversions such as colouring books and crayons, bouncy castles or children's DVDs at weekends.

It's rare to find cafés and restaurants, even in remote areas, that don't offer some vegetarian options. Even in some high-end hotel restaurants, a dish of vegetables and a bowl of champ (a leek and potato mix) accompany meals even when not needed. You can get chips, of course, but you still get the bowl of champ.

Overall, prices are not widely variable, and are always value for money.

FAST FACTS: IRELAND

Baby Services Most hotels and guesthouses can provide a cot, usually free. A growing number can also provide baby listening or babysitting, the second usually by a member of staff or a reliable local. You would be wise to check that this is advance, and, if you know you will need it, book ahead.

Banks Banking hours are generally 10am–4.30pm, Monday–Friday. Some banks open on Saturdays. ATM (cash) machines are located at most banks and accept all major credit and debit cards.

Beaches 'Blue Flags' are awarded to European beaches with clean, unpolluted water, safe access, lifeguards on duty, toilet facilities, wheelchair access and an information centre nearby.

Not all beaches are suitable for swimming because of strong currents and tides. Few are near catering facilities, so visitors to the remoter ones need to take their own refreshments.

The Blue Flag rating is valid only during the bathing season, which runs from June to the end of August. But this does mean that beaches are cleaned on a regular basis, daily in the peak season, and have sufficient lifeguards or lifesaving equipment to ensure a response in an emergency.

Breastfeeding Breastfeeding in public is not especially frowned on in Ireland and although rates have been a little lower than Britain, they are beginning to rise, particularly in cities, which means attitudes should be becoming more relaxed.

Car Rental Most of the major car rental companies have desks at airports, ferry terminals and in cities across Ireland. As a rule, these companies don't rent cars to drivers aged under 21 or over 70. All drivers must hold a valid full licence.

If you intend to rent a car, it is advisable to book in advance, especially if you intend to travel during the peak season. Booking in advance can often work out cheaper. The majority of rental cars are standard manual, but automatic cars are available for an additional fee, as are child seats.

For insurance reasons, you should inform your car rental company if you intend to travel between the Republic of Ireland and Northern Ireland.

Climate Ireland has a mild, temperate climate with summer temperatures generally ranging from 15°C to 20°C (60–70°F). Temperatures in spring and autumn are generally 10°C (50°F), and in winter between 5°C and 8°C (40–45°F). Snow, other than on mountain summits, is rare, but there is rain year round.

Consulates See 'Embassies and Consulates', p. 36.

Currency See 'Money', p. 16.

Customs Visitors to Ireland from the UK and other EU countries are not required to make a declaration to Customs at their place of entry. But certain goods are prohibited or restricted to protect health and the environment. These include meat and poultry.

For overseas visitors, such as US and Canadian citizens, the limit on duty-free and VAT-free items that may be brought into the EU for personal use are as follows: 200 cigarettes, one litre of liquor, two litres of wine, and other goods (including beer) not exceeding the value of €150 ($181) per adult. There are no restrictions on bringing currency into Ireland.

US Travellers
What You Can take Home from Ireland:

Onboard the flight back to the United States, you'll be given a Customs declaration to fill out. Returning **US citizens** who have been away for at least 48 hours are allowed to bring back, once every 30 days, $800 worth of merchandise duty-free. You'll be charged a flat rate of duty on the next $1,000 worth of purchases. Any dollar amount beyond that is dutiable at whatever rates apply. On mailed gifts, the duty-free limit is $200. Be sure to have your receipts or purchases handy to expedite the declaration process. ***Note:*** If you owe duty, you are required to pay on your arrival in the United States, by cash, personal cheque, government or traveller's cheque, or money order, and in some locations, a Visa or MasterCard.

To avoid having to pay duty on foreign-made personal items you owned before you left on your trip, bring along a bill of sale, insurance policy, jeweller's appraisal, or receipts of purchase. Or you can register items – think laptop computers, cameras, and CD players – with Customs before you leave. Take the items to any Customs office or register them with Customs at the airport from which you're departing. You'll receive, at no cost, a Certificate of Registration, which allows duty-free entry for the life of the item.

For specifics on what you can bring back and corresponding fees, download the invaluable free pamphlet *Know Before You Go* online at **www.cbp.gov**. Or contact the **U.S. Customs & Border Protection (CBP),** 1300

Pennsylvania Ave., NW, Washington, DC 20229 (☎ 877/287-8667) and request the pamphlet.

Canadian Travellers

For a clear summary of Canadian rules, send for the booklet *I Declare*, issued by the **Canada Border Services Agency** (☎ *800/461-9999* in Canada, or ☎ *204/983-3500*; *www.cbsa-asfc.gc.ca*). Canada allows its citizens a C$750 exemption, and you're allowed to bring back duty-free 1 carton of cigarettes, 1 can of tobacco, 40 imperial ounces of liquor, and 50 cigars per adult. In addition, you're allowed to mail gifts to Canada valued at less than C$60 a day, provided they're unsolicited and don't contain alcohol or tobacco (write on the package 'Unsolicited gift, under $60 value'). All valuables should be declared on the Y-38 form before departure from Canada, including serial numbers of valuables you already own, such as expensive foreign cameras. *Note:* The C$750 exemption can only be used once a year and only after an absence of seven days.

Dentists and Doctors

Information about local dentists and doctors is most easily obtained at your hotel or guest house, and many hotels will make appointments for you. You may also be able to get a list from tourist information centres or the local police.

Directory Enquiries To call Directory Enquires in the Republic of Ireland, ☎ *11811*; to do so in Northern Ireland, ☎ *118 500*. International Directory Enquiries, ☎ *118 505*. See also 'Telephone' on p. 38.

Driving in Ireland As in Britain, you drive on the left, and observe all the usual signs and courtesies. Northern Ireland is exactly the same as Britain, but the Republic of Ireland differs in a few details, notably that speed limits and road distances use kilometres rather than miles – something to remember when crossing the border between the two. A few road signs differ slightly but their meaning is clear.

In Northern Ireland, the speed limit in built-up areas is 30mph, on the open road 60mph, and unless shown otherwise, on motorways 70mph. In the Republic of Ireland, the speed limit is 80kph on non-national roads, 100kph on national roads, and 120kph on motorways.

As a word of warning, although roads are being improved at a remarkable rate all across Ireland, many of the remote roads are less than perfect. It is therefore wise to drive cautiously on country lanes and side roads.

Seat belts must be worn at all times, both in the front and the back of vehicles. In both the Republic of Ireland and Northern Ireland the law requires that all children travelling in cars use an appropriate child restraint or adult seat belt. Rear-facing child seats may not be used in the front passenger seat if the car has an airbag fitted unless the airbag is removed or deactivated. It is the driver's responsibility to ensure that children under the age of 14 are using an appropriate child restraint or an adult seat belt.

In September 2006, the law in the UK, and therefore Northern Ireland, changed so that it becomes necessary for children under 1.36 metres in height (and under 12 years), to use a special seat for their age, other than in certain mitigating circumstances. For information on car seat types, see *www.childcar seats.org.uk*.

As in Britain, there are very strict laws in Ireland on drinking and driving, making the best advice 'Don't drink and drive'.

Visitors to Ireland must bring a valid national driving licence, issued in the country of their permanent residence; in the Republic of Ireland the law requires that you carry your driving licence at all times, and, if the vehicle is not registered in your name, you will need a letter of authorisation from the owner.

Your British insurance will give you the minimum legal cover while driving in the Republic of Ireland, but the usual full cover while in Northern Ireland. It is advisable to ensure that you are covered to drive the car outside Britain. Green card cover is almost a thing of the past, and most insurance companies will automatically include cover for travel abroad – but check.

Some form of European Breakdown Cover such as the AA and RAC offer would be wise.

Electricity The standard electricity supply is 220 volts AC in the Republic of Ireland, and 240 volts AC in Northern Ireland. Visitors from outside Britain may need a transformer and/or adaptor to convert 2-pin plugs to the standard 3-pin plug. These can usually be bought at airports or electrical suppliers.

Email See p. 21.

Embassies and Consulates

Republic of Ireland: For further information, contact the Department of Foreign Affairs ℡ *01 478 0822*, or the Passport and Visa Office, Embassy of Ireland, Montpelier House, 106 Brompton Road, London SW3 1JJ ℡ *020 7225 7700*. For a list of Irish embassies, visit *www. dfa.ie*.

Northern Ireland: Further information is available from your local British Embassy or Consulate. For British details, contact the Foreign and Commonwealth Office at *www.fco.gov.uk*.

The **American Embassy** is at 42 Elgin Rd, Ballsbridge, Dublin 4 (℡ *01 668-8777*); the **Canadian Embassy** at 65–68 St. Stephen's Green, Dublin 2 (℡ *01 678-1988*); the **Australian Embassy** at Fitzwilton House, Wilton Terrace, Dublin 2 (℡ *01 676-1517*). In addition, there is an **American Consulate** at 14 Queen St., Belfast BT1 6EQ (℡ *028 9032-8239*).

Emergency Telephone Numbers

Republic of Ireland: Emergency services (police, fire, ambulance) ☎ *112* or *999*

Northern Ireland: Emergency services (police, fire, ambulance) ☎ *999*

Internet See p. 21.

Language Irish (Gaelic – pronounced Gay-lic) and English are the official languages of the Republic of Ireland, and street and road signs are bilingual. In Gaeltacht areas, road signs may be displayed only in Irish, and Irish is spoken daily, although everyone also speaks English. In Northern Ireland, English is the official language, though Irish is taught in many schools.

Pay Phones Easy-to-use country calling cards are widely available at many outlets across Ireland.

Postal Services Post offices are generally open from 9am–5.30pm, Monday to Friday both in Northern Ireland the Republic. Main post offices, i.e. in towns and cities, also open on Saturdays between 9am–12.30pm in Northern Ireland, and 9am–5pm in the Republic of Ireland. Exact opening hours may vary depending on the size and location of the post office branch.

Postal charges

	ROI	NI
Within Ireland	€0.48	£0.32
To Britain	€0.75	£0.32
To other countries in EU	€0.75	£0.44

In Northern Ireland post is priced on a system based on both size and weight, as in Britain.

Pubs The legal drinking age in Ireland is 18. Some pubs insist that patrons are over 21 and carry some form of ID.

Legislation in the Republic of Ireland stipulates that children under 18 are not allowed in premises that serve alcohol after 9.30pm.

Pubs in the Republic of Ireland are open seven days a week, usually from 10.30am. Opening hours in Northern Ireland are generally 11.30am–11pm, Monday to Saturday, and 12.30pm–10pm on Sunday. But many pubs have extended opening hours, especially at weekends.

Closing times vary through the week, but usually range from 11.30pm Monday to Thursday, and from 12.30am Friday and Saturday. Sunday opening hours are 12.30pm–11pm.

Shopping Hours Shops are generally open Monday to Saturday from 9am to 6pm, with late night shopping until 8pm or 9pm on Thursdays at many large stores. Sunday opening hours are generally midday until 5pm or 6pm (1–5pm in Northern Ireland).

Smoking Restrictions Smoking is not allowed in public areas, such as pubs, restaurants and hotels in both the Republic of Ireland and Northern Ireland.

Taxis In Belfast, Dublin, Galway, Limerick and Cork, taxis are metered. In other areas, fares should be agreed beforehand. Taxis are usually found at ranks in central locations, and do not usually cruise the streets.

Telephone See also 'Directory Enquiries', p. 35; 'Mobile phones', p. 20, and 'Pay Phones', p. 37.

If calling the Republic of Ireland from abroad, all telephone numbers must be prefixed with +353 (drop the first 0 of the telephone number called).

If calling Northern Ireland from abroad (but not from within Britain), all telephone numbers must be prefixed with +44 (drop the first 0 of the telephone number called).

Time Ireland is on **Greenwich Mean Time (GMT).** Clocks are put forward one hour in mid-March, and back one hour at the end of October. This means that during the summer months it can still be light at 11.30pm, although in winter it is usually dark around 4pm.

Tipping In restaurants, when a service charge is not included, 10–15% of the bill is an appropriate tip. Taxi drivers are usually tipped 10% of the fare, and porters about €1 (£0.75) per bag. In pubs, tipping bar staff is a discretionary matter.

Water It is perfectly safe to drink water in Ireland, and many restaurants automatically serve you with a jug of iced water. On the rare occasions when there have been problems with water supply, hotels have supplied complimentary bottles of water for cleaning your teeth.

3 Dublin

DUBLIN

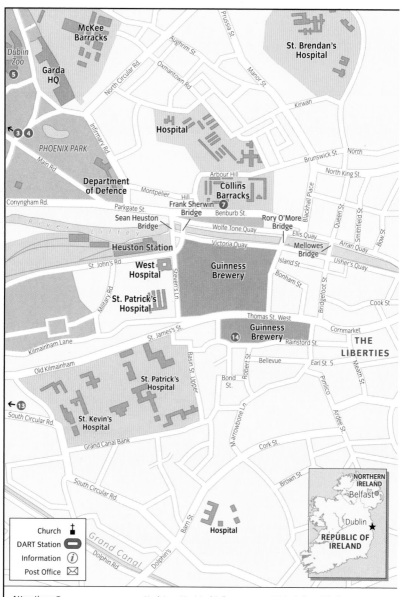

Attractions ●

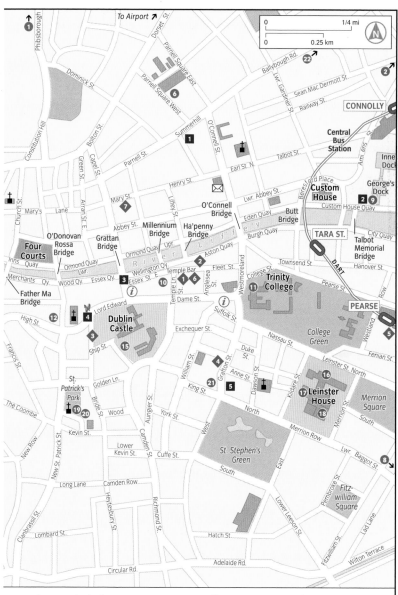

To Airport ↗

CONNOLLY

Central Bus Station

Custom House

George's Dock

TARA ST.

Talbot Memorial Bridge

Four Courts

O'Donovan Rossa Bridge

Grattan Bridge

Millennium Bridge

Ha'penny Bridge

Father Ma Bridge

Trinity College

PEARSE

Dublin Castle

College Green

Leinster House

Merrion Square

St. Patrick's Park

St. Stephen's Green

Fitzwilliam Square

National Museum of Ireland – Archaeology & History **17**
Natural History Museum **18**
St Patricks Cathedral **19**
Marsh's Library **20**
National Wax Museum **21**
GAA Museum **22**

Accommodation ■
Jurys Inn Parnell Street **1**
Jurys Inn Custom House **2**
The Clarence Hotel **3**
Jurys Inn Christchurch **4**

E89-107₂
454 0000

Dining ◆
Elephant and Castle **1**
Botticelli **2**
Leo Burdock **3**
Bewleys Café **4**

Dublin offers everything, from pure childish fun to historic sites that both inform and entertain. Not surprisingly, Ireland's capital is one of Europe's most popular city destinations, bursting with enthusiasm and pride, and absorbing all kinds of influences, while remaining essentially Irish. This charmingly chaotic blend makes the home of U2 and Westlife ideal for families.

There are excellent museums here, such as the notably child-friendly Dublinia and the Museum of Childhood, but also haunted castles, priceless treasures, ghost tours, a chance to play at invading Vikings, and the great green lung of Phoenix Park – perfect for a family picnic.

Massive investment has funded regeneration, sweeping aside the jaded past and replacing it with stylish cafés, bars and restaurants – many with a distinctly Continental flavour – alongside new designer shops.

At the same time the traditions of the Molly Malone era live on. Moving into the 21st century, Dublin's heritage remains alive and well with an enviable list of galleries, venues, museums and centres creating and presenting art in every conceivable form.

Geographically compact and relatively easy to get around, as well as being relaxed and friendly, Dublin offers impressive buildings, and there's always something new and often unusual around the corner. Quiet backstreets provide welcome relief from the bustle of the lively thoroughfares, and in most areas a small park is never far away.

VISITOR INFORMATION

Dublin Tourism, St Andrew's Church, Suffolk Street, Dublin 2 (☎ 01 605 7700; *www.visitdublin. com*) provides a wealth of local travel, accommodation and tourist information. The main information centre, which also offers currency exchange, is in the city centre on Suffolk Street between Dublin Castle and Trinity College. The centre is open Monday to Saturday, during June and September, 9am–7pm, during July and August, 9am–8pm, and October to June, 9am–5.30pm. Sundays and bank holidays throughout the year it is open 10.30am–3pm.

There are satellite offices in Upper O'Connell Street, Dublin 1 (open Monday to Saturday 9am–5pm) and Baggot Street, Dublin 2 (open Monday to Friday 9.30am–noon and 12.30pm–5pm), as well as at Arrivals in Dublin Airport (open daily 8am–10pm) and Dun Laoghaire Ferry Terminal (open Monday to Saturday 10am–1pm and 2pm–6pm).

INSIDER TIP

Details of local attractions and events are listed in the free 'Tourism News' and a bi-weekly 'Event Guide' *www.eventguide.ie*.

ORIENTATION

Dublin lies in the middle of Ireland's eastern seaboard, and is the main ferry terminal for England and Wales. Road and rail networks centre on the city, providing efficient links to most parts of the country and into Northern Ireland.

Getting to Know Dublin

Wherever you are in the city, water is never far away; the River Liffey cuts through the heart of the centre to Dublin Bay and a series of bridges span the river, stitching the two halves together. The most endearing is the 19th-century cast-iron Ha'penny Bridge, once a toll bridge, but today the illuminations of the nearby Millennium Bridge outshine it at night.

The Royal Canal and Grand Canal encircle the city north and south. Most of Dublin's main attractions lie within this flattened circle, just 2.4km across, which can be broken down into even more manageable chunks.

O'Connell Street

The theatre district along and around O'Connell Street is home to shops such as the elegantly charming Clery's on Lower O'Connell Street, or Arnotts, the largest department store in Dublin, on Henry Street. This area north of the river witnessed much turmoil in the country's struggle for independence and,

although once fashionable, it declined during the 19th and 20th centuries to the point where it was considered to feature Europe's worst city slum. That image is long-gone and its redevelopment is fast mirroring that on the south bank of the river.

Trinity College

The extensive campus of Ireland's oldest university, Trinity College, lies just south of the Liffey (see p. 41). Its august buildings cluster round a succession of hallowed quadrangles in the best of scholarly traditions, and it is here that you find the famed Book of Kells. Get children to keep an eye open for Molly Malone, affectionately known to Dubliners as 'The Tart with the Cart', as you walk towards Grafton Street.

Temple Bar

Heading west takes you into Temple Bar, once threatened by demolition but now the pulsating hub of nightlife. This colourful maze of cobbled streets has also become one of the city's cultural centres, with theatres, art and photographic galleries and the Irish Film Centre all here. On Saturdays, head here for the organic food market selling fresh fish and organic produce from local farms and suppliers.

Georgian Dublin

Among the elegance of the Georgian terraces with their

Georgian Doors

brightly coloured doors and rows of gleaming windows you find many of Dublin's most important, child-friendly museums. Here too is Leinster House, seat of the **Oireachtas** (the National Parliament) and the Queen Anne-style Mansion House, which since 1715 has been the official residence of Dublin's Lord Mayors.

Open spaces and squares punctuate the buildings, including St Stephens Green, one of the prettiest parks in the city, although it has a gruesome past – the gallows formerly stood here. On the pond are ducks to feed with leftover sandwiches and there's also a children's playground. It's easy to see how this was once prime pram-pushing territory among the lovely willows and flowerbeds.

The Old City & Liberties

Centred on Dublin Castle and surrounded by remnants of the city walls, this is the oldest part of the city, location of the two medieval cathedrals of Christchurch and St Patrick's.

Lying just outside the walls, Liberties historically enjoyed freedom from the taxes and jurisdiction imposed on the city, but today it's the place for antique shops and bargains.

Phoenix Park & Kilmainham

Both Kilmainham and the green of Phoenix Park lie to the west of the city, flanking the river as it enters. Phoenix Park is the largest city park in Europe and home to roaming herds of wild deer, Dublin Zoo (see p. 51) and Áras an Uachtaráin, the official residence of the Irish President. Kilmainham Gaol (see p. 53), south of the Liffey, has a dark past: it was here that the freedom leaders of the 1916 Rising were taken for execution.

Getting Around

Like any major city, Dublin can be a headache to drive round. Trying to find parking is even more frustrating, so don't even think about it. During the day virtually all available street parking is 'Pay and Display' and illegally parked vehicles may be clamped or towed away, with hefty charges for release.

If staying in the city centre with a car, find a hotel with its own parking. If your accommodation is outside the centre the public transport system provides good and frequent services to all areas. If just visiting for the day, park in the suburbs and use public transport or a taxi to travel into the centre.

By Bus Busáras, the central bus station is on Store Street. Services are operated by Dublin Bus (☎ *01 842 0000*; *www.dublinbus.ie*) and Luas (☎ *01 461 4910*; *www.luas.ie*).

Services operate from 6am (10am on Sunday) to 11.30pm with an additional late **Nightlink** service from midnight to 3am on Thursday, Friday and Saturday. Fares are based on the number of stages travelled and you must tender the exact money (in coins only) as you board, so make sure you have plenty of change.

Both companies offer **Rambler Passes**, which represent a saving against individual journey fares.

By Tram Dublin's tram network, **LUAS** (☎ *01 461 4910*;

www.luas.ie), is an alternative for getting about. The Red Line runs from Connolly Station via Busáras and Heuston Station out to the south eastern suburb of Tallaght, and the Green Line from St. Stephen's Green south to Sandyford.

Unfortunately the two systems don't connect, and although providing a handy bus link between the central bus and two train stations, it's not very convenient if you then want to travel south.

Buy tickets before boarding, either from vending machines at the stops themselves, which take credit cards, notes, coins and give change, or at certain shops. You can purchase one- and seven-day passes (the seven-day pass is also valid on the buses), which might save you money. On weekdays, the trams run between 5.30am and 00.30am, beginning a little later at weekends and with the last tram at 11.30pm on Sundays.

By DART The **Dublin Area Rapid Transport** (☎ *1850 366222*; *www.irishrail.ie*) is Dublin's underground rail system, although it stays largely in the open. The line runs between Greystones, Bray and Dún Laoghaire to the south and Howth, Malahide and Balbriggan in the north. There are three stations in the city centre: Connolly near the bus station, Pearse and Tara Street.

Obtain tickets at the station before you board and enquire about saver and family passes if you're likely to make several journeys. The frequent service

Rope Bridge

Dublin's O'Connell Bridge was originally made of rope and could carry only one person and a donkey at a time. It was replaced with a wooden structure in 1801. The current concrete bridge was built in 1863 and is the only traffic bridge in Europe that is wider than it is long.

operates Monday to Saturday between 7am and midnight and on Sundays from 9.30am until 11.30pm.

By Taxi There are taxi ranks at rail and bus stations, by the main hotels, and around the city centre. If you want to book a taxi, companies include the following:

Co-Op ☎ 01 676 6666, Shamrock Radio Cabs ☎ 01 855 5444, VIP Taxis ☎ 01 478 3333.

Seeing the Sights of Dublin

Bus Tours

We found that the open-top city bus tours are a great way for the family to get a taste of the high spots, and because they link all the main sites and you can simply get on and off the green and cream buses at any one of 20 stops, they're great for getting between the attractions you want to visit.

Dublin Bus (☎ 01 873 4222; *www.dublinbus.ie*) runs a 75-minute tour complete with entertaining commentary.

Tours *adults €14, children €6 (20% discount for on-line booking); valid for 24 hours.*

Gray Line (☎ 01 605 7705/01 458 0054; *www.girlfriday.com*)

offers a similar, slightly longer 90-minute tour of Dublin's great tourist attractions.

Tours*: adults €15, children €6 with tickets valid for 24 hours.*

Both companies – and there's little to choose between them – offer discounts and a complimentary town map.

Dublin Bus also operates a selection of themed trips, but it's a good idea to book these in advance, particularly during the summer months, at the Dublin Bus office in Upper O'Connell Street or alternatively at the Dublin Tourism Centre on Suffolk Street:

Dublin Ghost Bus

Not for the young (the under-14s or impressionable), the darker side to Dublin is explored by the spooky **Dublin Ghost Bus**, a two-and-a-quarter hour trip that unearths tales of body snatchers, glides past haunted houses and digs up Dracula's origins.

Tours *from Upper O'Connell Street Mon–Fri 8pm; weekends 7pm and 9.30pm.* **Fare** *€25.*

Viking Splash Tour

64–65 Patrick Street, Dublin 8. ☎ 01 707 6000; www.vikingsplash.com

This goes down a treat. Yelling war cries at passers by, you ride through the city streets past the main sites in a 'duck', a bullet-holed WWII landing craft, before a splashing finale back along the Grand Canal (squeals galore as the tank enters the water). Children (and adults if they wish) get to wear Viking helmets for the 75-minute tours, which leave Patrick's Street and St. Stephen's Green. Advance booking is advisable at weekends, and under-3s are not permitted on the water section.

Tours *Half-hourly departures (Feb) Wed–Sun 10am–4pm, (Mar–Oct) daily 9.30–5pm, (Nov) Tue–Sun 10am–4pm.* **Fare** *adults €20, children (under13) €10, family (2+3) €60.*

Dublin Bus North Coast & Castle Tour

Taking you farther afield is the **Dublin Bus North Coast and Castle Tour**, a three-hour trip taking in Howth and Malahide, where there's an opportunity to visit the castle included in the admission price.

Tours *daily at 10am and 2pm.* **Fare** *adults €22, children (under 14) €12 (10% discount for on-line booking).*

Gray Line, Keatings Park, Rathcoole, County Dublin (☎ 01 458 0054; www.grayline.com) also runs half- and full-day excursions throughout the year, taking in the nearby sights and beauty spots such as the Wicklow Mountains, Valleys and Lakes Tour.

Children-friendly Attractions & Entertainment

The Irish love festivals and events, and activities take place throughout the year. To check what's on during your stay, pick up the arts and entertainment magazine 'In Dublin' (€3) from newsagents, or have a look at www.dublinevents.com.

Bloomsday

On 16th June, thousands come to Dublin to re-enact the journey of Leopold Bloom as described in James Joyce's *Ulysses*. If you want to really get in the mood, kit yourselves out in striped blazers and boaters, and begin the day with a breakfast of 'liver and lights' at Sandycove before making for the city centre where readings, street theatre, music events and the ultimate costume parade are what it's all about.

The Docklands Maritime Festival

Graceful Tall Ships easing into Dublin's harbour are the centrepiece of this weekend-long gala at the beginning of June, and it's a superb sight – and one to trigger dreams of pirates. The Festival also includes music performances at various locations, and street theatre with a maritime. (☎ 01 818 3300; www.dublindocklands.ie)

St Patrick's Festival

Wander through Dublin's streets on 17th March and you'll be greeted by 'Beannachtaí Na Féle Pádraig' – Happy St Patrick's Day! The unashamedly, infectious fun lasts for a whole week with pageants, carnivals, street theatre and music. The centrepiece is a spectacular parade

Dublin Pass

With so much to see in the city, it might be worth purchasing a Dublin Pass (**www.dublinpass.ie**). It gives free entry into over thirty of the city's top attractions as well as discounts in a range of shops, restaurants, theatres and other entertainment venues. They are available online or from any of the city's Tourist Information Centres.

Prices: adult 1-day pass €31, 2-day pass €49, 3-day pass €59, 6-day pass €89; children (5–15) 1-day pass €17, 2-day pass €29, 3-day pass €34, 6-day pass €44.

through the city with bright costumes, colourful floats, bands, singing, dancing – you name it, concluding in a spectacular firework show (**www.stpatricks festival.ie**)

FAST FACTS: DUBLIN

Emergencies The emergency telephone numbers for the fire, police and ambulance are free of charge. Simply dial 999 or 112 and ask for the service you require and be able to give the location of where help is needed.

Hospitals Medical treatment for British visitors to the Republic of Ireland is covered under an agreement with the Department of Health. You will need a European Health Insurance Card (which came into effect on 1st January 2006 to replace the **E111** form) for each family member. You can get these by applying online at **www.ehic.org. uk**, or call (**0845 606 2030** or pick up a form at your local post office. However, this will only provide necessary treatment and does not cover repatriation, cancellation or the costs of extended accommodation (for example, if your child has to be hospitalised), and so it's a good idea to take out appropriate travel insurance as well the EHIC card.

Most of the larger towns and the cities have a hospital offering accident and emergency services. Within Dublin, the main hospitals are **St James's Hospital**, St James's St, Dublin 8, (**01 410 3000**, which can be found in the city centre just south east of Phoenix Park; The **Adelaide and Meath Hospital** at Tallaght, Dublin 24, (**01 414 2000**, signed from the N81 south west of the city and **St Vincent's University Hospital**, Elm Park, Dublin 4, (**01 221 4000**, which lies off the N11 to the south east of the city centre towards Dún Laoghaire.

Internet Access Many hotels throughout the country now offer Internet access, either within each room or from a general public area by reception. Internet cafes are opening in many of the larger towns and one place to get a list of these is **www.cybercafe.com**. Within the centre of Dublin, two of the main cafes are: **Central Cyber Café** on Grafton Street opposite Weirs Jewellers, ☏ *01 677 8298*, open Mon–Fri 9am–10pm, Sat and Sun 10am–9pm, and on the other side of the river, **Global Internet Café** at 8 Lower O'Connell Street, ☏ *01 878 0295*, open Mon–Fri 8am–11pm, Sat 9am–11pm and Sun 10am–11pm.

Safety Personal safety and security of possessions is no more of a problem in the Republic than in Britain. Away from the main towns and cities, crime is rarely a significant problem, but in Dublin and other large towns, particularly at night, incidents do sometimes occur. You should therefore be vigilant and exercise the same common sense precautions during your trip that you would normally observe when travelling at home. Basically don't go to places or areas that you wouldn't feel comfortable in or appropriate in your own country.

The risk of opportunist theft can be minimised by not leaving baggage unattended, locking your car, putting valuables out of sight and keeping hand and shoulder bags zipped shut. Don't carry excessive amounts of money or allow credit and cash cards to be taken away during payment transactions. Most hotels have security deposit facilities for guests.

In a strange place with a lot to see, you can become distracted and it's not always easy to keep an eye on the children. Youngsters, particularly when fascinated by something new, have a habit of wandering off, so make sure they know to keep by your side at all times. Hold onto their hands if necessary or invest in a wrist strap so that they can't stray. It's a good idea when visiting parks, museums and other places where children might go exploring on their own to show them an easily recognisable central spot where you can all go to meet up again should you become separated.

WHAT TO SEE & DO

Children's Top 10 Attractions

❶ **Meet Dracula** – if you dare – at the Bram Stoker Dracula Experience. See p. 50.

❷ **Discover Dublin's Viking History** at Dublinia and the Viking World. See p. 50.

❸ **Find out** how a middle-class 19th-century family lived at Number 29. See p. 55.

❹ **Suffer imprisonment** in the notorious Kilmainham Gaol. See p. 53.

❺ **Have fun** delving into history, art, natural history and much more in Dublin's superb National Museums. See p. 54.

❻ **Get arty** at The Ark children's cultural centre. See p. 50.

❼ **Get to know** the animals at Dublin Zoo and have a fun day in Phoenix Park. See p. 51.

⑧ Wonder at Tara's Palace and the Fry Railway Exhibition at Malahide Castle. See p. 60.

⑨ Bounce the waves in Dublin Bay on the exciting Sea Safari. See p. 56.

⑩ Be transported back to the past with vehicles at the National Transport Museum. See p. 61.

Children-friendly Attractions

The Ark ⭐⭐ ALL AGES

11A Eustace Street, Dublin 2, ☎ 01 670 7788, www.ark.ie.

Described as Europe's first custom-built children's cultural centre, The Ark runs workshops, exhibitions and concerts specifically for children. Tucked away in Temple Bar, this former Presbyterian Meeting House (1728) houses an indoor theatre, an outdoor amphitheatre, gallery spaces and workshop.

A fun, bright venue, this is chock-full of entertainment and for any given event, an advised age range is given.

Weekday sessions are usually for school groups, but there are public workshops for 3–14 year-olds on Saturdays and sometimes Sundays, and Bank Holiday Mondays. In school holidays and during the summer there are performances most days that might be based around music, story-telling or drama. Children's events during the Fringe and Dublin Writers festivals are also shown here.

Check the website for the upcoming programme and prices and it's a good idea to book in advance.

The Bram Stoker Dracula Experience ⭐ AGES 8 AND UP

Bar Code, Westwood Club, Clontarf Road, Dublin 3, ☎ 01 805 7824, www.thebramstokerdraculaexperience.com.

Born here in Clontarf in 1847 and educated at Trinity College, Bram Stoker ended up in London working as secretary to the actor Sir Henry Irving, when he wrote the world's most famous horror story. This interactive experience exploring his life and the creature he created is entertaining and educational, but above all, scary.

Open Fri 4–10pm, Sat–Sun noon–10pm. Adm adults €8.50, children €4.50.

Dublinia and the Viking World ⭐⭐ AGES 3 AND UP

St. Michael's Hill, Christchurch, Dublin 8, ☎ 01 679 4611, www.dublinia.ie.

Located in a stunning neo-Gothic Victorian building, a series of tableaux recreate something of life in Viking and medieval Dublin, complete with the sounds of fighting and smells of everyday life.

There are real-life archaeological finds on display, including the skeleton of a woman found buried near the city walls. Was she a Viking slave, perhaps?

The recreated fair features more sound effects, medicine stalls (open the drawers to see the cures), and a chance to throw balls at the man in the stocks.

Dublinia and the Viking World

The Viking World exhibition vividly tells the story of Scandinavian raids and eventual settlement; from the bloodthirsty attacks on monastic communities to the establishment of trading ports around the coast. There's a section on the language of the runes where youngsters can make a rubbing of their name, and if it's not raining, older children can climb the 96 steps to the top of the viewing tower in the adjacent St Michael's Church for a panoramic view of Dublin's medieval heart.

Open Apr–Sep daily 10am–5pm, Oct–Mar Mon–Fri 11am–4pm, Sat–Sun and bank holidays 10am–4pm. *Adm* adults €6, children €3.75, family (2+3) €16, under-5s free.

Dublin City Gallery – The Hugh Lane ★ AGES 6 AND UP

Charlemont House, Parnell Square North, Dublin 1, ☎ 01 222 5550, www.hughlane.ie.

The throngs of eager children here make it clear that this collection of modern art has a genuine appeal for youngsters.

Moved to its present location in 1933, it has become one of Ireland's most important collections of modern and contemporary art and has more than 2,000 works ranging from the French Impressionist masters – Renoir, Monet and Manet – to leading contemporary artists.

There are regular themed exhibitions, but the most appealing draw for children by far is the gallery's recent acquisition of Sir Francis Bacon's chaotic Reece Mews Studio from London. Reconstructed in its entirety it offers a fascinating insight into the artist's inspirations and the way he worked.

Open Tue–Thu 10–6pm, Fri–Sat 10–5pm, Sun 11–5pm. *Adm* (to permanent collection) free.

Dublin Zoo ★ ★ ★ ALL AGES

Phoenix Park, Dublin 8, ☎ 01 677 1425, www.dublinzoo.ie.

Ten million glasses of Guinness – the 'famous black pint' from Dublin – are produced daily all over the world.

With more than 700 species of animals and birds spread over some 59 acres in Phoenix Park, Dublin Zoo is part of a worldwide network helping to protect endangered species. The zoo undertakes research and breeding programmes for the Moluccan Cockatoo and the beautiful Golden Lion Tamarin.

You'll be pushed to see everything in a single day and separate areas explore the worlds of cats, primates, birds and reptiles, even taking you to the fringes of the Arctic and the African plains. World of Primates features the Orang-utan family, whose history reads like something from a soap opera.

In summer there are several daily 'Meet the Keeper' sessions,

Dublin Zoo

which are great for children who can't stop asking questions (weekends only in winter). You can also chat with staff at feeding times (check the information board for details as you go in, or look for signs at the enclosures). There's also a city farm, where you can pet some less exotic species.

*Open Mon–Sat from 9.30am, Sun 10.30am until around 3.30–6.30pm dependant upon time of year. **Adm** adults €14, children €6.50, under-3s free.*

GAA Museum ★ ★ AGES 5 AND UP

Croke Park, Drumcondra, Dublin 3, ☎ 01 819 2323, http://museum. gaa.ie.

Any child who loves football, or is a fan of any sport, will love the challenge of trying to hit the ball with the hurley (like a polo stick), or kick the Gaelic football over the post. Many of the exhibits are interactive, the stadium tour is a real buzz, and the novelty of standing on the pitch of a huge stadium with a capacity of nearly 90,000 gets anyone tingling. The 15-minute video at the start of the tour shows the furious pace of hurling in action, leaving football and rugby looking like soft options in comparison.

*Open July and August 9.30am–6pm Mon–Sat; rest of year Mon– Sat 9.30am–5pm, Sun 12–5pm **Adm** (museum only) adults €5.50, students/seniors € 4, under-12s €3.50, family (2+2) €15.00; (museum and*

Kilmainham Gaol

Croke Park Stadium Tour) adults €9.50, students/seniors €7, under-12s €6, family (2+2) €24.00.

Kilmainham Gaol ⭐⭐ ALL AGES

Inchicore Road, Kilmainham, Dublin 8, 📞 01 453 5984, www.heritage ireland.ie

This is where reality hits home. From 1792 until it was closed in 1924, Kilmainham was the scene of some of the blackest moments in Ireland's fight for independence. Although now empty, the audio-visual show, guided visit and exhibition give a real sense of what it was like to be imprisoned here. Leaders of successive rebellions against English rule were incarcerated in its open-view cells, and those leading the 1916 Uprising were executed here.

Open Apr–Sep, daily 9.30–5pm, Oct–Mar Mon–Sat 9.30–4pm, Sun 10–5pm Adm adults €5.30, children €2.10, family €11.50. Heritage Card.

National Botanic Gardens

⭐⭐ ALL AGES

Glasnevin, Dublin 9, 📞 01 857 0909, www.botanicgardens.ie.

Established in 1795 to promote the study of plants for food, medicine and the dyeing industry, the Botanic Gardens have grown to accommodate Ireland's leading collection of plants.

Sloping to the banks of the River Tolka, the gardens extend over 19 hectares and house more than 20,000 different species from across the world. Some of the more exotic specimens are housed in the four glasshouses, the centrepiece being the restored palm house.

Children may be amazed by the staggering variety and can explore areas demonstrating how some of the more unusual plants can grow quite happily in their own gardens.

Botanic Gardens

Open summer daily 9am–6pm, winter daily 9am–4.30pm *Adm* free, charge for car park €2.

National Gallery of Ireland ☆
AGES 6 AND UP

Merrion Square West and Clare Street, Dublin 2, ☎ 01 661 5133, *www.nationalgallery.ie.*

This is a place to introduce children, however young, to the greats of art – and might even inspire them. Discovered hanging innocuously in a Rectory in 1990, Carravagio's 'The Taking of Christ' is just one of the highlights in a collection of paintings and sculpture that includes Dutch, French and Italian masters from the past six centuries along with some splendid portraits by famous British artists such as Reynolds, Gainsborough and Hogarth.

Of course, it's the Irish paintings that hold pride of place, with a splendid exhibition from the country's most important 20th-century artist, Jack B. Yeats, brother of the poet, William Butler Yeats. You can pick up a family pack from the Millennium Wing information desk and there are family events – check the website for details.

Open Mon–Sat 9.30–5.30pm (8.30pm Thu), Sun noon–5.30pm. *Adm* to permanent collection free.

National Museums of Ireland
☆ ☆ ☆ **AGES 5 AND UP**

☎ 01 677 7444, *www.museum.ie.*

Split across three separate sites in the city, with a fourth at Castlebar in County Mayo, Ireland's national museum is a hugely diverse collection charting almost every aspect of the country's historical, cultural and natural life. The children's programme is constantly updated, making sure that youngsters stay intrigued – and informed.

The oldest part is the **Natural History** collection on Merrion Street, which covers not only native Irish wildlife but also hundreds of animal species from around the world. Skeletons of Irish deer, a basking shark, a whale and even a giraffe, are among the larger exhibits, but there are many smaller animals to attract inquisitive minds as well.

Nearby on Kildare Street is the **Archaeology and History** building, which houses a collection of artefacts tracing the settlement of Ireland from the Bronze Age including some extraordinary Celtic objects in gold.

Beautiful treasures from the Great Age of Christianity include the recently restored Tully Lough Cross, plus later Viking finds. A range of hands-on experience, interactive activities and multimedia packages are available to help you explore the vast collection.

The **Museum of Decorative Arts and History** is across the river towards Phoenix Park on Benburb Street and contains an eclectic range of objects from costume to coinage and weaponry to porcelain.

A programme of special exhibitions and events runs throughout the year and free themed family tours are occasionally offered. Call in advance for

Nursery at No 29 House Museum

details of any that coincide with your trip.

Open *Tue–Sat 10–5pm, Sun 2–5pm.* **Adm** *free.*

National Wax Museum ★ ★ ★
ALL AGES

Grafton Street, Dublin 2, ☎ *01 872 6340.*

Famous figures from Madonna and Michael Jackson to the scene of da Vinci's 'Last Supper' sit alongside a World of Fairytale and Fantasy where children can search for the genie's magic lamp.

Open *Mon–Fri 10–5pm, Sat 10–2pm.* **Adm** *free.*

Number 29 ★ ★ AGES 3 AND UP

29 Lower Fitzwilliam Street, Dublin 2, ☎ *01 702 6165.*

This elegant four-storey house stands at the heart of the fashionable Georgian quarter and children can get a feel for the era thanks to the colourful tour describing typical middle-class family life. Going from the basement through to the attic, the rooms have retained original artefacts since 1800.

The house was first occupied by the widow of a prominent local wine merchant, so this really is how the middle class lived. Young visitors are fascinated by the toys displayed in the nursery, tucked away at the top of the house. Highlights are two early 19th-century dolls houses complete with miniature furniture, a far cry from today's gizmos. And of course no well-to-do family would be complete without a governess teaching them needlepoint.

The comforts are in sharp contrast to the poverty and deprivation suffered by the poor existing at the other end of town, related in the introductory video.

Open *Tue–Sat 10–5pm, Sun 2–5pm.* **Adm** *adults €3.50, children free.*

Phoenix Park ★ ★ ★ ALL AGES

Once a royal hunting estate established under Charles II,

Trinity College

Phoenix Park is the largest urban park in Europe, and a magnet for rollerbladers. Its forests and open grasslands extend over 712 hectares and fallow deer roam wild in the woods.

The city's green lung, it's a popular place of recreation for Dubliners, with flower gardens, a range of sports pitches hosting polo and cricket matches most weekends – weather permitting – and miles of paths and formal tree-lined avenues to explore.

Ashtown Castle, a restored medieval tower house, is the oldest building in the park, right next to the Visitor Centre (see below). The Irish president's home is based here too, as is Dublin Zoo (see p. 51).

Phoenix Park Visitor Centre
ALL AGES

Phoenix Park, Dublin 8, 📞 *01 677 0095, www.heritageireland.ie.*

Near Ashtown Gate, this centre offers an audio-visual presentation on the park's history from the Bronze Age to the present day, with displays on the Viking grave discovered here plus a hugely enjoyable guided tour of the ancient castle. There's also an interactive wildlife section for youngsters and a decent café.

Open Nov–mid-Mar, Sat–Wed 10–5pm, mid-Mar–end Mar and Oct, daily 10–5.30pm, Apr–Sep, daily 10–6pm. Adm adults €3, children €1.50, family €7.50. Heritage Card.

Sea Safari ★ ★ ★ AGES 8 AND UP

Dublin City Moorings, Custom House Quay, Dublin 1, 📞 *01 855 7600, www. seasafari.ie.*

Book online, by phone or from the Dublin Tourist Offices for this hour-long trip on a rigid inflatable in Dublin Bay. It combines adventure and high speed thrills with magnificent scenery and the chance to see something of the coastal bird and wildlife.

The boats take you past the lighthouses and around the islands of the Skerries, Lambay, and Irelands Eye, with dolphins,

porpoises and seals regularly sighted.

Trips daily throughout the year, dependent on weather and demand, advance booking essential. **Price** adults €30. Not suitable for under-8s.

Trinity College Library ★
ALL AGES

College Street, Dublin 2, 📞 *01 896 1661, www.tcd.ie.*

Founded by Queen Elizabeth I in 1592, Trinity College houses the 'Book of Kells', which takes its name from Abbey of Kells in County Meath, its home in the Middle Ages. The significance of this beautifully illuminated manuscript completed in 800 AD, often eludes visitors, especially young ones. To get the most out of a visit do a little prepping first, for example using *www.bookofkells.com*, looking at the pictures and discussing who might have painted them, and why.

Open Mon–Sat 9.30–5pm, Sun (May–Sep) 9.30–4.30pm, (Oct–Apr) noon–4.30pm. **Adm** adults €8, children (under 12) free, family (2+4) €16.

Activities & Entertainment

Beaches

Not many capital cities have splendid beaches on their doorstep, but Dublin does. There are several fine stretches to choose from, particularly at Howth and Malahide to the north, and Sandycove at Dún Laoghaire, where the beach is backed by a fine promenade.

Theatre

Lambert Puppet Theatre and Museum ★ ★ **ALL AGES**

5 Clifton Lane, Monkstown, County Dublin, 📞 *01 280 0974, www. lambertpuppettheatre.com.*

More than just Punch and Judy, there are shows here every weekend, usually of popular fairy stories with the occasional Oscar Wilde children's tale thrown in. For the last 35 years all puppets have been handmade on site by the Lambert family and the theatre is also the venue for September's International Puppet Festival. After the show, visit the museum's permanent collection of puppets from around the world. There's also a shop where you can buy a whole range of different puppets and marionettes, plus videotapes of some of the shows.

Open Shows daily (May–Jun) and weekends during the rest of the year. **Adm** adults €12.50, children €9.50.

Walking

You don't have to leave the city to find great places to walk. Phoenix Park has miles of quiet woodland paths and tracks, or you can wander the towpaths beside the Grand Canal and Royal Canal. Farther afield from the top of Dalkey Hill, there are fine views of Killiney Bay and inland to the Wicklow Mountains.

To the south there's an enjoyable cliff-top walk from Bray across the headland to Greystones, the DART providing

a convenient link between the two places.

Horse Riding

You'll never get all round Phoenix Park in a day on foot, but you stand a better chance on horse-back. The family-run **Ashtown Riding Stables** (☎ *01 838 3807*; open daily 9.30am–5pm), is right next to the park on Navan Road, and offers scenic treks through the woodland for all ages and ability levels.

Days Out from Dublin

Reached by the DART, the pretty seaside village of Howth sits on the northern cusp of Dublin Bay overlooking a fine stretch of beach and a harbour where children can spend hours watching the comings and goings of fishing boats.

If you're feeling energetic, the walk on to the rugged **Howth** Head is recommended, for the views north over the Eye of Ireland and to the distant Wicklow Mountains.

At the northern terminus of the DART is the attractive sea-side village of Malahide, also known for its splendid sandy beaches and an historic (and haunted) castle set in extensive parkland. To the south the DART passes through the ferry harbour town of Dún Laoghaire along a beautiful stretch of coast known as the 'Irish Riviera' through Bray to Greystones.

Airfield House & Farm ★ ★
ALL AGES

Upper Kilmacud Road, Dundrum,
☎ *01 298 4301.*

In the mid-town suburb of Dundrum, this gorgeous farm cottage built in the 1820s has been updated as an urban farm with a wonderful café. A good all-weather option, there are year-round activities, opportuni-ties to meet the goats, geese and cows, and flower-filled grounds that are good for picnics.

A small Car Museum has vin-tage vehicles belonging to two feisty sisters who lived in the house, including a 1923 Peugeot and 1927 Rolls Royce. It's excel-lent value and will take half a day if the weather is good.

Open *Tue–Sat 10am–5pm, Sun and bank holidays 11am–5pm.* **Adm** *adults 6€, children 3€, family 18€.*

Dalkey Castle ★ **ALL AGES**

Castle Street, Dalkey, County Dublin
☎ *01 285 8366, www.dalkeycastle.com.*

With spectacular views from the tower to the mountains and across the bay to Dalkey Island, Dalkey Castle was the medieval port for Dublin and had seven 15th-century tower houses where the cargoes from incoming ships were taken for safe keeping. One of them, Goat Castle, was used during the Victorian period as a meeting room for the Town Commissioners. It now contains a heritage centre that tells the history of the port, including strange tales such as the Dalkey Gold Rush.

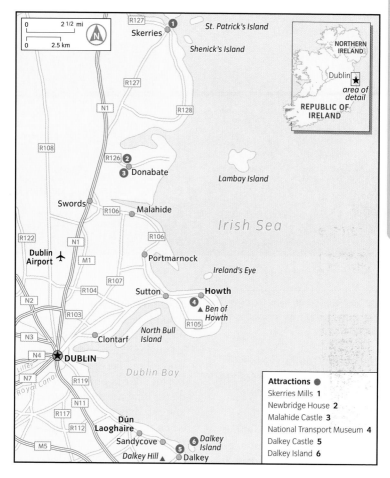

Attractions ●

Skerries Mills **1**
Newbridge House **2**
Malahide Castle **3**
National Transport Museum **4**
Dalkey Castle **5**
Dalkey Island **6**

Open Mon–Fri 9.30am–5pm, Sat, Sun and bank holidays 11am–5pm. **Adm** adults €6, children €4, family €16.

The Fry Model Railway ★★

ALL AGES

Malahide, Co Dublin.

In the grounds of Malahide Castle is the Fry Model Railway, one of the largest in the world. It was begun in the 1920s by Cyril Fry, a railway engineer who painstakingly assembled these beautifully crafted scale replicas of engines and rolling stock. Tracing the development of Irish railways from 1834 right up to the DART, the track layout covers some 232 square metres and has the River Liffey at its heart. Stations, tunnels, bridges, buildings and countryside add to the realism.

Open Apr–Sep Mon–Thu and Sat 10am–1pm and 2–5pm, Sun and bank holidays 2–6pm. **Adm** adults

Coliemore Harbour at Dalkey

€7, children €4.40, family €20 or combined ticket with Malahide Castle.

Malahide Castle ⭐ ALL AGES

Malahide, Co Dublin, 📞 *01 846 2184; www.malahidecastle.com.*

No castle is really complete without a ghost or two, but at Malahide you get your money's worth with five. The oldest, Sir Walter Hussey, was killed in battle on his wedding day, and is followed by his wife and her third husband, whom she chases around the bedrooms at night. Next is Miles Corbet, who was granted the castle during the Roundhead occupation of Ireland, but in punishment for desecrating the castle chapel, was hanged, drawn and quartered when the estate returned to the Talbots at the Restoration. Chance upon him in a dark corner and he will fall into four pieces before your very eyes. Finally, from the 16th century is

MOMENTS 》 Dalkey Island 《

A bare 300 metres from the land is Dalkey Island. Deserted today, archaeological excavation has revealed traces of Bronze Age and Viking settlements, though the current ruins are of a small 7th-century church dedicated to St Begnet and a 'Martello' tower built in 1804 as part of the defences against a Napoleonic invasion. Now the island's only inhabitants are a herd of goats and ubiquitous rabbits, while seals bob in the water offshore. It can be reached by rowing boat from the small harbour.

Not so Fun Fact <<

On the morning of the Battle of the Boyne in 1690, 14 members of the Talbot family breakfasted together in the Great Hall of Malahide Castle. All 14 were dead by nightfall!

Puck, a love-lorn jester, who vowed to haunt the castle until its lord took a commoner for his bride.

Originally a moated defensive Norman tower house, Malahide Castle also features superb period furnishings spanning the 17th–19th centuries.

You can get children interested in Malahide's story by pre-downloading a podcast that guides you round Malahide Castle from *www.visitdublin.com*. Once downloaded, copy to an mp3 player and do your own thing when you visit the castle.

Open Apr–Sept Mon–Sat 10am–5pm, Sun and bank holidays 10am–6pm, Oct–Mar Mon–Sat 10am–5pm, Sun and bank holidays 11am–5pm. *Adm* adults €7, children (under 12) €4.40, family (2+3) €20 or combined ticket with Fry Model Railway.

National Transport Museum
⭐ ⭐ ALL AGES

Heritage Depot, Howth Demesne, Howth, County Dublin, 📞 01 832 0427, *www.nationaltransport museum.org*.

Home to around 160 commercial, public service and military vehicles, this is the most comprehensive transport collection in the country, with about 60 vehicles on show. A highlight for children is the 1883 horse-drawn Merryweather firefighter,

though the buses, including Routemasters, go down well too. There's also a great assembly of trams as well as military personnel carriers that did duty during World War II. Less romantic, but just as necessary are vehicles that carried sludge and emptied cesspits.

Open Sep–May Sun, bank holidays and 26 Dec–1 Jan 2–5pm, Jun–Aug Mon–Sat 10am–5pm. *Adm* adults €3, children €1.25, family €8.

Newbridge House and Farm
⭐ ALL AGES

Donabate, County Dublin, 📞 01 843 6534.

Across the estuary to the north, the centrepiece of the Newbridge Demesne Regional Park is Newbridge House. A superb Georgian mansion built in 1737 by Archbishop Charles Cobbe. The Red Drawing Room features a beautiful white marble chimney piece and rococo plaster ceiling attributed to William Stuccoman.

Children however might prefer the family museum, which contains curiosities collected by the family on their travels, and the kitchen where they can have fun trying to decide what some of the utensils were used for.

The courtyard contains a blacksmith's forge, carpenter's shop, dairy and working horse stables, and the property's working farm is stocked with animals of the period.

Open Apr–Sep Tue–Sat 10am–1pm and 2–5pm, Sun and bank holidays 2–6pm, Oct–Mar Sat, Sun and bank holidays 12–5pm. **Adm** (house) adults €6.50, children (under 12) €3.70, family (2+2) €17.50; (farm) adult €3.50, children (under 12) € 2.50, family (2+2) €10.50.

Tara's Palace ★ ★ ALL AGES

Malahide, Co Dublin, ☎ 01 846 3779.

Part of the Malahide Castle estate, and inspired by Sir Neville Wilkinson's Titania's Palace, which he built in 1907 for his daughter Gwendoline, Tara's Palace is a masterpiece. Located in the castle courtyard, it's the centrepiece of a unique collection of antique toys that also includes 'Portobello' one of the earliest doll's houses to survive. Based on one of Ireland's greatest 18th-century mansions, its private apartments and grand staterooms are meticulously furnished with miniature replicas of antique furniture and masterpiece paintings.

Open Apr–Sep Mon–Thu and Sat 10am–1pm and 2–5pm, Sun and bank holidays 2–6pm. **Adm** €2.

FAMILY-FRIENDLY ACCOMMODATION

Dublin Tourism (☎ 01 605 7700; www.visitdublin.com) offers a full accommodation service and has a comprehensive listing of all types of establishment from

self-catering and bed and breakfast to luxury hotel. Moreover, if you keep checking the daily updated website you'll discover worthwhile special offers for short breaks in the city.

The hotels listed below are a selection specifically offering facilities for families.

EXPENSIVE

The Clarence ★ ★ ★

6-8 Wellington Quay, Dublin 2, ☎ 01 407 0800; www.theclarence.ie.

Hip and award-winning, but truly child-friendly too – what more could you ask?

Overlooking the River Liffey on the edge of the Temple Bar area of town this is genuine luxury, owned by Bono and The Edge of the Irish rock group U2, whose rock lifestyle has doubtless inspired much of what is on offer, with elegant comfort and attention to detail throughout. They go out of their way to make younger guests welcome, with 'Clarence Kids Cocktails', special gifts, Playstation and family movies. For mums-to-be, check out the special packages offered at www.baby-moon.eu.

Rooms 43 superior and deluxe double rooms, 3 one and two bedroom suites, 1 junior suite and 1 Penthouse suite (two bedrooms). **Rates** (room only) from €350–2600 if you want the Penthouse Suite. Full breakfast €27.50, Continental €20.50, extra bed or cot free of charge for children under 12. **Credit** all major cards accepted. **Amenities** 24-hour room service, 24-hour laundry and dry

The Clarence Hotel

cleaning, treatment room for massage, disabled access, wireless Internet access in all public hotel areas, Children's VIP gifts (Clarence Donkey for up to 12s or Clarence baseball cap for up to 16s), 'Clarence Kids Cocktails' (non-alcoholic) on arrival, Playstation, family movies, milk and cookies on turndown for 3–12 years, early turndown for younger children, baby-changing facilities in public areas, highchairs, children's menu and activity pack in restaurant, cot, bottle steriliser, baby bath, baby monitor, bottle warmer, babysitting services – charged per hour. **In Room** *fully interactive TV and entertainment system, with high-speed broadband Internet/email access (€20 for 24 hours unlimited access), latest films (€7.50 per movie for 24 hours) and music (€6 for 24 hours), DVD/CD player, safe (large enough for a laptop), stereos (in the suites only).*

EXPENSIVE

Radisson SAS St Helen's Hotel ★★★

Stillorgan Road, Dublin 4, ☏ *01 218 6000, www.dublin.radissonsas.com.*

One of Ireland's most important historic houses, in formal gardens surrounded by established woodland, doesn't sound like the place to take children. But the considerable elegance of this 5-star luxury hotel belies its very real welcome for younger guests.

Despite its location on the main southern road into the city the hotel is very peaceful, making it a perfect place to begin (or end) your visit to Ireland. And there's everything you might hope for, from light meals, afternoon teas in the ballroom lounge and Orangerie Bar, to the excellent Talavera Italian Restaurant in the basement, a draw in its own right. There are also facilities such as a fitness room and even snooker.

Rooms 151. **Rates** double from €250. **Credit** all major credit cards accepted. **Amenities** guest parking, snooker room, fitness room, inter-connecting rooms. **In room** tea/coffee-making facilities, in-room safe, iron/ironing board, PC modem line, cable and sat TV and 24-hour room service.

EXPENSIVE-MODERATE

Jurys Inn ★★

The **Jurys Inn** group has nine hotels in the city, ranging from luxury (the Ballsbridge Hotel on Pembroke Road, for example, *www.jurysdoyle.com*) to more moderately priced accommodation including the three 3-star hotels, mentioned below. Predictable but comfortable family rooms can accommodate 2 adults and 2 children, and there are restaurants on the premises if you don't want to go out again for an evening meal.

Room rates are from around €100 per night.

Custom House

Custom House Quay, Dublin 1, ☎ 01 607 5000; www.jurys-dublin-hotels. com.

Overlooking the River Liffey, the hotel is only a couple of minutes walk from the Busáras and Connolly station, and near the main shopping areas.

Christchurch

Christchurch Place, Dublin 8, ☎ 01 454 0000; www.jurys-dublin-hotels. com.

Right in the city centre opposite Christchurch Cathedral, this is close to many of the attractions including Temple Bar, the cathedrals and Trinity College.

Parnell Street

Moore Street Plaza, Parnell Street, Dublin 1, ☎ 01 878 4900; www.jurys-dublin-hotels.com.

By O'Connell Street on the north side of the river, this hotel is close to the main shopping district of Henry Street and the theatre area.

CAFÉS & FAMILY-FRIENDLY DINING

Dublin has a great reputation for food, and there's no shortage of places to eat, with everything on offer from fast food to a leisurely dinner.

INEXPENSIVE

Captain America's Cookhouse ★★

AMERICAN DINER CUISINE

Grafton Court, 44 Grafton Street, Dublin 2, ☎ 01 671 5266; www. captainamericas.com

A wacky kind of place – something of a rock and roll institution – this diner has wall-to-wall music, and children love its noisy chaos. It's a bit less frantic at lunchtime than in the early evening. Pampers to children's junk food whims with burgers, pasta and American dishes.

Open daily noon–midnight. **Main courses** €6.95–14.95. **Credit** V, MC. **Amenities** activity sheets and

FUN FACT ⟫ **U2 Buskers** ⟪

Ireland's most famous rockers, U2, started out busking for small change on Grafton Street. Did they eat in Bewley's, perhaps?

crayons for the children, children's menu, highchairs, and, sometimes, a clown on Sundays.

INEXPENSIVE

Leo Burdock ★★
FISH AND CHIPS

2 Werburgh Street, Dublin 8, 📞 01 454 0306.

With a reputation as the best fish and chip shop in town, Leo Burdock is patronised by everyone from the rich and famous to visiting families. You may have to queue, but the portions are generous. As it's only a take-away, you'll have to find a nearby bench on which to sit and eat.

Open Mon–Sat noon–midnight, Sun 4pm–midnight.

INEXPENSIVE–MODERATE

Bewley's Café ★★
PIZZA AND PASTA

78 Grafton Street, Dublin 2, 📞 01 635 5470; www.bewleyscafe.com.

Bewley's has become a Dublin institution and serves everything from a hearty breakfast onwards, and even throws in lunchtime drama and an evening cabaret.

For a snack visit the Mezzanine where you can watch the world go by on Grafton Street while tucking into tea and delicious cakes. The Café Bar Deli serves pastas, pizzas and salads,

or you might try something from the fish menu in the Mackerel.

Open daily 7.30am–11pm. **Main courses** €6.96–10.95. **Credit** V, MC. **Amenities** highchairs available.

INEXPENSIVE–MODERATE

Bad Ass Café ★
BURGERS AND PASTA

9 Crown Alley, Temple Bar, Dublin 2, 📞 01 671 2596; www.badasscafe. com

The wide range of dishes in this diner-style eatery includes chicken wings, homemade burgers, and pastas served with tasty, fresh salads. The singer Sinéad O'Connor used to be a waitress here.

Open daily, 11.30am–midnight. **Main courses** €6.95–14.95. **Credit** V, MC. **Amenities** children's menu, baby-changing facilities, highchairs.

MODERATE

The Church ★★ VALUE
MODERN IRISH

Former St. Mary's Church Junction of Mary Street and Jervis Street, 📞 01 828 0102; www.thechurch.ie.

You could spend all day here, and the children would love it, especially the Cellar Bar and Café, which dishes up salads, seafood, burgers, frittata and beef fillet – good quality and good value. Try the baked fish pie, fresh salmon, and prime Irish beef fillet.

The place is separated into a long, sleek pewter bar on the ground floor, two basement café-bars, and a dramatic choir-gallery restaurant with original stained-glass windows and pipe organ as the focal point. A simple space by day, it becomes altogether more atmospheric at night.

Music is eclectic: a classical string trio plays Saturday afternoons, a resident DJ spins records until late Friday and Saturday nights, and live bands perform on Sundays from 6pm.

Food served Mon–Sat noon–10pm, Sun 12.30–8pm. **Main courses** €9.95–23.95. **Credit** V, MC. **Amenities** children's menu.

MODERATE

Ouzo's Ranelagh ★ ★ ★ FIND
VALUE **SEAFOOD**

1 Sandford Road, Ranelagh, Dublin 6, ☏ 01 491 2253; www.ouzos.ie. Also at 11 Upper Baggot Street, Dublin 4, ☏ 01 667 3279.

When this restaurant opened in the increasingly boho Ranelagh, the owners decided to ensure they served only the best seafood and bought their own fishing boats, based in Dingle Bay, to catch it before racing it across country for same day freshness.

Arrive before 7pm any day or Sunday for the Great Crab and Lobster Feast, two courses of seafood heaven – seafood chowder, crab claws, crab cakes, skewers of lobster and shrimp, sirloin

with crab claws. If you miss that, there's always a catch of the day or big pots of mussels with fresh bread or lobster and crab salad.

You can do advance research on the website, which is packed with fascinating fish facts, and they expect children to participate with the Kid's Menu including lobster chops, crab cakes, chargrilled sirloin, tagliatelle carbonara, and sausage and chips, just in case.

Their advice? Never stop a child from playing with their food – he or she could be the next Gordon Ramsey. And children – Santa will come even if you don't eat your dinner.

Food served noon–late (lunch menu only at Baggot Street). **Main courses** €9.95–24.95. **Credit** V, MC. **Amenities** children's menu.

MODERATE

Botticelli ★ ★ ITALIAN

3 Temple Bar, Dublin 2, ☏ 01 672 7289.

This highly regarded Italian restaurant serves an array of pastas and pizzas as well as chicken and meat dishes, and interesting vegetarian options too. Homemade bread and colourful salads accompany the food, and to finish, children will probably want to try a little of everything from the ice cream parlour next door.

Open from lunchtime onwards. **Main courses** €7.95–13.95. **Credit** V, MC. **Amenities** children's menu, highchairs.

4 The East Coast: Louth, Meath & Wicklow

EAST COAST IRELAND

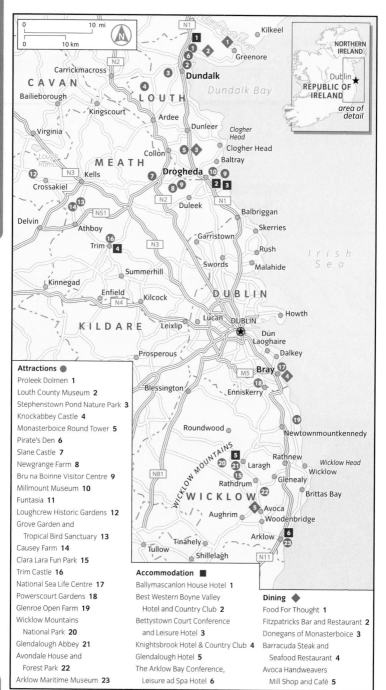

Attractions ●

Proleek Dolmen **1**
Louth County Museum **2**
Stephenstown Pond Nature Park **3**
Knockabbey Castle **4**
Monasterboice Round Tower **5**
Pirate's Den **6**
Slane Castle **7**
Newgrange Farm **8**
Bru na Boinne Visitor Centre **9**
Millmount Museum **10**
Funtasia **11**
Loughcrew Historic Gardens **12**
Grove Garden and
  Tropical Bird Sanctuary **13**
Causey Farm **14**
Clara Lara Fun Park **15**
Trim Castle **16**
National Sea Life Centre **17**
Powerscourt Gardens **18**
Glenroe Open Farm **19**
Wicklow Mountains
  National Park **20**
Glendalough Abbey **21**
Avondale House and
  Forest Park **22**
Arklow Maritime Museum **23**

Accommodation ■

Ballymascanlon House Hotel **1**
Best Western Boyne Valley
  Hotel and Country Club **2**
Bettystown Court Conference
  and Leisure Hotel **3**
Knightsbrook Hotel & Country Club **4**
Glendalough Hotel **5**
The Arklow Bay Conference,
  Leisure ad Spa Hotel **6**

Dining ◆

Food For Thought **1**
Fitzpatricks Bar and Restaurant **2**
Donegans of Monasterboice **3**
Barracuda Steak and
  Seafood Restaurant **4**
Avoca Handweavers
  Mill Shop and Café **5**

The east coast of Ireland is about the outdoors, with the carefree pleasures of the seaside, fine beaches and bubbly resorts. Alternatively try the rather less frenetic whaleback Wicklow Mountains, a grand theatre for outdoor exploration from strenuous hill-walking to gentle strolls through woodland filled with birdsong. Or there's more of the same on the Cooley Peninsula, a neck of land that gazes across Carlingford Lough to the Mourne Mountains, and even closer to Dublin along the coast path around Bray Head.

Looking out across the Irish Sea, the counties of Louth, Meath and Wicklow, together with Co Dublin, form the eastern seaboard of the Republic. Between the more mountainous areas of Wicklow in the south and the Cooley Peninsula in the north, the high ground backing the coast is broken by the rivers Liffey and Boyne, natural passageways to inner Ireland.

This 'gateway' has attracted settlers and conquerors for centuries, all of whom have left their stamp, and a legacy that includes some of Ireland's most outstanding prehistoric sites. Not least among these are the 5,000-year old passage grave complex at Newgrange, and many monastic sites founded by the Celtic monks in the 5th and 6th centuries. At Trim, you'll find the largest Anglo-Norman castle in the country, whereas upriver from Drogheda at Oldbridge, signboards help interpret the action between the opposing armies of James II and his son in law, the future William III, at the site of the infamous Battle of the Boyne.

ESSENTIALS

Getting There

By Sea The ferry ports of Dublin and Dún Laoghaire are central to the area, but Belfast provides an alternative way in to Ireland, particularly if you intend to visit Louth or Meath. Likewise, to the south, Rosslare is well-placed for visitors to Wicklow.

By Air The nearest airport is Dublin, to which there are frequent flights from most British and all Irish airports (see Chapter 2).

VISITOR INFORMATION

There are websites covering the whole region, and at a number of differing levels: see in particular *www.eastcoastmidlands.ie* and *www.ireland.ie*. Within the individual counties, check out *www.louthholidays.com*, *www.meath.ie/tourism* and *www.visitwicklow.ie*.

The main Tourist Information Offices are found at:

Louth

Drogheda Tourist Information Office, Drogheda, Co Louth.
📞 *041 983 7070*; *www.drogheda.ie*

Dundalk Tourist Office, Dundalk, Co Louth. ☏ 042 933 5484.

Carlingford, Cooley Peninsula Tourist Office, Old Dispensary, Co Louth. ☏ 042 937 3033; *www.carlingford.ie*

Meath

Brú na Bóinne Visitor Centre, Donore, Co Meath. ☏ 041 988 0305.

Kells Tourist Office, Kells Heritage Centre, Navan Road, Kells. ☏ 046 924 7840.

Trim Visitor Centre (seasonal), Castle Street, Trim, Co Meath. ☏ 046 943 7227.

Wicklow

Wicklow Tourist Information Office, Rialto House, Fitzwilliam Square, Wicklow Town, Co Wicklow. ☏ 0404 69117; *www.visitwicklow.ie*

Arlkow Tourist Information (seasonal), The Coach House, Arklow, Co Wicklow. ☏ 040 232 484.

ORIENTATION

Dundalk, Co Louth, is 90km (56 miles) N of Dublin, 244km (152 miles) N of Rosslare, and 82km (51 miles) S of Belfast.

Navan, Co Meath is 55km (34 miles) NW of Dublin, 196km (122 miles) N of Rosslare, and 139km (86 miles) S of Belfast.

Wicklow Town is 46km (29 miles) S of Dublin, 100km (62 miles) N of Rosslare, and 227km (141 miles) S of Belfast.

Louth, Meath and Wicklow all boast fine beaches, and proximity to Dublin makes them popular weekend destinations for Dubliners as well as visiting tourists.

Getting Around

Exploring the east coast, as with most places in Ireland, is best done by car, which gives far greater flexibility. The major north–south route through the region follows the coast from Dundalk through Dublin to Arklow. National roads radiate from Dublin and divide Meath like slices of pie; at the time of writing (2007) a motorway is under construction along the course of the N3 towards Kells. Elsewhere, particularly through the Wicklow Mountains, the road network consists of quiet lanes between the villages. It's fun to drive these ancient highways, but they were not built with tourists in mind, and do feature sudden twists and turns.

INSIDER TIP ⟩⟩

On car journeys across Ireland, get young children to keep an eye out for farm animals, feral ponies and birds; simple diversions have the ability to reduce wall-to-wall in-car bickering.

Bus Éireann runs services from Dublin to the main towns, with a link across the border to

The Saga of Táin Bó Cuailgne

One of Ireland's greatest legends is rooted in the landscape; the epic saga of Táin Bó Cuailgne, in which Queen Maeve of Connaught sent her armies to capture the great Brown Bull of Cooley. A cycling trail traces the sites of the many ferocious battles that took place, culminating in the tragic single combat between Cúchulainn and his lifelong friend Ferdia. Maeve had bewitched Ferdia to do battle on her behalf, but when Cúchulainn finally slew him in the River Dee after three days of fighting, the water ran with tears as well as blood.

Belfast (☏ 01 836 6111; *www. buseireann.ie*). If you are sticking to the coast, Irish Rail, (☏ 01 836 6222; *www.irishrail.ie*) operates useful services north from Dublin through Dundalk and across the border. To the south, the line runs to Wicklow before describing an inland curve via Rathdrum to Arklow. However, unless you intend to stay in just one spot, a car is the only realistic way to get about. If you arrive by air, you'll find all the main car rental companies at Dublin Airport.

Discover the Counties

Louth

Occupying the coastal margin between the River Boyne at Drogheda and the Cooley Peninsula, Louth is the smallest of Ireland's counties, and duly dubbed the 'Wee County'. Where the land gathers in a mountainous tongue containing Dundalk Bay the scenery is at its most dramatic and wild.

The towns of Drogheda and Dundalk stand at opposite ends of the county and have imaginative museums, and at Millmount there's a superb view over Drogheda from the top of the Martello Tower.

The town trail in the attractive old town of Carlingford, overlooking the lough, links its many medieval buildings.

Inland, the woodland walks, lake and children's playground of Stephenstown Pond nature park (see p. 75) make a great family day out, while quiet lanes offer stress-free cycling or horse riding.

Meath

Meath is rich in ancient sites, and a heritage trail, available from the tourist office, leads you along the Boyne Valley to places at the root of Ireland's history. The awe-inspiring passage graves at Brú na Bóinne (see p. 75) and Loughcrew, the massive castle at Trim (see p. 82) and the atmospheric monastic site of Kells are all awe-inspiring.

Of the three counties, Meath has the shortest stretch of coastline but size isn't everything and

With over 65km of coastline, there is no shortage of places to spend time by the sea. Particularly noteworthy are the Blue Flag beaches at Templetown on the Cooley Peninsula and Clougherhead, not far north of Drogheda.

there are splendid beaches fronting the holiday resort of Bettystown and at Laytown.

Wicklow

Wicklow, known as the 'Garden of Ireland', rises over 915m from the sea into a rugged mountain chain that dominates the county. Much of it is within the **Wicklow Mountains National Park**, an area of outstanding scenic beauty. Deep glens cut into the wild heath and bog of the rounded uplands, introducing a softer landscape of woodlands, sparkling streams and crystal lakes that offer superb opportunities for walking and wildlife watching.

For a spectacular car journey, take a route over Sally Gap and Wicklow Gap, two of the highest road passes in the country. Other sights not to miss in the park are the monastic settlement at Glendalough (see p. 80) and the Powerscourt Estate (see p. 81), where a pleasant walk leads to a popular beauty spot beneath Ireland's highest waterfall.

Wicklow's coastline takes some beating and there are Blue Flag beaches at Arklow and Greystones, the latter accessible by DART from Dublin.

Children-friendly Events & Entertainment

INSIDER TIP >>

If you are planning to stay in a town or village for a few days, get the local newspaper; that's where you'll find what's happening, and when.

Kells Summer Festival

Kells, Co Meath, 📞 *046 924 0683;* **www.kellsfestivals.com**

The summer festival at Kells lasts for five full days in July, with music, comedy and drama events every day plus fireworks displays, fancy dress and fairground amusements.

Rathdrum Fireworks Festival

Rathdrum, Co Wicklow, 📞 *040 446 262.*

Each August, musical entertainment in the town's Market Square precedes a sparkling evening firework display in the Parnell Memorial Park.

Greystones Arts Festival

Greystones, Co Wicklow, 📞 *01 287 6466;* **www.greystonesartsfestival. com**.

Street theatre, music and comedy are just some of the events packed into the weekend August festival at Greystones. Keep an eye open for the silver Sau'rusus that communicate through noisy, incomprehensible sounds, filled with both rhythm and humour. The colourful costumes and workshops are great: learn how to stilt walk, play an Irish drum, hip hop or belly dance. But be sure to stay for the dazzling fireworks display at the end of the day.

Moynalty Steam Threshing

Moynalty, Kells, Co Meath, ☏ 046 924 4390; www.community.meath.ie/ moynaltysteamthreshing.

This festival with a difference celebrates country life of a bygone era and centres around the traditional harvesting and threshing of a crop of oats using horse and steam power. Displays of vintage farm equipment and rural crafts form the heart of the festival, but there's also plenty of traditional Irish food cooked on open fires. Watch butter being churned, or learn about spinning, basketry, woodturning, tin smithing and more. There's a water wheel on the river and a thatched house on the hill. Sparks fly at the forge where the anvil rings as the blacksmith shapes iron to shoe horses.

WHAT TO SEE & DO

Children's Top 10 Attractions

❶ **Discover the 5,000-year old Neolithic tombs** of Brú na Bóinne. See p. 75.

❷ **Look for wildlife** in the Wicklow National Park. See p. 72.

❸ **Let your inhibitions go** and be Irish for the day with the Murtagh family at the Causey Farm. See p. 76.

❹ **Gaze upon Ireland's highest waterfall** at the Powerscourt Estate. See p. 81.

❺ **Explore the passage grave** of Loughcrew. See p. 77.

❻ **See Ireland's biggest Norman castle** at Trim. See p. 82.

❼ **Find out about** Wicklow's sea-going heritage at the Arklow Maritime Museum. See p. 79.

❽ **Soak up the lonely atmosphere** of St Kevin's monastic settlement at Glendalough. See p. 80.

❾ **Meet the animals** at Glenroe Open Farm. See p. 80.

❿ **Come face to face** with creatures from the deep at the National Sea Life Centre. See p. 81.

Children-friendly Attractions

Louth

County Museum ★★
AGES 3 AND UP

Jocelyn Street, Dundalk, Co Louth, ☏ 042 932 7056; www.dundalktown. ie/dundalktown/museo1.htm.

The sometimes-turbulent story of Louth since the Stone Age is told in this celebrated museum set in a restored 18th-century warehouse, where treasures and artefacts are displayed in three separate galleries. A favourite exhibit with children is a bubble car, designed by the German aircraft manufacturer Heinkel and produced here in Dundalk during the 1960s. A small cinema, which also doubles as a concert venue during the summer, shows a short film on the archaeology and history of the area.

Open May–Sep Mon–Sat 10.30am–5.30pm, Oct–Apr Tue–Sat 10.30am–5.30pm, Sun and bank holidays all year 2–6pm. **Adm** adults €3.80, children €2.50, family €10.15. **Credit** V, MC. **Amenities** disabled access, public toilets, parking, picnic area.

Knockabbey Castle and Garden ★ ALL AGES

Louth Village, Co Louth, ☎ 01 677 8816; www.knockabbeycastle.com. N of Tallanstown along R171.

This 14th-century castle used to be a simple tower house, but has been extended and embellished over the years to create a magnificent rambling home. Centrepiece is the 30-hectare garden, lovingly restored over the last 10 years so that you can stroll through a medieval water garden, Victorian greenhouse, and shrubberies as well as extensive parkland.

There's a treasure hunt you can download from the website – along with the answers so cheating is rife.

Open May and Sep Sat and Sun 10.30am–5.30pm, Jun–Aug Tue–Sun and bank holiday 10.30am–5.30pm. **Adm** (house) adults €6, children €4, family €16; (garden) adults €6, children €4, family €16, (combined ticket) adults €10, children €8, family €28. **Credit** V, MC. **Amenities** toilets, coffee shop, interpretative centre, wheelchair friendly.

Millmount Museum ★★
AGES 5 AND UP

Millmount, Drogheda, Co Louth, ☎ 041 983 3097; www.millmount. net.

Among the exhibits at Millmount that intrigue children is a 19th-century kitchen, a world apart from today's high-tech gadgetry. But you may be surprised to discover that they had vacuum cleaners and washing machines even then.

Millmount was the scene of one of the bloodiest episodes of the Civil War, in September 1649. After a bombardment lasting three days, Oliver Cromwell stormed the town, slaughtering not only the 2000-strong garrison, but thousands of women and children as well. Located

Millmount Museum

within the 18th-century Millmount Fort, the Millmount Museum offers a fascinating glimpse into the troubled history of the area. But the displays cover less gory topics too, such as geology, archaeology and local life.

Open *Mon–Sat 10am–6pm Sun and bank holiday 2.30pm–5.30pm.* **Adm** *(museum and tower) adults €5.50, seniors/children €3, students €4, family €12.* **Credit** *V, MC.* **Amenities** *limited disabled access, toilet.*

Monasterboice Round Tower and High Crosses ★ ALL AGES

Monasterboice, Co Louth, 📞 *041 982 2813. 10km NW of Drogheda.*

This collection of ruins stands on the site of a 5th-century monastery that flourished until the 10th century when the Vikings razed it to the ground. An air of peace now rests over the graveyard and ruined churches, where you will find three impressive high crosses. The round tower served as a refuge for the monks in case of attack and is the tallest in Ireland, impressive in its sheer size rising over you, although it has lost its conical cap.

Open *daily.* **Adm** *free.*

Stephenstown Pond Nature Park ★★ ALL AGES

Knockbridge, Dundalk, Co Louth, 📞 *042 937 9019. 6km SW of Dundalk.*

The ponds were built in the 19th century to pound water for driving the grinding mills of the Stephenstown Estate. Today they are a haven for wildlife, and can make a really rewarding half-day

out. If you approach quietly you may see a fox, squirrel, hedgehog or bat as well as the birds and butterflies in the two hectares of woodland, willow copse, flower meadows and lake shore – so bring binoculars.

Open *daily May–Sep 8.30am–8.30pm, Oct–Apr 9am–5pm.* **Adm** *€2 per car.* **Amenities** *toilets, coffee shop, craft shop.*

Meath

Brú na Bóinne ★★★ ALL AGES

Donore, Co Meath, 📞 *041 988 0300; www.heritageireland.ie. Signposted W from Drogheda.*

If you have only limited time in the area, do not miss Brú na Bóinne, Ireland's most intriguing archaeological site. Older than Egypt's pyramids and Stonehenge, the Boyne burial complex is one of the most important prehistoric sites in Europe and includes more than 40 separate monuments.

The most spectacular is the Newgrange tomb, a huge mound, 80 metres in diameter and 110 metres high, built 5,000 years ago, and fronted by a brilliant white façade of quartz quarried in the Wicklow Mountains. From the entrance a long, low passage leads to a cruciform chamber deep in its heart, where cremated remains were laid to rest.

Intricate carvings line the passage and adorn the massive block at the entrance. You might hazard guesses as to what they mean but no one really knows. That its builders had a precise knowledge

Brú na Bóinne

of astronomy as well as highly sophisticated construction skills is demonstrated at the winter solstice. A shaft of light creeps slowly along the passage to illuminate the inner chamber for just 17 minutes, and is thought to represent the rebirth of the deceased.

Because the Earth's position has shifted since the mound was built, and the spectacle is not quite what it is, an artificial sunrise is simulated daily for visitors. But be warned: at one point the guide plunges the chamber into darkness to heighten the effect.

Before seeing the tombs themselves, look at the displays at the Visitor Centre. Vivid reconstructions portray the way of life followed by these early farmers. A skeleton shows some of the injuries and illness suffered by our Neolithic ancestors, and even evidence of surgery on his skull.

> **INSIDER TIP** >
>
> Tickets for Brú na Bóinne are sold on a first come-first served basis, so arrive early in the morning, particularly during the summer months. This is a mainly outdoor site, so bring adequate protection against the weather. Allow two hours to see the visitor centre and one of the sites, three hours for both.

Open *Mar–Apr and Oct 9.30am–5.30pm, May and late Sep 9am–6.30pm, Jun–early Sep 9am–7pm, Nov–Feb 9.30am–5pm.* **Adm** *(visitor centre) adults €2.90, seniors €2.10, children €1.60, family €7.40; (with Newgrange) adults €5.80, seniors €4.50, children €2.90, family €14.50; (with Knowth) adults €4.50, seniors €2.90, children €1.60, family €11; (with Newgrange and Knowth) adults €10.30, seniors €7.40, children €4.50, family €25.50, OPW Heritage Card.* **Credit** *V, MC.* **Amenities** *parking, toilets, baby-changing facilities, disabled access within visitor centre, exhibition, audio-visual display, gift shop, restaurant, tourist information.*

The Causey Farm ★ ★ ★
AGES 6 AND UP

Girley, Fordstown, Navan, Co Meath, 📞 *046 943 4135; www.causey experience.com, booking E: info@causey.ie. 15km W of Navan.*

The Murtaghs invite you to be Irish for one unforgettable day. The family have farmed here for a thousand years so they know a bit about the business, and their home has long been a centre for music and dancing – the traditional céilídh.

This is more than just visiting a farm because you spend the day with a group learning a whole new bag of tricks. Digging turf, milking cows and working sheepdogs are just some of the jobs to be done, and there's culture too, playing the bodhrán (the Irish drum), learning a few words of the language, trying your skill at hurling, and dancing a jig.

But don't come in your Sunday best. Each day is different and you might end up exploring in the woods learning to live off the land, feeding the pigs, or wallowing about in the bog.

If the weather forces you indoors, there's plenty to keep children occupied – wall painting, clay modelling, rope weaving and baking bread.

Open *most days Mon–Sat through the season. Advance booking is essential, by phone or preferably email.* **Cost** *varies dependent upon activities available – adults around €30 for the day, reductions for children.* **Credit** *V, MC.* **Amenities** *parking, toilets, refreshments.*

Grove Garden and Tropical Bird Sanctuary

Grove Garden and Tropical Bird Sanctuary ★ ★ ALL AGES

Fordstown, Kells, Co Meath, ☎ 046 943 4276. Between Kells and Athboy on R164.

Come and meet Billy the Ferret along with white rabbits, white peacocks, ponies, lemurs, llamas and deer. Crammed into the 1.6 hectares of garden are more than 400 different types of roses and more than 300 varieties of hybrids in the clematis walk. The garden is a life's labour by the present owner and paths lead through distinct settings from lawns, borders and shrubs to vegetable plots.

Dotted throughout are cages of exotic birds, including talking cockatoos that call out as you pass. It's a great place for a family picnic with indoor and outdoor tables, and open areas for running about in.

Open *Easter–Oct daily 10am–6pm.* **Adm** *adults €7, seniors/children €5, family (2+4) €25.* **Credit** *V, MC.* **Amenities** *parking, toilets, teas and coffees available, indoor and outdoor picnic areas.*

Loughcrew Historic Gardens ★ ALL AGES

Oldcastle, Co Meath, ☎ 049 854 1356; www.loughcrew.com. 5km SE of Oldcastle.

Loughcrew Historic Gardens caters specifically for young children in something of a wonderland with a 'Celtic Legend Trail', watermill cascade, nature and history trails, larger than life toadstools, hidden fairies, giant bugs and characters from Alice in Wonderland. These pleasant restored gardens date from the

In the old Celtic calendar, the year is divided into two: Beltaine, the eve of 1st May, and Halloween at the end of October. On these two nights, gateways between this world and another of fairies are opened. One gateway is the Hill of Tara.

17th century and young visitors are kept amused with a quiz sheet (available in the café) encouraging them to hunt for the wooden sculptures and other features along the walks. And if that's not enough, there's a playground with climbing frames.

Open Apr–Sep daily 12.30–6pm, Oct–Mar Sun and bank holidays 1–4pm. **Adm** adults €7, seniors €5, children €3.50, family €20. **Credit** V, MC. **Amenities** parking, toilets, tearoom, gift shop, children's play area.

Newgrange Farm ★★
ALL AGES

Newgrange, Slane, Co Meath, 📞 041 982 4119; www.newgrangefarm. com. 6km W of Drogheda.

If the children have not been overawed by the prehistoric monuments at nearby Brú na Bóinne, they will enjoy wandering around the 135-hectare Newgrange Farm. Although a fully working farm, everything is geared up to showing just what goes on in running the operation.

There's plenty of 'hands on' stuff for youngsters, including getting to know and feeding some of the animals, and workload permitting, Farmer Bill will take you out on the tractor-trailer to see what's happening in the fields. On Sundays there's even more fun to be had in the

Newgrange Farm Stakes Sheep Race with teddy bear jockeys.

Open Easter–end of Aug daily 10am–5pm. **Cost** (event days) €8 per person, family (2) €12, (3) €18, (4) €24, (5) €30. **Credit** V, MC. **Amenities** toilets, baby-changing facilities, indoor and outdoor picnic areas, coffee shop, gift shop.

Proleek Dolmen ★ ALL AGES

Dundalk, Co Louth, 📞 042 933 5484. 10km N of Dundalk off R173.

Standing in the grounds of the Ballymascanlon Hotel is this spectacular dolmen. It's a 10-minute walk from the hotel car park – open to visitors – and signs direct you around the back of the hotel and past the stables.

The dolmen consists of a huge boulder miraculously balanced on three slender uprights, placed there 5,000 years ago by sheer brute force. Originally it would have been covered by a mound of stones and served as a ceremonial burial chamber.

Legend has it that anyone who can toss a pebble on to the top without it falling off will be granted a wish, and as there aren't many lying around nearby, it's good to bring a few along with you.

Open during daylight hours. **Adm** free. **Amenities** parking, morning coffee and bar meals at the Ballymascanlon Hotel.

Proleek Dolmen, Dundalk

Slane Castle ★ AGES 5 AND UP

Slane, Co Meath, 📞 *041 988 4400,* *www.slanecastle.ie. W of Drogheda along R163.*

U2, Madonna, Bruce Springsteen, Robbie Williams, REM, and the Rolling Stones have all headlined Slane's annual rock concert, and if you'd rather enjoy the place without the company of 80,000 others, don't come in the middle of August.

Just up-river from the site of the Battle of the Boyne, the castle looks impressive with an array of battlements and turrets. Painstakingly restored after a disastrous fire in 1991, it houses one of Ireland's finest art collections and you can wander around some of the principal rooms including the King's Room and the Ballroom.

George IV was a visitor in 1821, when he paid visits to his mistress Lady Conyngham, the great, great, great, great grandmother of Lord Henry Mount Charles, the present owner. It is said that the road linking it to Dublin was built arrow straight so that the King wasted no time on the journey.

Open May–Aug Sun–Thu 12–5pm. *Adm adults €7, seniors/children €5 (under-5s free), family €20. Credit Most major cards.*

Wicklow

Arklow Maritime Museum
★★ AGES 4 AND UP

St Mary's Road, Arklow, Co Wicklow, 📞 *0402 32868.*

Arklow has a great sea-faring tradition and in 1826 it was the first town in Ireland to have a lifeboat. The town celebrates the theme with a fascinatingly diverse collection, which ranges from a model of *Gypsy Moth III*, built in Arklow and the boat that brought Sir Francis Chichester victory in the first solo transatlantic yacht race, to a lady's shoe from a passenger on the *Lusitania*. There's a display on how the ship was sunk, as well as a range of safety and navigation equipment, shipwright's tools, and even a working model of a trawler's wheelhouse.

Open summer months Mon–Fri 10am–1pm and 2–5pm and occasional weekends. Adm adults €7, seniors/students €3, children (under-12s) free. Credit V, MC. Amenities toilets.

Avondale House and Forest Park ★ ALL AGES

Rathdrum, Co. Wicklow, 📞 *0404-46111; www.coillte.ie.*

Avondale House was the birthplace and home of leading 19th-century Irish politician Charles Stewart Parnell and is set in a wonderful 200-hectace forest park, which includes tree trails and walks taking from one to five hours plus two orienteering courses and events such as autumn mushroom hunts.

For those who want culture, the Georgian house is introduced in an audio-visual presentation.

Facilities include a restaurant, bookshop, picnic areas, and children's play area.

Open *(house) mid-March to end October daily 11am-6pm, house closed Mondays in Mar, Apr, Sept and Oct except Bank Holidays.* **Adm** *adults €6.00/concessions €5.50, family €16.00 (2+3).*

Glendalough Abbey ★ ★ ★

ALL AGES

Visitor Centre, Glendalough, Co Wicklow, ☎ 0404 45325 or 0404 45352; www.heritageireland.ie.

You don't have to be religious to appreciate the setting and beauty of Glendalough. St Kevin came here, the 'Glen of the Two Lakes', in the 6th century seeking a place of solitude for prayer and contemplation. His spirituality soon attracted a growing community and from a simple hermitage developed this rambling abbey, a great centre of religious study, and one of Ireland's most important sacred sites. Success also attracted the attention of the Vikings, and for three centuries Glendalough suffered repeated pillaging.

Today, ruins scatter this hauntingly beautiful valley, paths winding from the visitor centre past the two lakes. The most striking building is the slender round tower, over 31 metres high, in which a lantern was lit to guide pilgrims. Kevin himself lived in a tiny cave, known as St. Kevin's Bed.

Younger children will enjoy exploring the ruins, whereas older ones may appreciate the exhibition and audio-visual presentation in the visitor centre.

Open *(visitor centre) daily mid-Oct–mid-Mar 9.30am–5pm, mid-Mar–mid-Oct 9am–6pm.* **Adm** *(abbey) free, exhibition and audio-visual presentation: adults €2.90, seniors €2.10, children €1.30, family €7.40, OPW Heritage Card.* **Credit** *V, MC.* **Amenities** *toilets, baby-changing facilities, disabled access in visitor centre, restricted on abbey site, picnic area, walks. Refreshments and meals available at nearby Glendalough Hotel.*

Glenroe Open Farm ★ ★

AGES 10 AND UNDER

Ballygannon, Kilcoole, Co Wicklow, ☎ 01 287 2288; www.glenroefarm. com. 4km S of Greystones.

A family-run farm where children get to meet farm animals – sheep and their lambs, goats, cattle, pigs and even Sika deer. There are plenty of birds pecking about as well, including hens and chicks, geese, turkeys, ducks and some impressive peacocks.

In the pets' corner youngsters can get up close with rabbits, gerbils, guinea pigs and chipmunks.

The farmhouse museum casts an eye over the past hardships of farm life, while the wildlife education area, nature walk, secret garden and children's playground give the children plenty to do until lunchtime when you can have an indoor picnic in the piggery or choose from home-cooked food in the coffee shop.

Open Mar–Apr and Sep–Oct Sat–Sun 10am–5pm, May–Aug Mon–Fri 10am–5pm, Sat–Sun and bank holidays 10am–6pm. **Adm** adults €6, seniors/children €5. **Credit** V, MC. **Amenities** toilets, picnic tables, coffee shop, children's playground, nature walk, gift shop.

National Sea Life Centre ★★
ALL AGES

Strand Road, Bray, Co Wicklow, ☎ 01 286 6939; www.sealife.ie.

Sharks, octopus, seahorses, crabs and starfish all swim in lifelike habitats here, and there's a special 'touch' pool where youngsters can meet some of the more polite ones that don't bite. There are more than 90 species from rivers, estuaries and the ocean, many of which live in Ireland's native waters. There are also brightly coloured tropical fish and piranhas from the Amazon.

The subtle emphasis is on education and conservation and there are 'magic glasses' with which children can read questions and find answers. There's a soft play area too, to get rid of surplus energy.

Open Jan–Mar and Oct–Dec Mon–Fri 11am–5pm Sat–Sun and school holidays 10am–6pm, Apr–Sept Mon–Fri 11am–6pm Sat–Sun and bank holidays 10am–6.30pm. **Adm** adults €10, children €6.50, family from €29. **Credit** V, MC. **Amenities** toilets,

baby-changing facilities, ice creams, small children's gift shop.

Powerscourt Gardens, House, and Waterfall ★★
ALL AGES

Enniskerry, Co Wicklow, ☎ 01 204 60000; www.powerscourt.ie. Signed from N11, W of Bray.

There are two major reasons to visit Powerscourt; the views to the Wicklow Mounts and the interiors of this magnificent 18th-century mansion, run down by the time the family moved out in the 1950s and then gutted by fire in 1974.

It is once again a resplendent stately home, a few of the rooms open to show, including the grand entrance where there's an exhibition on its fascinating history, and the ballroom, which is an opulent setting for weddings and functions.

It also houses a number of specialist shops and a terrace café with that wonderful view.

The gardens fall to ornamental lakes, where corners, walled gardens and shrubberies offer rambling walks. A 2km drive or walk across the estate takes you to the highest and most spectacular waterfall in the country, the River Dargle cascading almost 120 metres down the cliffs.

There is also a nature trail, pet cemetery, Japanese and Italianate gardens and a well-equipped children's playground, making this good for family picnics.

Open (house and garden) daily 9.30am–5.30pm (gardens close at dusk in winter); (waterfall) May–Aug

9.30am–7pm, Mar–Apr and Sep–Oct
10.30am–5.30pm, Nov–Feb
10.30am–4pm. **Adm** (house and
garden) adults €9, students €7.50
children €5 (under 5 free); (waterfall)
adults €5, children €3.50 (under 5
free). **Credit** V, MC. **Amenities** toilets, café, disabled access, speciality
shops, garden centre.

Louth

Pirate's Den ★★ AGES UNDER 12

Coes Road, Dundalk, Co Louth, 📞 042
932 7454; www.pirates-den.com.

In Dundalk there's the Pirate's
Den for when children just want
to play, with different zones for
babies, toddlers and the over-5s.
You sit in the café while they
have fun clambering over rope
bridges, wallowing in ball pools
or whizzing down slides, and
there's a learning area too.

Open summer and school holidays
Mon–Fri 11am–6.30pm, Sat–Sun
10.30am–6.30pm, low season
Mon 2–6pm, Tue, Thu, Sat, Sun
10.30am–6.30pm, Wed, Fri
11am–6.30pm. **Adm** €8 for 90
minute-session.

Irish Cycle Hire (see By Bike
in Chapter 2 on p. 29) has
depots in Drogheda, Dublin,
Cork, Killarney, Ennis, Galway,
Westport.

Meath

Funtasia ★★ ALL AGES

Bettystown, Co Meath, 📞 041 982
8301; www.funtasia.ie.

One of Ireland's top indoor family entertainment centres; a
bowling alley, multi-media play

area and children's disco com-
pete with snooker tables, a
monorail and train rides, and
even a casino for the over-23s,
plus fast food restaurant.

Open daily 10am–midnight. **Adm**
free but charges apply for activities
and rides.

Trim Castle ★★ ALL AGES

Trim, Co Meath, 📞 046 943 8619;
www.heritageireland.ie/en/Historic
Sites/East/TrimCastleMeath/.

The massive keep, which featured in Mel Gibson's *Braveheart*,
took 30 years to build, creating
in the process the largest Anglo-
Norman castle in the country. It
was designed to curb Richard de
Clare, known as Strongbow, and
is in the shape of a 20-sided
tower, further fortified with a
ditch, curtain wall and moat.

After extensive excavation and
restoration completed in 2000,
access to the keep is by 45-minute
guided tour only. Some of the
stairs are very steep, and so
unsuitable for buggies and small
children. The space however is
great for running about.

Open November–March Sat and Sun
10am to 5pm, April–end Sept 10am
to 6pm, October 10am–5.30pm daily.
Adm (castle) adults €1.50, children
€0.75, families €4.25; (castle and
keep) adults €3.50, children €1,
families €8.25.

Wicklow

Clara Lara Fun Park ★★★
AGES UNDER 16

Vale of Clara, Rathdrum, Co Wicklow,
📞 0404 46161; www.claralara.com.

On Yer Bike

The Táin Trail follows the saga of Maeve in her attempt to gain the great brown bull of Cooley, defended by the legendary Celtic hero, Cúchulainn. Stretching between Rathcrogan and the Cooley Peninsula, it dogs the route taken by her army, passing resting-places and battle sites, and taking in plenty of other places of interest too. The whole tour is 584km long and makes a splendid cycling holiday for really energetic families. However, broken into shorter stretches, such as those passing through County Louth, it offers a leisurely route through the countryside.

Set in 12 hectares of beautiful countryside beside the Avonmore River valley, Clara Lara is a great outdoor activity park where the sole objective is family fun. Rowing boats, rafts, tree houses, go-karts, water slides, Tarzan swings and mini-golf are all there. Everything's outdoors, and even if it doesn't rain, with all the water about, they're going to get wet. But, as that's half the fun, come in suitable footwear and bring a towel and change of clothes. And when they get hungry, there's a restaurant serving hot and cold food and plenty of picnic space as well as barbecues you can use.

Open May Sat–Sun, Jun–Sep daily 10.30am–6pm. *Adm* adults and children €9 (under-5s and seniors free), 'Gold Bracelet' (covers unlimited access to additional charge rides) €9. *Credit* V, MC, Amex.

Trim Castle

Simply Wicked

Walking in the Wicklows is wicked, wonderful and wild. There are many well-marked long-distance footpaths, and plenty of scope for free range exploration moving from glen to glen. If you haven't visited before, a short-cut is to contact one of the agencies that provides guided walks:

Barry Dalby, 1555 Beachdale, Kilcoole, Co Wicklow, ☎ 01 287 5990.

Damien Cashin Outdoor Activities, Tomdarragh, Roundwood, Co Wicklow, ☎ 01 281 8212.

Footfalls Walking Holidays, Trooperstown, Roundwood, Co Wicklow, ☎ 0404 45152; *www.walkinghikingireland.com*.

FAMILY-FRIENDLY ACCOMMODATION

MODERATE–EXPENSIVE

Ballymascanlon House Hotel
★★★

Carlingford Road (R173), Dundalk, Co Louth, ☎ 042 935 8200; www.ballymascanlon.com.

52 hectares of private parkland and extensive gardens surround this 4-star luxurious family-run hotel. It's a blend of old and new with, at its heart, a Victorian mansion, extended to provide additional accommodation, and a health club incorporating a 20-metre deck-level swimming pool plus children's pool, Jacuzzi, steam room, and gym.

Fresh local produce forms the basis of the high quality cuisine.

Children are welcome to use the hotel's leisure facilities under supervision, including the tennis courts and golf course, and during the holiday season, they have their own summer camp activities. The hotel can also organise horse-riding and the Blue Flag beach of Templetown is only a short drive away.

Rooms 96. *Rates* double €160–180, children to age 3 free, to age 7 €25, to age 12 €35, but check for special offers. *Credit* all major credit cards accepted. *Amenities* guest parking, laundry service, baby-sitting service available. *In room* tea/coffee-making facilities, in-room safe, iron/ironing board, WiFi throughout hotel, sat TV, room service.

MODERATE–EXPENSIVE

Boyne Valley Hotel and Country Club ★★★

Stameen, Drogheda, Co Louth, ☎ 041 983 7737; www.bestwestern.ie. On the outskirts of town off the main Dublin to Belfast road.

This restyled 18th-century mansion is a relaxed but high quality hotel in 6.5 hectares of well-tended gardens. The food draws on Irish and French traditions and uses only the best local produce. There's a crèche and for energetic youngsters, a swimming pool with children's pool, sauna, Jacuzzi, steam room and fitness suite plus beauty salon.

Older children can use the tennis court and nearby golf course; other close attractions include the tombs at Newgrange.

Rooms 72. **Rates** double €160, children to age 6 €23, to 12 €35, but check for special offers. **Credit** all major credit cards accepted. **Amenities** laundry service, babysitting service available. **In room** tea/coffee-making facilities, in-room safe iron/ironing board, Internet connection, TV, room service.

Bettystown Court Conference and Leisure Hotel ★★★

Bettyscourt, Co Meath, ☎ *041 981 2900; www.bettystowncourt.com.*

This smart modern hotel is ideal for enjoying the traditional seaside resort of Bettystown with its splendid beach, funfair and crazy golf, and during the summer period the hotel runs a children's club.

Facilities include a pool incorporating a child's pool, sauna, Jacuzzi, steam room and fitness suite. A carvery serves Sunday lunch and evening dinner is in the restaurant whereas lunch and a more informal menu is available from the bar.

Rooms 120. **Rates** room (2 adults and up to 2 children under 12 sharing) €99–150, but check for special offers. **Credit** all major credit cards accepted. **Amenities** cots, babysitting, bottle service, children's menus and small portions available, laundry service. **In room** tea/coffee-making facilities, iron/ironing board, broadband and WiFi connections, TV, room service.

Knightsbrook Hotel and Golf Resort Meath ★★★

Dublin Road, Trim, Co Meath. ☎ *01850 554400; www.knightsbrook.com.*

Sporting a championship golf course, this resort offers a choice of hotel or self-catering holiday accommodation in the grounds of the 67-hectare estate, both types of accommodation with access to extensive leisure facilities. The restaurant offers Irish and international cuisine, or in the more informal Terrace Lounge food is served from 10.30am each day.

Local attractions include Trim Castle, Newgrange, the Hill of Tara with its grand views and space for running about, and Bective Abbey, a Cistercian monastery founded in 1147.

Rooms 134. **Rates** €170–210, children under 3 free, ages 3–14 €20, but check for special offers. **Credit** all major credit cards accepted. **Amenities** WiFi in public areas, guest parking, cots, baby-sitting, bottle service, children's menus and small portions available, laundry service, pool incorporating child's pool, sauna, Jacuzzi, steam room, crèche, health and beauty spa, fitness suite. **In room** tea/coffee-making facilities, iron/ironing board, Internet connection, sat TV, room service.

Glendalough Hotel ★★

Glendalough, Co Wicklow, ☎ *0404 45135, www.glendaloughhotel.com.*

In stunning scenery next to the spot chosen by St Kevin for his 6th-century monastery, this comfortable family-run hotel is the ideal place from which to explore the Wicklow Mountains. In a charmingly refurbished and extended Victorian house, rooms take full advantage of the surrounding views. À la carte and table d'hôte menus are offered in the restaurant, with more informal eating in the bar or on the outside terrace, where barbecues take place during the summer months – weather permitting.

Just a short walk away is Abbey Wood and there are moors and lakes on the doorstep.

Rooms *44.* **Rates** *€160–180, child under 12 free, age 12–15 50% reduction, but check for special offers.* **Credit** *all major credit cards accepted.* **Amenities** *cots, baby-sitting, bottle service, children's menus and small portions available.* **In room** *tea/coffee-making facilities, iron/ironing board available, safety deposit at reception, sat TV, room service.*

MODERATE

The Arklow Bay Conference, Leisure and Spa Hotel ★★★

Arklow, Co Wicklow, 📞 *0402 32309;* **www.arklowbay.com.**

Just outside town, this hotel with an attractive location overlooking a lake and Arklow Bay, is part of a small family-owned chain known for good service.

During the school holidays there's a children's club with a range of games and activities to keep youngsters amused for morning and afternoon sessions, plus an evening video club.

The leisure centre includes a pool, child's pool, sauna, Jacuzzi, hydrotherapy pool, steam room, family changing room, beauty spa, and a fitness suite.

Youngsters are welcome in the restaurant where they can select from their own menu or choose small portions from the extensive main menu.

Rooms *92.* **Rates** *room (2 adults and up to 2 children under 12 sharing) €99–150, but check for special offers.* **Credit** *all major credit cards accepted.* **Amenities** *cots, baby-sitting, bottle service, children's menus and small portions available, laundry service, WiFi in reception.* **In room** *tea/coffee-making facilities, iron/ironing board available, Internet connections in some rooms, sat TV, room service.*

CAFÉS & FAMILY-FRIENDLY DINING

MODERATE

Donegans of Monasterboice
★★ MODERN IRISH

Monasterboice, Co Louth, 📞 *041 983 7383;* **www.donegans.net.** *Just off the M1.*

This attractive roadside inn is well-placed for eating after visiting the Monasterboice Round Tower. On a fine day, you can sit outside in the beer garden or on the deck patio, but children are equally welcome in the lounge and dining areas until 9pm. Tuck into steak and scampi, homemade burgers, Thai curry or fresh tortellini pasta. Children can have smaller portions of adult dishes or choose from their own menu. Soup and sandwiches are available all day in the bar.

Open *daily from 12.30pm, lunch until 3.30pm (2.30 on Sun), evening menu 4.30–10pm (5–9.30pm on Sun).* **Main courses** *€13.95–31.* **Credit** *V, MC.*

Amenities children's menu and small portions, bottle warming, highchairs, baby-changing facilities.

Food For Thought ★★ FIND
MODERN IRISH

Dundalk Street, Carlingford, Co Louth, ☎ 042 938 3838. At the top end of the town.

This inviting deli is the place to check out the packets and smells of good food including cheeses, breads, salads and meats plus snacks and dishes such as home-made lasagne, chicken and bacon pie and the 'catch of the day', served with potato and side salad. For a lighter meal, there are pizzas, toasted savouries and sandwiches. Drinks include a few wines, soft drinks and speciality teas and coffee, or freshly-made smoothies. Most items are available to take-away, and given notice, staff will make up hampers of food to take home or stock self-catering cupboards.

Open Mon–Sat 9am–7pm, Sun 10am–7pm. *Main courses* €7.95–10.95. *Credit* V, MC. *Amenities* small portions, bottle warming, highchairs.

Fitzpatricks Bar and Restaurant ★★★ FIND
MODERN IRISH

Rockmarshall, Jenkinstown, Co Louth, ☎ 042 937 6193; www.fitz-patricks-restaurant.com. On main R173 Dundalk-Carlingford road.

From the sea of flowers surrounding the car park to the chamber pots festooning the toilets, you might be forgiven for thinking Fitzpatricks should have been included as an 'attraction' rather than a place to eat. It's jam packed with antiques, curiosities and bygone objects, even in the loos, and children will be endlessly distracted by a plethora of old cameras, flat irons, telephones, weighing scales and other items too numerous to mention. Outside is just as characterful, with ancient ploughs, bicycles, milk churns and even an old car sprouting a garden under its bonnet. The food is equally interesting, with steaks, grills and local fish and seafood the house specialities, though children might be upset to learn that the lobsters in the display tank are not there just for show.

You need to book for evening meals but the same menu is served in the bar where you will generally get a table, even if you have to wait a little.

Open for food: Mon 12–8pm, Tue–Sat, 12–10pm, Sun 12.30–3.30pm and 5.30–9pm. *Main courses* €13.95–29.50. *Credit* all main credit cards. *Amenities* children's menu and healthy eating options, small portions, bottle warming, baby menu, highchairs, baby-changing facilities, drawing books and children's games, car park.

Avoca Handweavers Mill Shop and Café ★★
MODERN IRISH

Avoca Village, Co Wicklow, ☎ 0402 35105; www.avoca.ie.

Fans of Ballykissangel will recognise the village as the setting for location shots in the TV series, but this mill shop and café is another reason for visiting. The pretty valley was once the scene of extensive ore mining and is shown on Ptolemy's map of the world drawn around 150 AD. It is now the site of Ireland's oldest working mill, established in 1723. Visitors can wander round the workshops to see throws, blankets and scarves being woven before heading for the country-style café.

Homemade hot and cold dishes include honey roast ham, orange and apricot chicken breast or sweet chilli salmon, served with interesting salads. Or you can opt for a freshly baked scone, cookie or cake and a drink.

Open *daily summer 9.30am–5pm, winter 10am–4.30pm.* **Main courses** *€13.95–29.50.* **Credit** *All major cards accepted.* **Amenities** *children's special at weekends, small portions, bottle warming, highchairs, baby-changing facilities, wine licence, car park.*

Barracuda Steak and Seafood Restaurant ★
SURF AND TURF

Strand Road, Bray, Co Wicklow, ☎ *01 276 5686; www.barracuda.ie.*

Upstairs from the Sealife Centre, booking is advisable for Friday and Saturday evenings at this popular restaurant overlooking the beach. Among the specialities are Dublin Bay prawns, Dover sole meunière, vegetarian frittata, and T-bone steak. Many dishes are available as child-size portions, or children can choose from their own menu, and the layout allows families their own space.

Open *daily from 9am for coffee and light snacks, lunch Mon–Fri 12–3pm, evening menu from 5–11pm, Sat–Sun brunch 12–5pm, evening menu from 6pm.* **Main courses** *€9.95–23.95.* **Credit** *all major cards accepted.* **Amenities** *children's menu, small portions, highchairs, bottle warming, baby-changing facilities, wine licence.*

Fitzpatricks Bar & Restaurant

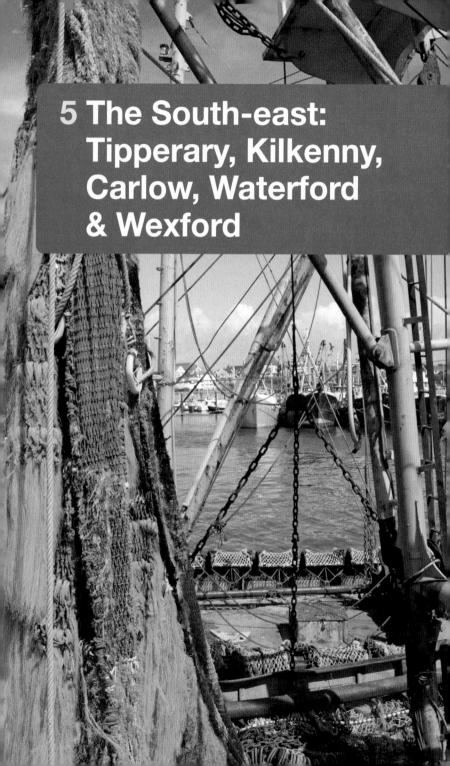

5 The South-east: Tipperary, Kilkenny, Carlow, Waterford & Wexford

SOUTH-EAST IRELAND

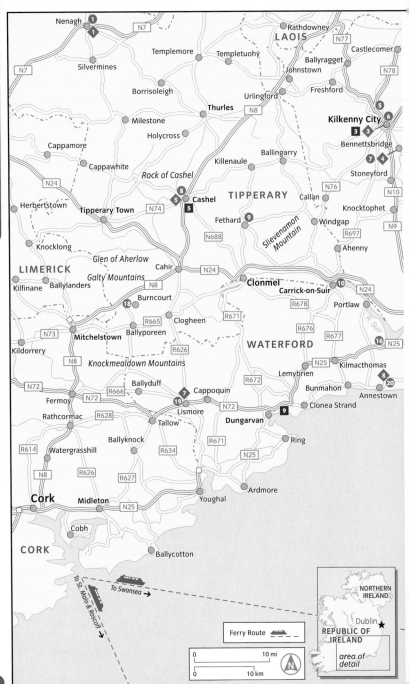

Attractions ●

Nenagh Heritage Centre **1**
Browneshill Dolmen **2**
Altamont Gardens **3**
Huntington Castle **4**
Dunmore Cave **5**
Newpark Fen **6**
Nore View Folk and
   Heritage Museum **7**
Brú Ború Cultural Centre
   and Cashel Folk Village **8**
Fethard Folk Farm and
   Transport Museum **9**
Ormond Castle **10**

SS Dunbrody Emigrant Ship **11**
Irish National Heritage Park **12**
Wexford Wildfowl Reserve **13**
Irish Agricultural Museum and
   Famine Exhibition **14**
Waterford Treasures at
   the Granary Museum **15**
Waterford and
   Suir Valley Railway **16**
Waterford Crystal Visitor Centre **17**
Mitchelstown Cave **18**
Lismore Castle Gardens **19**
Copper Coast Mini Farm **20**
Hook Lighthouse **21**

Accommodation ■

The Mount Wolseley **1**
Lord Bagenal Inn **2**
Springhill Court **3**
Courtown Hotel **4**
Clonmel Park Hotel **5**
Tower Hotel and Leisure Centre **6**
Hotel Curracloe **7**
Kelly's Resort Hotel **8**
Clonea Strand Hotel **9**

Dining ◆

Pepes Café Bar **1**
The Forge **2**
Kilkenny Design Centre **3**
Nicholas Mosse Pottery **4**
Ryan's Daughter **5**
Granary Café **6**
Foley's on the Mall **7**
Copper Kettle **8**
The Strand Inn **9**

Known as the 'Sunny South-east', a mild climate and long hours of sunshine make the craggy coastline and Blue Flag beaches of this part of Ireland popular with families who want time by the sea. Pretty fishing villages and harbours dot the coastline, while the country inland has a gentle, rural charm, with green, rolling hills and mountains split by the rivers Blackwater, Suir, Nore, Barrow and Slaney, each reaching the sea in deep-set bays.

Both towns and villages are fun to explore and there always seems to be something going on, from annual festivals to music and dance gatherings that happen anywhere at the drop of a hat.

The five counties of the southeast fit snugly together and any of the main towns makes a good base for exploration. However, as long as you have a car, there's no shortage of comfortable hotels and homely bed and breakfasts in the countryside.

The area is proud of its heritage, which at the Browneshill Dolmen in County Carlow reaches back more than 5,000 years. Celtic, Viking and Norman influences have also left their mark, and their fascinating, sometimes bloody, history is told in heritage centres across the region.

ESSENTIALS

Getting There

By Sea The most convenient ferry port for the area is Rosslare (Rosslare Europort, Co Wexford, ☏ *053 915 7929; www.iarnrodeirann. ie/rosslare*), with sailings from Pembroke and Fishguard in Wales. **Irish Ferries** run a service from Pembroke Dock with a sailing time of 3 hours 45 minutes (☏ (UK) *08705 171 717* (Ireland) *0818 300 400; www.irish ferries.ie*).

StenaLine operates ferries from Fishguard, with the crossing times from as little as 2 hours (☏ (UK) *08705 70 70 70* (Ireland) *053 916 1590; www.stenaline.ie*). There is also a service from Swansea into Cork operated by **Swansea Cork Ferries** (☏ (UK)

01792 456116; www.swansea corkferries.com). Arrivals from other British Ports disembarking at the Dublin and Belfast ports will of necessity face a significant drive.

By Air The regional airport at **Waterford** is central to the whole area and operates daily flights between London, Luton, Birmingham and Manchester Airports (☏ *051 875 589; www. flywaterford.com*).

Cork International (☏ *021 431 3131; www.corkairport.com*) is reasonably convenient for the western corner of the region and receives scheduled flights from most British airports.

Shannon Airport (☏ *061 712 000; www.shannonairport.com*) is the closest for visitors to County Tipperary and handles flights from Britain's main airports.

There are **taxi services** into the nearest town or you can arrange to pick up a **rental car** from one of the several companies operating at each of the airports.

VISITOR INFORMATION

You can get comprehensive visitor information for all the south-eastern counties of Ireland from the Discover Ireland website *www.ireland.ie* or *www.southeast ireland.com*.

The main tourist office for the area is **Fáilte Ireland South East** at 41 The Quay, Waterford City, Co Waterford, ☏ *051 876 720*.

The northern part of Tipperary lies in the **Shannon Tourist Region** (*www.shannon regiontourism.ie*).

For further information on the individual counties, the websites *www.tipperary.com*, *www. kilkenny.ie*, *www.carlowtourism. com*, *www.waterfordtourism.org* and *www.wexfordtourism.com* are all useful sources.

The main **Tourist Information Offices** for each of the counties are located as follows:

Tipperary

Cashel Heritage Centre, Main Street, Cashel, Co Tipperary. ☏ *062 62511*.

Carrick-on-Suir Tourist Office Heritage Centre, Carrick-on-Suir, Co Tipperary. ☏ *051 640 200*.

Cahir Tourist Office (seasonal), Castle Car Park, Castle Street, Cahir, Co Tipperary. ☏ *052 41453*.

Nenagh Tourist Office (seasonal), Connelly Street, Nenagh, Co Tipperary. ☏ *067 31610*.

Kilkenny

Kilkenny Tourist Office, Shee Alms House, Rose Inn Street/ Mary's Lane, Kilkenny City, Co Kilkenny. ☏ *056 775 1500*.

Carlow

Carlow Tourist Office, Tullow Street/College Street, Carlow Town, Co Carlow. ☏ *059 913 1554*.

Waterford

Waterford Tourist Office, Waterford Granary, The Quay, Waterford City, Co Waterford. ☏ *051 358 397 / 051 875 823*.

Dungarvan Tourist Office, The Court House, Dungarvan, Co Waterford. ☏ *058 41741*.

Waterford Crystal Tourist Office (seasonal), Cork Road, Waterford City, Co Waterford. ☏ *051 358 397*.

Tramore Tourist Office (seasonal), Railway Square, Tramore, Co Waterford. ☏ *051 381 572*.

Wexford

Wexford Tourist Office,
Crescent Quay, Wexford Town,
Co Wexford. ☎ *053 912 3111.*

Gorey Tourist Office, Main
Street, Gorey, Co Wexford.
☎ *053 942 1248.*

New Ross Tourist Office,
Dunbrody Heritage Centre,
New Ross, Co Wexford. ☎ *051
421 857.*

Enniscorthy Tourist Office,
Castle Museum, Enniscorthy,
Co Wexford. ☎ *053 923 4699.*

ORIENTATION

Tipperary is 182km (113 miles)
SW of Dublin, 157km (98
miles) W of Rosslare and 347km
(216 miles) SW of Belfast.

Kilkenny is 133km (83 miles)
SW of Dublin, 90km (56 miles)
NW of Rosslare and 299km
(186 miles) S of Belfast.

Carlow is 83km (52 miles) SW
of Dublin, 92km (57 miles) NW
of Rosslare and 250km (155
miles) S of Belfast.

Waterford is 182km (113 miles)
S of Dublin, 73km (45 miles) W
of Rosslare and 348km (216
miles) S of Belfast.

Wexford is 129km (80 miles) S
of Dublin, 17km (11 miles) N
of Rosslare and 309km (192
miles) S of Belfast.

Main roads link the major towns
in the area and are fine if getting
from A to B is what matters. But
the minor roads offer quieter
and more attractive if occasionally bumpy driving, passing
through villages and backwaters.
Coast roads are especially attractive and lead you past innumerable inviting bays.

As elsewhere in Ireland, the
larger towns are sometimes con-
gested but can often be avoided
by attractive detours. For example, travelling between Waterford
and Wexford the N25 crosses
the river Barrow at New Ross,
because there is no other bridge
farther down river. However, the
R733 to Ballyhack and the
Passage East Car Ferry (☎ *051 382
480* or *051 382 488*) across
Waterford Harbour can save up
to an hour's driving.

Getting Around

Bus (☎ *01 836 6111; www.
buseireann.ie*) and rail (☎ *01 836
6222; www.irishrail.ie*) services
link the main towns in the area
but to explore the area properly
you will need a car and can
arrange to collect one from the
various car hire firms at the airports or ferry terminal.

Discover the Counties

Tipperary

Tipperary is a straggling county,
reaching from the shores of
Lough Derg to the Galty and
Knockmealdown Mountains and
the River Suir in the south. It goes
from lush green dairy pastures in
the Golden Vale to more dramatic
scenery among the uplands.

Rock of Cashel

Many farms open their doors to visitors, offering a chance to meet the animals – not just cattle but also horses, including those at the country's biggest stud at Fethard.

The whole county is a place for relaxing away from the crowds, the exception being Cashel, which is spectacular, but very busy in the height of the season.

Kilkenny

Kilkenny is famed for its beauty, particularly along the valleys of the River Nore and the River Barrow. Winding into the heart of the country, these rivers were highways for the first settlers, who have left evidence of their passing in the dolmens and earthworks dotting the landscape.

The county was named after the county town, which was for a time the medieval capital of the country. The first Anglo-Saxon lord, Strongbow, built his castle there in 1172 but Ireland's smallest city was old even then, having grown up around a monastery founded in the 6th century.

Among the highlights is picnicking on the riverbank by the mill at Kells, visiting the spectacular cave at Dunmore (see p. 100), and watching wildlife at Newpark Fen (see p. 100).

Carlow

Set back from the coast behind the Blackstairs Mountains and the tail of the Wicklows, County Carlow's rich agricultural plains reach down to the River Barrow. It's good walking country and small, rural villages lend it an idyllic air.

The river offers excellent fishing and is a great place for cruising. Elsewhere, there are monasteries, Anglo-Norman tower houses and castles to be explored.

One thing children shouldn't miss is the massive Browneshill Dolmen (see p. 101), They'll be awed at its capstone, which weighs a staggering 100 tonnes or more.

Wexford & Waterford

Wexford and Waterford border Ireland's south-east coast, which, protected from the prevailing Atlantic weather but receiving the full benefit of the Gulf Stream, has a reputation as the sunniest corner of Ireland. A serpentine and pretty coastline runs for miles, alternating cliffs and secluded bays with great expanses of unbroken beach. As well as sandcastles, paddling and swimming there's scope for surfing, sea-fishing and endless coastal walks.

There is much to see as well: find out about the mass emigration on the *SS Dunbrody* (see p. 105) that followed the Great Famine, or learn how our Stone Age ancestors lived at the National Heritage Park. Take a train ride along the Suir Valley, or climb Hook Lighthouse for the dramatic view along the jagged coast.

Child-friendly Events & Entertainment

Tipperary

The Irish Conker Championships (end of October)

Freshford, Co Kilkenny; 📞 *056 883 1845; www.irishconker championships.com.*

Encourage the children away from Gameboys and Playstations to spend an afternoon discovering the low-tech joys of conkers. There are even prizes to be won – for adults as well as children. Other attractions include pony rides, bouncy castles, a treasure hunt, with food and entertainment happenings throughout the streets.

Carlow

Éigse Carlow Arts Festival

Forresters' Hall, College Street, Carlow Town, Co Carlow; 📞 *059 914 0491; www.eigsecarlow.ie.*

In early June, the streets of Carlow come alive to a massive programme of entertainment that draws artists and performers from across Europe and farther afield. The 10-day spectacle includes dance, theatre, music, visual arts, comedy and a host of children's events.

Tullow Agricultural Show (August)

Tullow, Co Carlow, 📞 *059 918 0755.*

Cattle and sheep, displays of horsemanship and exhibitions by working horses are just some of the attractions at an agricultural show that always has plenty going on.

Waterford

Sprog Festival (July)

Garter Lane Arts Centre, O'Connell Street, Waterford City, Co Waterford, 📞 *051 855 038.*

This festival is designed especially for 5 to 8-year-olds, but the rest of the family is equally welcome to join in. Entertaining and educational, there's a programme of shows and workshops as well as exhibitions to keep young minds entertained.

Wexford

Bannow and Rathangan Agricultural Show (July)

Killag, Duncormick, Co Wexford, 📞 *053 914 8847.*

More cattle and sheep, displays of riding, and exhibitions by working horses feature at another traditional agricultural show.

International Sand Sculpting Festival (July)

Duncannon, Co Wexford, 📞 *087 205 8491; www.visitduncannon.com/ sand_festival.htm.*

Sandcastle building is taken to the extreme in the International Sand Sculpting Festival when the beach is transformed into one of the strangest and most intriguing galleries ever seen. This is serious stuff and fantastic figures and structures are wrought out of the sand but there's plenty of fun too, with amateur sculpting competitions, face painting, street theatre, a teddy bears' picnic and inevitably music, singing and dancing.

Kilmore Quay Seafood Festival (July)

Kilmore, Co Wexford, 📞 *053 912 9922.*

If you're trying to persuade the children that healthy eating can be fun, take them to Kilmore during the seafood festival. The charming fishing village, noted for its lobsters, really gets into party mood for a two-day celebration of the fruits of the sea. There's plenty of opportunity to try out something new and lots more going on besides with traditional music, song and dance lasting well into the evening.

WHAT TO SEE & DO

Children's Top Attractions

❶ Experience what it was like leaving home in search of a fresh life in the New World aboard *SS Dunbrody*. See p. 105.

❷ Puzzle at how ancient humans built the Browneshill Dolmen. See p. 101.

❸ Visit one of the world's first beacons set to warn shipping, at the Hook Lighthouse. See p. 103.

❹ Learn about Waterford's Viking past at Waterford Treasures. See p. 103.

❺ Wonder at the rock formations in Mitchelstown and Dunmore caves. See p. 99.

❻ Discover life in the Bronze Age at the Irish National Heritage Park. *www.inhp.com.*

❼ Unearth how rocks are formed – and have fun on the beach along the Copper Coast. See p. 105.

8 Chug along on the Waterford and Suir Valley Railway. See p. 103.

9 Understand one of the tragic turning points in Irish history at the Irish Agricultural Museum and Famine Exhibition. See p. 104.

Children-friendly Attractions

Tipperary

Brú Ború Cultural Centre ★★
AGES 4 AND UP

Rock Lane, Cashel, Co Tipperary, ☎ *062 61122; www.comhaltas.com. 20 km NE of Tipperary.*

Literally the 'Palace of Brian Boru', this cultural centre is devoted to and passionate about traditional Irish music and dance. From the *geantraí* or lively dance tunes to the softer *goltraí* (laments) and *suantraí* (lullabies), Ireland has a rich musical heritage, which is still very much an integral part of Irish life.

The 'Sounds of History' exhibition in the subterranean exhibition hall tells the story of Irish music through the centuries.

A short film in the theatre gives a real flavour of the subject, presenting highlights of the Fleadh Cheoil Na hEireann music festival, held at Enniscorthy in 2000.

During the summer, you can experience the excitement for yourself in a spectacular live show in the centre's theatre. There's a pre-concert dinner and

the music often continues with informal gatherings in the bar after the performance. Overall think Riverdance, but much more genuine.

Open mid-Sep–mid-Jun Mon–Fri 9am–5pm, mid-Jun–mid-Sep shows Tue–Sat at 9pm, exhibition then open until 8.30pm. Adm ('Sounds of History' exhibition) adults €5, children €3. (Show) adults €18, children €10. (Dinner and show) adults €48, children (under 12) €24. Credit V, MC. Amenities craft shop, toilet, refreshments, parking.

Cashel Folk Village ★★
AGES 3 AND UP

Dominick Street, Cashel, Co Tipperary, ☎ *062 62525.*

Just round the corner from Cashel Heritage Centre, the collection of artefacts in this folk museum really gives a picture of what rural life was all about in this reconstructed village, which includes a crofter's kitchen, a butcher's shop, blacksmith's forge, a village pub and a penal chapel.

A museum room is packed with paraphernalia including agricultural implements and bygone surgical instruments, many accompanied by diagrams illustrating their use – good for the gruesome. Another room contains memorabilia of the IRA, giving a graphic insight into Republican history and the struggle for Irish independence, while a small chapel recalls the period when Catholicism was repressed. The final exhibit is a traditional horse-drawn caravan,

Cashel Folk Village

its cosy interior complete with made-up beds.

Open *daily Mar–Oct 10am–6pm.* **Adm** *adults €5, children €3.* **Credit** *V, MC.*

Fethard Folk Farm and Transport Museum ★★
AGES 3 AND UP

Fethard, Co Tipperary, ☏ 052 31516, www.fethard.com/attra/Museum. html. 15km N of Clonmel.

More than 12,000 exhibits from penny-farthing bicycles to ancient horse-drawn carriages are housed in this absorbing museum in a century-old railway goods store. The multitude of items on show, including oddities such as a 19th-century washing machine and the scales to weigh jockeys prior to the Cashel races, will keep children guessing.

The site also hosts Ireland's biggest and best car boot sale, with traders and buyers travelling from all over the country, so you may pick up a bargain too.

Open *Sun and bank holiday Mon.* **Adm** *(grounds) adults €1.50, children €1; (museum) adults €1.50, children €1.*

Mitchelstown Cave ★★★
ALL AGES

Burncourt, Cahir, Co Tipperary, ☏ 052 67246. 10km SW of Cahir.

Discovered in 1833 and explored by the famous French speleologist Martel in 1895, Mitchelstown cave is considered one of the most spectacular in Europe. The tour follows almost a kilometre of passageways through a series of great caverns, two of which have been dubbed the 'House of Commons' and the 'House of Lords'.

Imaginative children will enjoy the shapes and colours of the stalactites, stalagmites and calcite columns, the largest of which is called the 'Tower of Babel'.

Open *daily Mar–Nov 10am–5.30pm, Dec–Feb 11am–4.30pm.* **Adm** *adults €6, children €2.* **Credit** *V, MC.*

Nenagh Heritage Centre ★★

AGES 5 AND UP

Nenagh, Co Tipperary, ☎ *067 33850. 41km NE of Limerick.*

In its time, the building has been a gaol, a convent and a school, but now opens its doors to visitors as a heritage centre. Children can experience a schoolroom of yesteryear and see a drapers and a traditional pub and grocery shop. There's a recreated dairy showing how real Irish butter is made, and the original kitchen has an unusual oven. There's also a model of the gaol, complete with condemned cells and execution area, and there are tales of the felons whose lives came to an untimely end.

Open *Mon–Fri 9.30am–5pm and also Sat mid-May–mid-Sep.* **Adm** *free.*

Ormond Castle ★ AGES 5 AND UP

Castle Park, off Castle Street, Carrick-on-Suir, Co Tipperary, ☎ *051 640787, www.heritageireland.ie.*

Lacking turrets and battlements, children will point out that, despite its name, this is definitely not a proper castle. Nevertheless two 15th-century towers of an earlier castle lie at its heart. Ormond is the finest example in Ireland of an Elizabethan manor house and was built in 1560 for the 10th Earl of Ormond. It has fine plasterwork in its rambling rooms, offering a glimpse of the sumptuous living of the time. A toilet and car park are nearby.

Open *daily mid-Jun–early Sep 10am–6pm.* **Adm** *free.*

Kilkenny

Dunmore Cave ★★★ ALL AGES

Ballyfoyle, Co Kilkenny ☎ *056 776 7726, www.heritageireland.ie. 10km N of Kilkenny off N78.*

A cave with a grizzly tale to tell, this is where in 928 AD a raiding party of Vikings herded the local people inside before massacring them, an event recorded in the Annals and supported by archaeological finds.

After a video and exhibition in the Visitor Centre, guided tours lead you through successive chambers, formed over millions of years by an underground river. The cave contains the most spectacular calcite formations known in Ireland, created by the slow evaporation of mineral-rich water percolating through the limestone bedrock.

Open *daily Mar–mid-Jun and mid-Sep–Oct 9.30am–5pm, mid-Jun–mid-Sep 9.30am–6.30pm, Nov–Mar Fri–Sun and bank holidays 10am–5pm.* **Adm** *adults € 2.90, children €1.30, family €7.40, OPW Heritage Card.* **Credit** *most major cards accepted.* **Amenities** *exhibition, toilets.*

Newpark Fen ★ ALL AGES

Kilkenny City, Co Kilkenny, ☎ *056 776 3995, 2km NE of Kilkenny off the Castlecomer Road.*

Young ornithologists love this wildlife reserve centred on a stretch of open water in a marsh. The diversity of plant species and habitats attracts a wide range of animal and insect species as well as birds, and the bird feeding area is a special attraction for children.

Open *daily.*

Nore View Folk and Heritage Museum ★ AGES 5 AND UP

Bennettsbridge, Co Kilkenny, 📞 *056 772 7749. 9km S of Kilkenny.*

On the edge of the village by the River Nore, this quirky, private museum is worth a look if you are passing or visiting the nearby Nicholas Mosse pottery and café. It's packed with a motley collection of exhibits from the daily lives of ordinary people, from Stone Age artefacts to old petrol pumps. Displays include an old forge, a carpenter's workshop and a traditional pub, while others explore the impact of turbulent periods in Irish history such as The Uprising, War of Independence and the Potato Famine.

Open daily 10am–6pm. Adm adults €5, children €4, family €12. Credit V, MC. Amenities toilets, limited parking. Refreshments nearby at the Nicholas Mosse Pottery.

Carlow

Altamont Gardens ★ ALL AGES

Tullow, Co Carlow, 📞 *059 915 9444. Near Ballon, signed off N81 between Tullow and Bunclody.*

A great place to come for a family picnic, these beautiful traditional gardens have been developed over several generations to bring together a wonderful and varied collection of rare trees in a natural landscaped environment. Yew-fringed lawns offer views across a tranquil lake, dug to provide work during the famine. Old rose gardens and herbaceous gardens fill the summer air with their delicate perfumes.

Open Apr–Oct Mon–Thu 9am–5pm, Fri 9am–3.30pm, Sat–Sun and bank holidays 2–5.30pm. Adm (guided tour) adults €2.75, seniors €2, children €1.25, family €7, OPW Heritage Card. Credit most major cards accepted. Amenities toilet.

Browneshill Dolmen ★★ ALL AGES

Hacketstown Road, Carlow Town, Co Carlow. 3km E of Carlow on R726.

There are dolmens scattered right across Europe, but this one is considered to have the largest capstone of all, estimated to weigh more than 100 tonnes. Older than the Great Pyramid of Egypt, these mysterious monuments were once thought to be the resting places of giants or portals to the underworld, and their true significance may never be fully understood. All we know for sure is that they contained burials, perhaps of great chieftains and important members of their clan.

Open any reasonable hour. Adm free.

Altamont Gardens

Dolmens

Irish folklore often refers to such monuments as 'Leaba Diarmaid agus Grainne', which means 'the bed of Diarmaid and Grainne' and it is said that they were built by Dermot for he and his lover to sleep in while they were on the run. Diarmaid and Grainne had eloped together, but the only problem was that Grainne was already married to Finn. Finn, being the jealous type, pursued the couple all over the land and this accounts for the great many 'beds' to be found.

Huntington Castle ★
AGES 6 AND UP

Clonegal, Co Carlow, 📞 *054 77552. 6.5km E of Bunclody.*

Today's castle has evolved from a defensive tower house, built in 1625. It stands on the site of a 14th-century abbey and an even older Druid temple.

Huntington's timeless setting and famous avenues lined with yew and lime have appeared as backdrops to period films, but children will be more interested in finding out about the ghosts that give it the distinction of being the most haunted castle in the whole of Ireland, with 10 resident spooks. If you're brave enough, you can rent a wing of the castle for a holiday.

Open *Jun–Aug daily 2–6pm (last tours 5.30pm).* ***Adm*** *adults €6, children €4.* ***Credit*** *V, MC.*

Waterford

Copper Coast Mini Farm ★★
AGES 12 AND UNDER

Fenor, Tramore, Co Waterford, 📞 *051 396 870. 15km S of Waterford on R675.*

A great place for younger children to play in a farm setting, with diggers, buckets and spades and toy tractors to drive. There's an indoor play area, where children will find a cosy crofter's kitchen, a great setting for story telling, and a small playhouse as well as more toys. Animals to make friends with include a shaggy donkey, goats, pigs, deer and even a pair of young zebras, and there's a collection of vintage farm memorabilia to investigate. The Copper Kettle Tea Rooms offer tasty homemade snacks.

Open *May daily 12–6pm, Jun–Aug Mon–Fri 10am–5.30pm weekends and bank holidays 12–6pm, Sep weekends 12–6pm.* ***Adm*** *adults €5, children €7.* ***Credit*** *V, MC.* ***Amenities*** *toilets, baby-changing facilities, light refreshments, picnic area, pocket-money gifts for sale.*

Waterford Crystal Visitor Centre ★★ **AGES 5 AND UP**

Kilbarry, Waterford City, Co Waterford, 📞 *051 332 500; www. waterfordvisitorcentre.com. SW suburb of the town.*

Crystal has been made in Waterford since 1783, when George and William Penrose established a glass factory in the port to produce a range of flint glassware 'plain and cut, useful and ornamental'. Waterford glass is now known worldwide and there is a glittering display of some of the finest pieces.

Children, however, will be more interested in a tour of the factory to see how it's made. Molten glass taken straight from the furnace is skilfully blown to shape, and when cool, expertly cut and polished.

Open (visitor centre) *daily Jan–Feb 9am–5pm, Mar–Oct 8.30am–6pm, Nov–Dec 9am–5pm; (factory tours) Jan–Feb Mon–Fri 9am–3.15pm, Mar–Oct daily 8.30am–4.15pm, Nov–Dec Mon–Fri 9am–3.15pm.* **Adm** *(factory tour) adults €9.50, seniors/students €7.50, children €6.50.* **Credit** *all major cards.* **Amenities** *restaurant, Bureau de Change, toilets, baby-changing facilities, wheelchair accessible, gift shop.*

Waterford Treasures at the Granary Museum ★★★
AGES 5 AND UP

Merchant's Quay, Waterford City, Co Waterford, ☎ 051 304 500; www.waterfordtreasures.com.

Waterford's history goes back a thousand years to the arrival of the Vikings and here, housed in a former granary, it's all brought vividly back to life. Interactive displays, multimedia shows and a 3D film take you through the centuries, showing the arrival of the Normans and how the city grew through medieval trade. An exhibition shows some of the beautiful treasures and artefacts found in the area, including a Viking kite broach in gold. There

are sound guides for children, and a café.

Open Oct–Mar Mon–Sat 10am–5pm Sun and bank holidays 11am–5pm, Apr–Sep Mon–Sat 9.30am–6pm Sun and bank holidays 11am–6pm. **Adm** *adults €7, seniors/students €5, children (under 16) €3.20, under-5s free, family (2+1) €15, (2+2) €18, (2+3) €21.* **Credit** *all major cards.* **Amenities** *café, public car park nearby, toilets, baby-changing facilities, gift shop, tourist information.*

Waterford and Suir Valley Railway ★★ ALL AGES

Kilmeadan, near Waterford City, Co Waterford, ☎ 051 384 058; www.wsvrailway.ie. W of Waterford between Kilmeadan and Portlaw on R680.

This heritage narrow-gauge railway offers 40-minute round trips along a particularly beautiful 6.5km stretch of the River Suir, following the course of the former Waterford–Dungarvin branch line, which operated from 1878 until closure in 1967. The booking office is a converted railway carriage and among the engines is a restored Simplex 60sp diesel locomotive, which pulls Edwardian-style carriages.

Open April–Sept Mon–Sat 11am–4pm Sun 12–5pm. **Price** *adults €7.50, children €3.50, family (2+2) €19.* **Credit** *V, MC.*

Wexford

Hook Lighthouse ★★
AGES 5 AND UP

Hook Head, Fethard-on-Sea, Co Wexford, ☎ 051 397055/4; www.thehook-wexford.com/hook_head_lighthouse1.htm. 35km S of New Ross.

Hook lighthouse

Hook Tower is one of the oldest working lighthouses in the world, serving mariners along this treacherous coast for more than 800 years. 115 steps wind inside the wall to the upper parapet, where in the 13th century, a blazing brazier of coals provided the light.

During the climb you'll learn about the light and its long line of keepers, a history that begins in the 6th century when Dubhán, a Welsh monk erected the very first light on this wild peninsula. The views from the top are truly exhilarating.

Open daily Mar–Oct 9.30am–5.30pm (guided tours only), Nov–Feb 10am–5pm (guided tours available only on Sun). **Adm** child/student €5.50, OAP €3.50, under 5 free, family (2+2) €15. **Credit** V, MC. **Amenities** toilet, café, craft shop.

Irish Agricultural Museum and Famine Exhibition ★★
AGES 4 AND UP

Johnstown Castle Research Centre, Bridgetown Road, Wexford Town, Co Wexford. ☎ 053 914 2888; *www.heritageireland.com*. 10km SW of Wexford.

On a 19th-century farm in the grounds of Johnstown Castle, and containing a whole range of tools and implements, this remarkable museum shows the development of Irish farming over two hundred years into the 1950s. Displays on dairying, rural transport and village crafts-people, such as the blacksmith, thatcher and wheelwright, show different aspects of country life.

There's also an exhibition explaining the country's dependence on the potato and the devastation caused by the terrible famines of the 1840s. Harry Ferguson, who made the first powered flight in Ireland in a plane designed by himself, but is perhaps better known in Britain for his tractors, is also featured.

Open Dec–May Mon–Fri 9am–12.30pm and 1.30–5pm, Sep–Nov 2–5pm, Jun–Aug Mon–Fri 9am–5pm Sat–Sun 11am–5pm. **Adm** adults €6, children €4, family €20. **Credit** V, MC.

SS *Dunbrody* Emigrant Ship ★★★ AGES 3 AND UP

The Quay, New Ross, Co Wexford, 📞 *051 425 239; www.dunbrody.com. 24km NE of Waterford.*

Find out what it was like for the 19th-century emigrants escaping famine-torn Ireland for the promise of a better life in America and Canada. The *SS Dunbrody* is a full-scale reconstruction of a three-masted barque built in Quebec.

Originally a cargo ship, it was converted to take passengers and was typical of the many that plied back and forth across the Atlantic. Up to 300 passengers were crammed between the decks, left to fend for themselves during the long and often storm-lashed voyage. The Dunbrody's captain did what he could to alleviate the terrible conditions and it is remarkable that most of his passengers survived the rigours of the trip.

The guided tour paints a vivid picture of the experiences of the passengers and crew, enhanced by actors who take up their parts and tell their individual stories, of the life they were leaving behind and their hopes for the future. A young deck hand brilliantly highlights the issues to children.

Open daily 9am–6pm. **Adm** *adults €7, children €4, family (2+3) €20.* **Credit** *V, MC.* **Amenities** *adjacent public car parking, toilets, baby-changing facilities, café, gift shop, genealogy centre, guided tour.*

Wexford Wildfowl Reserve ★★ ALL AGES

North Slob, Co Wexford, 📞 *053 912 3129; www.heritageireland.ie.*

Only a short drive from Wexford towards Curracloe, the reserve is internationally important as an over-wintering site for birds, and up to 10,000 white fronted geese (about one-third of the world's population) arrive from Greenland every winter. In summer there are plenty of other birds on the wide, shallow harbour where mud flats and sand dunes attract a wide range of waders and wildfowl, many of whom come to breed as well as feed, so there is always something of interest to see.

Exhibitions and an audio-visual show at the visitor centre tell you what to look out for from the several hides around the reserve.

Open daily 9am–5pm. **Adm** *free.*

Active Children

Beaches

The whole coastline is stunning by any standards, with a seemingly endless run of cliffs and bays stretching into the distance, punctuated by pretty fishing villages and harbours.

Copper Coast

The rugged coastline between Tramore and Dungarvan is not to be missed, miles of towering cliffs broken by sandy coves, caves, harbours and attractive villages. One of them, Annestown, is unusual in being the only village in the whole of Ireland without a pub. Fed up with the constant drunken brawls or 'donnybrooks' caused by soldiers from the nearby barracks, the landowner had them all closed down.

The area is known as the **Copper Coast** because it was the scene of considerable mining activity during the 19th century. Its outstanding geological heritage has led to its designation as a European Geopark, where the history of the land's creation is revealed in a series of marked trails and information boards. An introduction to the geology, complete with field trip collecting sheet, has been prepared especially for children and can be downloaded from the website, *www.coppercoast.com*.

The **Blue Flag beach of Bunmahon** is a great base from which to explore the region, a superb white sandy beach backed by spectacular rugged cliffs. **Waymarked trails** lead past relics of the old copper mining industry or head inland to the ruins of an ancient monastery.

Just up the road from the beach is a 'time trail', a short walk during which the evolution of life and the Earth's rocks is revealed, from the earliest microscopic amoeba through the emergence of insects, fish, dinosaurs, birds, and eventually mammals and humans.

Dunmore East

At the tip of **Waterford Harbour** and looking out across the sound to the Hook Peninsula with its lighthouse, Counsellors Strand is backed by sandstone cliffs and so can be a sun-trap. It is ideal for getting to work with buckets and spades or splashing about in the sea.

Bunmahon

During the mid-19th century the village was home to copper miners, but today the area is rich in wildlife. There are fine sandy beaches and dunes, or the headland cliffs offer an exhilarating walk with superb views.

The Copper Coast

Clonea

East of Dungarvan, tucked behind the headland at the mouth of the harbour is the sweeping beach of Clonea. The sands make a fine playground with the coast behind offering opportunities for a scenic walk.

Tramore

Even if it means a detour, approach Tramore along the road from Annestown to the west to appreciate the stunning panorama of the bay. Tramore lives up to its name, which means the 'Big Strand', a 5km sweep of golden sand almost cutting off the inner bay behind.

Facing the Atlantic rollers, it's a great place for surfers and you can hire equipment and even take lessons. The area is also good for beach and cliff fishing and Tramore's amusement and leisure park offers rides to suit all ages.

Courtown

The popular resort of Courtown has grown up round a 19th-century harbour village and offers a wide range of family facilities. The nearby **Forest Park Leisure Centre** (☎ 053 942 4849) has a splendid 25-metre pool as well as learner and children's pools and a flume, plus a health suite too.

Pirates Cove Adventure Park in Courtown Harbour (☎ 053 942 5555) includes radio-controlled model trucks, safari cars and pirate ships, adventure golf and computerised tenpin bowling. For youngsters there is also the fun caves play area. But if the sun is shining, you'll want to be outside, where the sweeping

beach backed by sand dunes stretches for miles and the water is great for bathing.

Curracloe

Farther south, above Wexford, is **Curracloe**, where the coast is particularly noted for its bathing, and sea fishing from the beach is a popular activity. Alternatively, **Curracloe House Equestrian Centre** (☎ 053 913 7582) offers everything from beach treks to cross country and farm rides plus an indoor arena.

Duncannon

Tucked in the long estuary of Waterford Harbour, Duncannon has been the site of battles and sieges for most of the last two millennia as invaders have tried to set foot on Irish soil.

The 16th-century fort, where there is a military and maritime museum dominates a small promontory above the harbour, and if you're there on the June bank holiday weekend, there's the excitement of the re-enactment of a battle for the fort. In July, sandcastle building is taken to the extreme in the **International Sand Sculpting Festival**.

Rosslare

Children can watch ferry boats coming and going to northern France and Wales as they play on Rosslare's splendid Blue Flag beach. The town itself is a lively resort with plenty going on and, if you're looking for a day out close by, try the **Yola Farmstead Park** just 1½km away at Tagoat (☎ 053 913 2611). Dotted round the two-hectare farm are thatched cottages, barns, a forge and a working windmill, and plenty of bygone farm machinery adding to the 18th-century colour. And if the nature walks and rare breed animals and poultry are not enough to keep the children fully occupied, there's an 'Alamo' playground as well.

Open *daily throughout the summer, but closed at weekends during the winter period.* **Adm** *family (2+4) €11.*

FAMILY-FRIENDLY ACCOMMODATION

Lord Bagenal Inn ★★

Leighlinbridge, Co Carlow; 📞 *059 972 1668; www.lordbagenal.com.*

Overlooking the River Barrow, the Lord Bagenal offers spacious family accommodation with a playroom for children and further facilities planned.

Centrally located for a touring holiday, it's equally suited for relaxing on the deck terrace watching boats go by, or taking youngsters for a walk along the delightful riverbank. Families can eat in the bar or traditional restaurant, or for parents there's the fine dining of the Waterfront Restaurant.

Rooms *40.* **Rates** *double €130–150, child sharing €10–25 dependent upon age, enquire for special deals.* **Credit** *all major credit cards accepted.* **Amenities** *cots, bottle service, children's menus and small portions available, highchairs, baby-sitting arranged.* **In room** *room service, tea/coffee-making facilities, sat TV,*

laundry service, irons and boards, hairdryer, air-conditioning.

The Mount Wolseley ★★★

Tullow, Co Carlow, 📞 *059 915 1674; www.mountwolseley.ie.*

Set in an 80-hectare park overlooking a lake and its own golf club, this luxury venue offers both hotel and self-catering accommodation.

The hotel leisure club includes a pool and fitness suites as well as a spa offering a full range of treatments, and in summer there's a children's club offering entertainments such as face painting. There is also a children's play room and play ground.

Nearby outdoor activities range from gentle walking to quad biking or even trekking on horseback.

Rooms *152.* **Rates** *double €109–189, reductions for child sharing, enquire for special deals.* **Credit** *all major credit cards accepted.* **Amenities** *cots, bottle service, children's menus and small portions available, highchairs, baby-sitting arranged.* **In room** *room service, tea/coffee-making facilities, sat TV, Internet access, laundry service, irons and boards, hairdryer, air-conditioning.*

Springhill Court ★★★

Waterford Road, Kilkenny City, Co Kilkenny, 📞 *056 772 1112; www. springhillcourt.com.*

On the edge of town, Springhill Court offers a range of facilities geared up to families. As with other hotels in the Brennan chain, the family-friendly focus includes a properly run and planned summer children's club.

Alongside the pool, there's a pool for youngsters, and for parents a fitness suite and spa.

There's a choice of dining in the Claddagh Restaurant or the Paddock Bar, and children have their own menu if they can't find anything they fancy eating on the main one.

Rooms 85. **Rates** room €99–150 (2 adults and up to 2 children under 12 sharing), enquire for special deals. **Credit** all major credit cards accepted. **Amenities** cots, bottle service, children's menus and small portions available, highchairs, baby-sitting arranged. **In room** room service, tea/coffee-making facilities, safe deposit at reception, sat TV, WiFi, laundry service, irons and boards.

MODERATE

Clonmel Park Hotel ★ ★ ★

Poppyfield, Clonmel, Co Tipperary, ☎ 052 88700; www.clonmelpark hotel.com.

As well as a play area, the Li'l Rascalls Kids' Club offers swimming, basketball and arty-crafty sessions, with an evening video club over the weekend. For parents, there's a well-equiped leisure club and spa with pool, steam room, and Jacuzzi.

The hotel is well situated for many of the local attractions, with Mitchelstown Cave, Cashel and Cahir only a short drive away.

Rooms 99. **Rates** room €99–150 (2 adults and up to 2 children under 12 sharing), enquire for special deals. **Credit** all major credit cards accepted.

Amenities WiFi in reception area, safe deposit at reception, cots, bottle service, children's menus and small portions available, highchairs, baby-sitting arranged. **In room** room service, tea/coffee-making facilities, sat TV, broadband connection, laundry service, irons and boards.

MODERATE

Courtown Hotel ★

Courtown Harbour, Gorey, Co Wexford, ☎ 053 942 5210.

The Courtown Blue Flag beach is just round the corner from this great family hotel, which has its own swimming pool and leisure centre with sauna, steam room, Jacuzzi, fitness suite and play area.

The resort features all the attractions of a traditional seaside holiday: a harbour, amusement centre, bowling alley and other facilities only a short walk away.

Eat in the bistro dining room or the bar, or try the beer garden, which is fully enclosed so that children can't wander off. At weekends, there's often a singer or musician providing entertainment in the bar (children welcome until 9pm), or if you want a quiet evening, try the resident's bar instead.

Rooms 20. **Rates** room €100–140, child sharing (3–16) 50%, enquire for special deals. **Credit** all major credit cards accepted. **Amenities** safe deposit at reception, cots, bottle service, children's menus and small portions available, highchairs, baby-sitting arranged. **In room** room service, tea/coffee-making facilities, TV, laundry service on request, irons and boards available.

Hotel Curracloe ★

Curracloe, Wexford Town, Wexford,
☏ 1053 913 7308; www.hotel
curracloe.com.

Wexford's coastline has some
splendid beaches and the one at
Curracloe boasts Blue Flag status
and is close to the North Slobs
bird sanctuary and nature reserve.

Only a few minutes walk
from the beach, this smaller
hotel offers families a handy base
for touring the area. There's a
children's outdoor play area and
during the summer family entertainment evenings are arranged,
with spot prizes guaranteed to
create a bit of fun; teenagers
have their own disco.

Rooms 29. **Rates** room €80–100,
child sharing (4–12) 50%, (13–14)
25%, enquire for special deals. **Credit**
all major credit cards accepted.
Amenities safe deposit at reception,
cots, bottle service, children's menus
and small portions available, highchairs, baby-sitting arranged. **In room**
room service, tea/coffee-making facilities, sat TV, irons and boards available.

Kelly's Resort Hotel ★★★ FIND

Rosslare, Co Wexford, ☏ 053 913
2114; www.kellys.ie.

Kelly's has been hosting family
holidays at Rosslare for more
than a hundred years, so they
probably know even more than
you do about what goes into
making a really great vacation.

For a start, the setting is perfect, a really top class hotel with
extensive gardens fronting a
superb beach plus a pool.

Service is honed to perfection
and there's a fully equipped baby
room and crèche to look after
the very youngest, while older
children have just about every
entertainment and activity they
could wish for with a play room,
outdoor play areas and games,
and a summer activity and entertainment programme.

With tennis, crazy golf, swimming, snooker and a host of
other games and sports, there's
never a shortage of things to do
but if you want to wander farther afield, the hotel can arrange
bike hire, horse riding and sailing. And for parents there's also
an extensive spa with sauna,
steam room, Jacuzzi, hot tub,
health club, and treatments.

Rooms 120. **Rates** room from €170,
child sharing to age 3 €25, to age 10
33%, (11–14) 25%, enquire for special deals. **Credit** all major credit
cards accepted. **Amenities** WiFi in
public areas, cots, bottle service,
children's menus and small portions
available, highchairs, baby-sitting
arranged, fully equipped laundry
room. **In room** room service, tea/cof-
fee-making available, safe, sat TV,
laundry service.

Tower Hotel and Leisure Centre ★★

The Mall, Waterford City, Co
Waterford, ☏ 051 862 2300; www.
towerhotelwaterford.com.

On the waterfront in the heart
of the city, the Tower Hotel is
well placed for attractions in the
area, as well as offering a full
range of facilities in its own
leisure centre, which includes a

pool, sauna, steam room, Jacuzzi and health club. There's a choice of restaurants or you can book a qualified babysitter and have an evening out on the town.

Rooms 144. **Rates** *room from €142–182, child sharing (over 3) €20, enquire for special deals.* **Credit** *all major credit cards accepted.* **Amenities** *guest parking, cots, bottle service, children's menus and small portions available, highchairs, baby-sitting arranged.* **In room** *room service, tea/coffee-making facilities, safe, TV, WiFi throughout hotel, iron and board, laundry service.*

Clonea Strand Hotel ★★

Clonea, Dungarvan, Co Waterford, 📞 *058 45555; www.clonea.com.*

With a Blue Flag beach on its doorstep, and offering a host of activities for all the family, this resort hotel makes a great holiday destination. There's a choice of accommodation arrangements, with holiday cottages and apartments available at the nearby Gold Coast Golf Resort and Hotel.

All have full access to the facilities that between the two sites include a fully equipped leisure centre, pool, sauna, steam room, Jacuzzi, health club, fitness centre, and massive children's soft play area as well as ten-pin bowling alley, tennis courts, football net and basketball hoop.

The hotel restaurant serves traditional and continental dishes, many of which use the fresh fish and seafood landed around the coast.

Rooms 59. **Rates** *room from €69–190, child sharing €10 – 50% reduction dependent upon age, enquire for special deals.* **Credit** *all major credit cards accepted.* **Amenities** *cots, bottle service, children's menus and small portions available, highchairs, baby-sitting arranged.* **In room** *room service, tea/coffee-making facilities, safe deposit facility at reception, sat TV, WiFi available (public areas only), iron and board, laundry service.*

CAFÉS & FAMILY-FRIENDLY DINING

The Forge ★★ TRADITIONAL IRISH

Kilbride Cross, Ballon, Co Carlow, 📞 *059 915 9939.*

The 18th-century granite building was originally built as a forge, but more recently has served as a shop and post office before becoming a coffee shop full of delicious smells.

Ideally placed for visits to Altamont Gardens, it's simply furnished with original flag floors and you won't be disappointed with Mary Jordan's home baking: her scones and loganberry jam are a delight.

Early callers can tuck into a hearty breakfast and daily specials can include roast beef, Irish stew or baked ham using seasonal local produce. There's a small display of local crafts, and the pieces of artwork and photography decorating the walls are for sale.

Open *daily 9.30am–5.30pm.* **Main courses** *€9.95–14.50.* **Credit** *V, MC.* **Amenities** *wine licence, children's* menu and small portions, highchairs, bottle warming, baby-changing facilities, car park.

MODERATE

Kilkenny Design Centre ★★★
FIND **LIGHT MEALS**

Castle Yard, Kilkenny City, Co Kilkenny, ☎ 056 771 2118; www.kilkenny design.com.

Facing the castle, in the former stables and coach house above the Design Centre, the staff have done a lot to make this a great place to bring children. Not only are the surroundings and food first class, but you also get help with tables, buggies and more.

There are colouring books and crayons, and while lots of places now have baby-changing facilities, this one will even provide you with a nappy for those unexpected emergencies. There's plenty of space around the tables for buggies, and all the food is freshly prepared in the kitchens, including an interesting selection of specials to supplement the menu.

You can get everything from breakfast to an early evening meal, or just wander in, browse round the craft shop downstairs, and then relax over a drink and pastry.

Open Mon–Sat 10am–7pm, Sun 11am–7pm. **Main courses** from €7.95. **Credit** V, MC. **Amenities** licensed, children's options, small portions, highchairs, bottle warming, baby-changing facilities.

MODERATE

Nicholas Mosse Pottery ★★
FIND SNACKS & MODERN IRISH

Bennettsbridge, Co Kilkenny, ☎ 056 772 7105; www.nicholasmosse. com.

This friendly eatery is in an old flourmill just downstream of the town bridge, and is home to the famous Nicholas Mosse Pottery and an extensive store selling a good range of household wares, fabrics and candles as well as the distinctive pottery.

Large windows open into the workshops, where children can watch the pots being thrown and decorated. Book in advance and you can all have a go at decorating your own pots, plates or cups, which after firing will be

Kilkenny Design Centre

posted on to you at home if you can't get back.

The café serves a tasty selection of freshly baked cakes, tarts and crumbles and light lunches such as quiche, cottage pie, lasagne and pork and apricot terrine.

Open (shop) 9am–6pm, Sun 1–5pm; (café) Mon–Sat 11am–5pm, Sun 1.30–4pm. **Main courses** €7.95–15. **Credit** V, MC. **Amenities** small portions, bottle warming, highchairs, baby-changing facilities.

MODERATE

Ryan's Daughter ★ LIGHT MEALS

Ladyswell Street, Cashel, Tipperary, 062 62688.

This comfortable, homely, country cottage style restaurant is at the top end of town towards the Rock of Cashel. Decorated with stills from the film 'Ryan's Daughter', it's friendly and popular with locals, who come for the plain, no frills Irish cooking, generous portions and friendly service. There are sandwiches and toasties, main courses such as lamb cutlets with mint sauce, pork chop with apple sauce or scampi, and afternoon tea with scone. There is also a Kiddies Corner menu.

Open summer Mon–Thu 9am–8.30pm Fri–Sun 9am–6.30pm, winter Mon–Thu 9am–8.30pm Fri–Sun 9am–6pm. **Main courses** €6.95–16.95. **Credit** V, MC. **Amenities** children's menu, small portions, bottle warming, highchairs.

MODERATE

Pepes Café Bar ★ ITALIAN

Kenyon Street, Nenagh, Co Tipperary, 067 43883; www.nenagh.net/main/pepes.htm.

This modern café bistro concentrates on Italian pizzas including fruity ham, corn and pineapple, and spicy pepperoni, onion and chilli, and pasta such as bacon, chicken, mushroom and onion in a creamy sauce, plus the more traditional spaghetti bolognese or lasagne. You can also opt for plaice and chips or a 100% Irish beef burger and for children there are also chicken goujons or burger with chips.

Open Mon–Thu 5–10pm, Fri–Sun 4–10pm. **Main courses** €8.95–16.95. **Credit** most cards. **Amenities** licensed, children's menus and portions, highchairs, bottle warming.

MODERATE

Granary Café ★★
SNACKS AND LIGHT MEALS

Merchant's Quay, Waterford, Co Waterford, 051 854 428.

This café is located in the same stone-and-brick built 19th-century granary as the Waterford Museum of Treasures, where there's also a tourist information centre. The airy modern café is a relaxed place that goes out of its way for children, and is popular for a coffee and cake or a light lunch with options including quiches, tarts, salads and soup and home-made bread all on show (so children can make their own selection).

Open summer Mon–Sat 10am–5pm Sun 11am–5pm, winter Mon–Sat 10am–4pm Sun 11am–4pm. **Main courses** from €6.95. **Credit** V, MC. **Amenities** children's portions, highchairs, bottle warming, baby-changing facilities.

Copper Kettle ★ LIGHT SNACKS

Copper Coast Mini farm, Fenor, Tramore, Co Waterford, 📞 *051 396 870.*

There's a mini-farm here for children to wander and it's a good place to know about when out exploring the coast, being not far from Tramore on the R675 towards Dungarvan, where there aren't too many places to drop into. On offer are assorted sandwiches and toasties, homemade fruit pies and cakes, and ice creams.

Open *May daily 12–6pm, Jun–Aug Mon–Fri 10am–5.30pm weekends and bank holidays 12–6pm, Sep weekends 12–6pm.* **Main dishes** *from €6.95.* **Credit** *V, MC.* **Amenities** *highchairs, bottle warming, baby-changing facilities.*

MODERATE

Foley's on the Mall ★
MODERN IRISH

Main Street, Lismore, Waterford. 📞 *058 53671; www.foleysonthemall. com.*

This is a bistro pub with a traditional bar and dining room downstairs and a bright and modern restaurant upstairs. Good pub food is what's on offer – open and club sandwiches, toasties, hot tortilla wraps, cod in batter and pasta dishes. Starters are also available as a large portion if you want to make a light meal of it. But firm favourites are the steaks and burgers served with different sauces

and relishes. There's a beer garden at the back for when the weather is fine.

Open *Mon–Thu 12–9pm, Fri–Sat 12–9.30pm.* **Main courses** *€10.50–23.90.* **Credit** *V, MC.* **Amenities** *licensed, children's menu and portions, bottle warming, highchairs, baby-changing facilities.*

MODERATE–EXPENSIVE

The Strand Inn ★ MODERN IRISH

Dunmore East, Co Waterford, 📞 *051 383 174; www.thestrandinn.com.*

A great place both to eat and stay, this residential inn is on the village seafront with a choice of bars, restaurant and a patio overlooking the bay. Fish takes pride of place but there's something for every taste. Lunchtime options include chowder, open crab sandwich, ploughman's platter or seafood pie with salad. In the evening a starter of pea and prawn risotto could be followed by rack of lamb with a mint reduction and there's always a blackboard of fish specials.

They have no separate children's menu but can provide small portions of most things. Children are welcomed in the restaurant until 8pm and on the patio until 10pm. Book for the restaurant in the evening.

Open *bar food from lunchtime, restaurant 6.30–10pm daily.* **Main courses** *€22.50–26.50.* **Credit** *V, MC.* **Amenities** *child portions, bottle warming, highchairs, baby-changing facilities.*

The 'Midlands' are less visited than other parts of Ireland, and so they remain uncrowded, even in peak holiday periods. The area is mainly rural, with few large towns or major tourist attractions but instead quiet lanes and attractive villages. Along with the innate friendliness of the locals it makes an ideal place for a relaxing, outdoors holiday.

Enclosed on the west by the natural boundary of the Shannon, the longest river in the British Isles, the geographical heartland of the country sweeps south from the border with Northern Ireland to the productive plains of the south. Fishing and boating are hugely popular, and cruising the lakes and the Shannon are great ways to relax.

Over time, many of these watery areas have filled with silt and vegetation to create extensive boglands and fens, a traditional source of fuel. Now recognised as an important environmental resource, providing rich habitats for wildlife, they've also yielded traces of Ireland's prehistoric past, with one of the most spectacular finds being the bog roads at Keenagh.

Beyond the bogs the green meadowlands have been a mainstay of Irish agriculture, ideal for cattle and, above all, horses. In sharp contrast the Slieve Bloom Mountains rise to define the border between Offaly and Kildare. Here, although the highest spots barely top the 520-metre contour, the views are spectacular. Wooded valleys sheltering fast-flowing streams and open moorlands provide a wealth of opportunities for walking, horse riding or simply picnicking.

ESSENTIALS

Getting There

By Sea The ferry ports of Dublin and Dun Laoghaire are conveniently placed for the whole area, though if you're holidaying in Monaghan or Cavan, driving across the border from Larne or Belfast is hardly a long journey. Similarly, Rosslare best serves Laois and Kildare.

By Air Like the ferry ports, Ireland's airports are scattered around the periphery of the country, and none lies within the Midlands area. Dublin is generally the most convenient because it has links with the majority of British airports. See Chapter 2 for details of airlines into Ireland.

VISITOR INFORMATION

The main website covering the region is the Discover Ireland site, *www.ireland.ie*. For Monaghan and Cavan also look at *www.irelandnorthwest.ie*, *www.monaghantourism.com* and *www.cavantourism.com*.

Visitors to Longford, Westmeath, North Offaly, Kildare and Laois should check out *www.eastcoastmidlands.ie*.

THE MIDLANDS

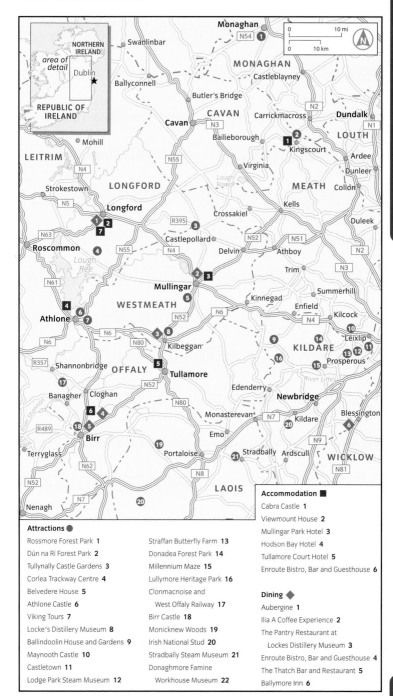

The southern half of Offaly comes under the Shannon Tourist Region *www.shannon regiontourism.ie*.

Information on the individual counties can be found at *www. longford.ie*, *www.westmeath tourism.com*, *www.offalytourism. com*, *www.kildare.ie/tourism* and *www.laoistourism.ie*.

The main Tourist Information Offices for each of the counties are located as follows:

Monaghan

Monaghan Tourist Office (seasonal) Mullacroghery, Clones Road, Monaghan Town, Co Monaghan. ☏ 047 81122.

Cavan

Cavan Tourist Office (seasonal) Farnham Street, Cavan Town, Co Cavan. ☏ 049 433 1942.

Longford

Longford Tourist Information Office (seasonal) 45 Dublin Street, Longford Town, Co Longford. ☏ 043 46566.

Westmeath

Mullingar Tourist Office, Dublin Road, Mullingar, Co Westmeath. ☏ 044 934 8650.

Athlone Tourist Information Office (seasonal) Athlone Castle, Athlone, Co Westmeath. ☏ 090 649 4630.

Clonmacnoise Tourist Information Office (seasonal) Via Shannonbridge, Athlone, Co Westmeath. ☏ 090 967 4134.

Offaly

Tullamore Tourist Information Office Bury Quay, Tullamore, Co Offaly. ☏ 057 935 2617.

Birr Tourist Office (seasonal) Castle Street, Birr, Co Offaly. ☏ 050 920 110.

Kildare

Kildare Tourist Information Office Market House, Kildare Town, Co Kildare. ☏ 045 521 240.

Laois

Portlaoise Tourist Office James Fintan Lawlor Avenue, Portlaoise, Co Laois. ☏ 057 862 1178.

ORIENTATION

Monaghan is 135km (84 miles) NW of Dublin, 290km (180 miles) N of Rosslare and 101km (63 miles) SW of Belfast.

Cavan is 118km (73 miles) NW of Dublin, 259km (161 miles) N of Rosslare and 150km (93 miles) SW of Belfast.

Longford is 123km (76 miles) NW of Dublin, 265km (164 miles) NW of Rosslare and 202km (126 miles) SW of Belfast.

Athlone

Mullingar is 83km (52 miles) W of Dublin, 225km (140 miles) NW of Rosslare and 191km (119 miles) SW of Belfast.

Tullamore is 103km (64 miles) W of Dublin, 163km (101 miles) NW of Rosslare and 263km (163 miles) SW of Belfast.

Kildare (not the county town) is 54km (34 miles) SW of Dublin, 126km (78 miles) NW of Rosslare and 220km (137 miles) S of Belfast.

Portlaoise is 83km (52 miles) SW of Dublin, 126km (78 miles) NW of Rosslare and 250km (155 miles) S of Belfast.

Ireland's major road system radiates out star-fashion from Dublin, providing convenient links from the capital to the main towns in each of the region's counties. Motorways follow the lines of the N4 and N7 to Mullingar and Portlaoise. Elsewhere, roads between the smaller towns and villages are generally quiet and traffic-free, the relatively few hills making this an excellent region for cycling.

Getting Around

A car is really the only practical way of getting around the wider region, and if you have arrived by air you can pick up a hire car from one of the companies at the airport.

However, if your holiday is largely at a single base, Bus Éireann runs regular services from Dublin to the main county towns (☎ *01 836 6111; www.buseireann.ie*). The rail service (☎ *01 836 6222; www.irishrail.ie*) will get you into any of the counties except Cavan, with routes leaving Dublin to the northwest through Mullingar and Longford and west via Kildare to Tullamore and Athlone. Trains also serve Portlaoise and Carlow.

Discover the Counties

Monaghan

Forming the upper tip of the Midlands region with much of its boundary shared by the Northern Province, Monaghan is one of Ireland's best-kept secrets. Although lacking major tourist attractions and sights, its scenery is a delight, speckled with rivers and lakes. The area is an angler's paradise, but its tranquil lanes and beautiful countryside also make it ideal for a leisurely exploration by bike or on horseback. The forest parks at Rossmore (see p. 123) and Bellamont are great spots for walks and to let the children run off a bit of energy, or spend a more relaxing afternoon picnicking under the trees. The county's small towns and villages have a quiet attractiveness, while Clones and Carrickmacross are famous for their lace making.

Cavan

To the south and west stretches Cavan, a watery landscape of meandering rivers, streams and sinuous small loughs, broken by low rounded hills called drumlins. It's said that there is a different lake for each day of the year, justifying the title Lake County. Nowhere is this description more apt than just to the northwest of Cavan Town, where the River Erne almost loses its way in a maze of interconnecting lakes and ponds. With so much water about, pre-historic settlers had to adopt a different approach to making their homes, building settlements on small artificial islands (crannogs) that gave them security from attack.

The rivers Shannon and Erne both have their source in the Cuilcagh Mountains to the northwest. The River Erne heads north to break from land in Donegal Bay, while the Shannon meanders south across the central plain for almost 330km before finding the Atlantic in the southwest.

There's enjoyable walking to be had in the forest park of Dún na Rí (see p. 123), or you can climb into the saddle (bike or horse) to explore the countryside from a different vantage point. Its scattered villages and hamlets add to the rural appeal, while Virginia, on the banks of Lough Ramor, is where Jonathan Swift reputedly got the idea for his Gulliver's Travels.

The county town is worth visiting too, and is the only medieval town that was actually founded by the Irish themselves, its narrow streets still following the original layout.

Longford and Westmeath

Bordering the northern shores of Lough Ree, where the River Shannon spills out across the land in a massive lake, are the counties of Longford and Westmeath. Traditional farming country, they have the laid-back pastoral charm of small villages and peaceful lanes.

The Royal Canal brought prosperity to the area in the 19th century, with Clondara in County Longford, where the canal meets the Shannon, developing as a small harbour. There was a flax mill and corn mill, which for a time served as a whiskey distillery, the produce being shipped to Dublin along the canal. But the Great Famine cut short the heyday, with many emigrants leaving for the New World from that same harbour.

The 19th-century St Mells Cathedral dominates Longford's county town and is a landmark from miles around, while to the south you find one of the country's most important archaeological sites, the Corlea Trackway Centre (see p. 124).

Athlone at the southern tip of Lough Ree lies almost at the geographical centre of Ireland and as the largest town along the river is a popular centre for cruising on the waters.

Offaly and Laois

Offaly and Laois are divided by the rise of the Slieve Bloom Mountains, which just top 518 metres and give wide-sweeping views across the central plain. They offer some of Ireland's finest walking and on a really clear day you can see the highest points of each of the country's four provinces. The 77km Slieve Bloom Way will be more than most families would contemplate, but there are several shorter walks exploring its many beautiful corners.

The whole area is rich in wildlife and, apart from the numerous birds, there's a good chance of seeing deer, wild goats and foxes – if you can persuade the children to stay quiet enough. To the west the ground falls across Offaly towards the Shannon, and one of the highlights is a visit to Birr Castle (see p. 127). During the 18th century, it possessed the world's largest reflecting telescope, which now restored, forms the centrepiece of an imaginative science museum that's well presented for children.

Another novel attraction is the Clonmacnoise Railway (see p. 127), which makes a noisy but fascinating journey of discovery into Ireland's boglands. To the east, Laois' attractions include the **Donaghmore Famine Workhouse Museum** and children will also enjoy the freedom of the parkland at Emo and Heywood.

Away from the main roads, hushed lanes encourage unhurried travel and you're likely to meet a horse-drawn caravan – just another way to chill out and enjoy the countryside.

Kildare

The Irish are passionate about many things, but near the top of any list are horses, and in Kildare, you're right at the very heart of horsiness. The rich green turf is fantastic grazing and has just the right bounce for training prize-winning mounts. It is therefore no surprise to find that one of the country's most successful industries is centred here – Kildare is 'Thoroughbred County'.

There are three top class racecourses in the area and a day at the races can be a fun outing, even if you're not into form. **The Irish National Stud** at Tully provides a fascinating insight into all aspects of the 'Sport of Kings', and is a chance to see some of the world's finest horses.

Other fun ideas for a children's day out include the Butterfly Farm at Straffan (see p. 130), and the Lullymore Heritage Park (see p. 129) in the heart of Allen Bog.

Children-friendly Events & Entertainment

Bord na Mona Water Festival

Lamesboro, Ballyleague, Co Longford, ☎ 043 27070.

A fun weekend for everyone, especially children, in this festival that celebrates all things wet, plus music, dancing and a great firework finale.

Phoenix Festival

Tullamore, Co Offaly, ☎ 057 932 4606; www.phoenixfestival.ie.

Hot air balloons, skydiving, canal barge trips and helicopter flights are just some of the big draws here with music and dancing in the square providing ongoing entertainment. For children, there's face painting, puppet theatres, mime artists and story telling. The whole weekend comes to a climax with a grand parade and firework display at which the phoenix is ceremoniously burnt.

Stradbally Steam Rally

Stradbally, Co Laois, ☎ 057 862 5154; www.irishsteam.ie.

At Stradbally Hall on August Bank Holiday Sunday and Monday (it's the first week of the month in Ireland) traction engines, road rollers and lorries come from all over Ireland (and a few from the UK as well) to trundle up and down in all their glory. There are plenty of stationary engines as well – such as threshing machines and stone crushers – and some fine working scale models as well as some more unusual contraptions that put steam to work in making music. Vintage cars and tractors come too, and the Stradbally narrow gauge railway will be running as well.

Tullamore and National Livestock Show

Tullamore, Co Offaly, ☎ 057 935 2141; www.tullamoreshow.com.

Billed as the country's largest one-day show and held in August, this is one of the great agricultural events of the year. Country children will love everything going on, while for townies, it's an eye-opening experience. They'll come face to face with pedigree breeding cattle and sheep and see some of the finest horses in the country. Show jumping, carriage driving and pony club events are just some of the events, and there are exhibits of farming produce so youngsters can see where their food actually comes from. There's music and food all day and plenty of amusements and games, especially for children.

WHAT TO SEE & DO

Children's Top 10 Attractions

❶ Watch thoroughbreds being trained at the Irish National Stud. See p. 122.

❷ Marvel at the Iron Age roadway at Corlea Trackway Centre. See p. 124.

❸ Discover the wonders of science at Birr Castle. See p. 127.

❹ Find out about the plight of the 19th-century poor in Donaghmore Famine Workhouse Museum. See p. 121.

❺ See how Irish whiskey is made at Locke's Distillery Museum. See p. 134.

❻ Wander through history at the Lullymore Heritage Park. See p. 129.

❼ Thrill to the engines and vehicles of another age at the Stradbally Steam Museum. See p. 130.

❽ Have a go at peat cutting and enjoy a ride on the Clonmacnoise and West Offaly Railway. See p. 127.

❾ Look for wildlife in the glens of the Slieve Bloom Mountains. See p. 121.

❿ Enjoy a picnic in the woods at Dún na Rí or Rossmore Forest Park. See below.

Children-friendly Attractions

Monaghan

Rossmore Forest Park ★
ALL AGES

The waymarked trails in this forest park are a great way of going birdwatching without fear of getting lost. Just a short distance south of Monaghan Town along the R189 in the direction of Newbliss, the Rossmore Forest Park has picnic sites, a nature trail and lake, and those lovely forest walks. The forest is centred on the ruins of Rossmore Castle, which dates from the late 18th century. Although little now remains, it provides a good viewpoint across the surrounding countryside, a landscape of small lakes, rivers and hillocks created by slowly flowing ice, which created the small egg-shaped hills called drumlins.

Open daily until dusk. *Adm* €5 per car. *Amenities* picnic areas.

Cavan

Dún na Rí Forest Park ★
ALL AGES

Kingscourt, Co Cavan, ☎ 049 433 1942; www.coillte.ie. 1.5km N of Kingscourt on R179 in the direction of Carrickmacross.

This pretty wooded glen follows the River Cabra through a dramatic gorge and offers a choice of short waymarked trails. Among the sights to look out for are an ice-house, the ruins of

Flemmings Castle, Cromwell's Bridge, and the famous Toba na Splinne wishing well.

Open daily until dusk. **Adm** €5 per car. **Amenities** toilet, picnic area.

Longford

Corlea Trackway Centre ★★
AGES 5 AND UP

Keenagh, Longford, Co Longford, ☎ 043 22386; www.heritageireland. ie. Off R397, 3km from Keenagh.

The bog roads of Keenagh are guaranteed to stir the imaginations of children old enough to grasp their age. A wooden trackway unearthed while cutting peat in 1984 led to the discovery of a whole network of bog paths in the area, known locally as *toghers*, dating from 5,500 years ago. The most startling is a kilometre-long stretch of Iron Age roadway leading to an island on higher ground. Wide enough to take a cart, it is made of wooden planks laid cross-wise on tree-trunks, rather like an upside-down railway track. An 18-metre section has been preserved and re-laid in its original position within a specially constructed hall, humidified to prevent the ancient wood from drying out. Axe marks left by its builders are still plainly visible but oddly, the road shows little signs of wear, and archaeologists have determined that within 10 years of its construction it began to sink into the bog.

An enthusiastic guide introduces you to the descriptive exhibition before leaving you to watch a film describing its discovery and preservation. You are then taken to see the trackway itself, when the guide explains more about the lifestyle of the people who built it and invites speculation as to its purpose.

The tour then moves outside on to the bog itself under which the ongoing track still lies, and the guide helps identify the flora and wildlife. The plants that most fascinate children are the insectivores, such as sundew, which survive in this harsh landscape by trapping and devouring small insects.

Open Apr–Sep 10am–6pm. **Adm** free. **Amenities** toilets, baby-changing facilities, picnic area.

Westmeath

Belvedere House Gardens and Park ★★★ **ALL AGES**

Belvedere, Mullingar, Co Westmeath, ☎ 044 934 9060; www.belvedere-house.ie. S of Mullingar off N52.

A restored 18th-century hunting and fishing lodge, the house stands in 65 hectares of beautiful gardens and parkland overlooking Lough Ennell, where there are picnic areas by the lake.

In the house, the ground floor rooms are open to view, including the lounge and dining room, while in the stable block a video and exhibition brings the history of the house and estate to life, telling stories of scandal and intrigue.

Belvedere House Gardens and Park

There's a walled garden and Victorian glasshouse, plus ponies and goats in the paddocks to befriend.

The park is particularly renowned for its collection of follies such as the Jealous Wall, the Gothic Arch, and a Gazebo, and there's also an ice-house, where winter ice from the lake was stored for use in the summer.

During the summer months, you can ride round the grounds on a tram, and for youngsters a Narnia trail leads through the woods passing creatures turned to stone by the wicked White Witch – look out for the unicorns and other creatures. And, if the children are still going strong after all that, let them loose in one of the three playgrounds, each designed for a different age group.

The Courtyard Café (accessible even if you don't visit the house and gardens) offers a range of snacks and light meals throughout the day including children's options and small portions.

Open (house) Mar, Apr, Sep and Oct 10.30am–5pm (garden 10.30–7), May–Aug 10am–5pm (garden 9.30am–9pm), Nov–Feb 10.30am–4.30pm. **Adm** adults €8.75, seniors/students €6.25, children €4.75, family (2+2) €24. Tram: adults €2, seniors/students/children €1. **Credit** V, MC. **Amenities** toilets, baby-changing facilities, disabled access, highchairs in restaurant.

Tullynally Castle Gardens ★
ALL AGES

Castlepollard, Co Westmeath, ☎ 044 966 1159; www.tullynallycastle.com. 1.5km NE from Castlepollard in the direction of Granard.

Gothic towers and turrets adorn this splendid 120-room castle, one of the largest in the country and home to the Earls of Longford for over 350 years. Although not generally open to the public, it stands as an imposing backdrop to the terrace and walled gardens.

Beyond a limestone grotto and Chinese gardens, woodland paths and lakeside walks take you farther afield. A quiz sheet, available in the courtyard, leads children on the Tullynally Treasure Trail, and youngsters can have fun looking for sculptures carved into the boles of trees. There's a crocodile lurking in the lake and a llama with babies in the kitchen garden, while on the forest walk is a Chinese house.

The Children of Lir: an Irish Legend

Tullynally means 'hill of the swan' and the present castle is said to be built on the site of the stronghold of King Lir.

Long ago the brave and noble Lir lived here happily in the heart of a forest with his wife Aeb and their four children, a daughter, Fionnuala, and three sons, Aodh, Fiachra and Conn. When Lir's wife died his children were still young and he married Aeb's sister, Aoife, to be a mother to them. But Aoife grew jealous of Lir's love for his children and plotted their riddance. She took the children to nearby Lough Derravaragh and, as they swam in the water, cast a spell turning them into swans and condemning them to spend 300 years on Lough Derravaragh, 300 years in the Straits of Moyle and 300 years on the Isle of Inish Glora in the western sea, only to be released when the ringing of a bell proclaimed the arrival of a new faith.

When Aoife returned without the children, Lir went off in search of them and standing on the shores of the lake he heard their voices and wept bitterly when he learned of the spell. Each day, Lir would speak to his children and they would sing sweetly in response, attracting people from far and wide to hear the peaceful, beautiful melody. In time the swans flew off to the cold and stormy Sea of Moyle and ultimately to Inish Glora to wait out the last age of the spell.

Eventually, the sun rose to the sound of a tolling bell that broke the enchantment, but on regaining human form they found they were no longer children, but old and frail. As the four sank to the ground in exhaustion, a monk named Kenoc from the church sprinkled holy water on them. That night he dreamed of four swans flying into the clouds, and knew that the children of Lir had finally returned to their mother and father.

Open *May–Jun, weekends and bank holidays, Jul–Aug daily 12–6pm.* **Adm** *adults €6, children €3, family €16.* **Credit** *V, MC.* **Amenities** *toilets, partial wheelchair access, tearoom serving light refreshments.*

Viking Tours ★ ALL AGES

7 St. Mary's Place, Athlone, Co Westmeath, ☎ *086 262 1136; www.iol.ie/wmeathtc/viking.*

In 796 AD, Viking raiders under Turgesius sailed up the Shannon to plunder the monastic settlements on the islands and around the shores of Lough Ree. But Turgesius got more than he bargained for and in the battles that followed, the Irish king Malachy sank half his fleet and drowned him in a neighbouring lake.

A reconstructed longboat tours the lake as a Viking crew tells entertaining tales of the battles fought and treasures won, and children can dress as Vikings for a memorable picture.

Open *May–Aug daily, Sep–Oct dependent upon minimum numbers – morning Clonmacnoise, afternoon*

Lough Ree. Prior booking necessary. **Fare** (Clonmacnoise) adults €20, children €15, family (2+4) €60; (Lough Ree) adults €12, children €10, family (2+4) €40. **Credit** V, MC.

Offaly

Birr Castle Demesne and Historic Science Centre
★★★ ALL AGES

Birr, Co Offaly, 📞 *05791 20336; www.birrcastle.com. In the centre of the town.*

Although the castle is not open, the demesne is one of the largest and finest in the country and you can spend an enjoyable day wandering through the formal gardens, terraces and extensive parkland. However, the real attraction for older children will be the Historical Science Centre, based round the outstanding scientific achievements of the family. The story begins with the third Earl of Ross, who constructed a massive 183-centimetre reflecting telescope in 1840. It remained the largest in the world for 75 years and enabled him and his son to undertake many remarkable observations and discoveries. Elsewhere are displays illustrating pioneering work in photography by Mary, Countess of Ross, and the invention of the steam turbine by her son Charles. A Junior Science Trail, downloadable from the website, highlights key exhibits.

The climax of the visit is undoubtedly the great telescope itself, restored to full working order and standing resplendent in the centre of an ancient meadow in the park.

Open daily 9am–6pm. **Adm** adults €9, seniors/students €7.50, children €5.50, family €25. **Credit** V, MC. **Amenities** parking near the visitor entrance, toilets, gift shop, partial disabled access, tea room (open daily March to Oct 11am–5.30pm, 12.30–5.30pm Sundays) serves light snacks.

Clonmacnoise and West Offaly Railway ★★ ALL AGES

Shannonbridge, Co Offaly, 📞 *090 9674450. Off R357 between Shannonbridge and Cloghan.*

The Blackwater Bog is part of the vast Bog Allen, which covers 8,100 hectares and extends across four separate counties. There's an 8km trip on a clickety-clackety narrow-gauge railway to discover how the bog was formed and learn something of its history, wildlife and fascinating flora. Much of the bog is given over to industrial harvesting to fuel power stations, but there are areas left untouched and others of more traditional forms of extraction. The machines once used to excavate the peat are there to be seen, and children can have a go at traditional turf cutting for themselves.

Open Apr, May and Sep Mon–Fri 10am–5pm, Jun–Aug daily 10am–5pm. **Fare** adults €6.50, children under 12 €4.80, family (2+3) €22. **Credit** V, MC. **Amenities** disabled access, gift shop, coffee shop, toilets.

Kildare

Ballindoolin House and Gardens ★ ALL AGES

Carbury (near Edenderry), Co Kildare, ☎ 046 973 1430; www.ballindoolin. com. 6km E of Edenderry.

Set in a 53-hectare park, this attractive early 19th-century house is complete with farmyard and gardens. After seeing the house, wander into the huge walled garden where there's an unusual 'melon pit' used for forcing and raising the plants, a limekiln and a dovecote. The museum with its old machinery and the farmyard are the big attractions for children, although there's also a play area and a whole range of small farm animals who are used to making friends with visitors, including Matilda, a ginger Tamworth pig. An interesting nature trail completes the attractions.

Open May–Jul Wed–Sun 12–6pm. Adm adults €6, children €4 (under-5s free). Credit V, MC. Amenities mostly disabled access, coffee shop, toilets, woodland walks.

Castletown ★ AGES 5 AND UP

Celbridge, Co Kildare, ☎ 01628 8252; www.heritageireland.ie.

Castletown, the grandest Palladian country mansion in Ireland, was built for the Speaker of the Irish House of Commons, William Connolly, in 1722. Extensively restored, its interiors revel in their former glory.

In the grounds are two delightful follies, commissioned by Connolly's wife Louisa to provide work for the starving poor during the Great Famine. One is a slender obelisk, the other an unusual corkscrew style barn with a stone stairway winding round the outside.

Open Easter–Sep Mon–Fri 10am–6pm, Sat, Sun and bank holidays 1–6pm, Oct Mon–Fri 10am–5pm, Sun and bank holiday 1–5pm. Adm adults €3.70, seniors €2.60, children €1.30, family €8.70, OPW Heritage Card. Credit V, MC. Amenities toilets, coffee shop, limited disabled access.

Donadea Forest Park ★★ ALL AGES

Co Kildare, www.coillte.ie. 8 km S of Kilcock.

Set around ruins transformed from medieval castle to 19th-century mansion, this is a perfect place for wood and parkland walks. The short lake walk is accessible to wheelchairs and buggies while longer paths wind into the forest where there's a nature trail.

Open daily. Adm day pass €4 (correct change required). Credit none. Amenities café, shop, picnic area, toilet.

Lodge Park Steam Museum ★★ AGES 3 AND UP

Lodge Park, Straffan, Co Kildare, ☎ 0162 73155/0162 88412. 13km NE of Naas.

Lodge Park is famous for its 18th-century walled garden, but youngsters will want to visit the atmospheric steam museum alongside, housed in a wonderful gothic building, originally owned by the Great Southern & Western Railway, and transported from Dublin.

The fascinating collection includes scale locomotives as well as some splendid examples of stationary engines used to provide industrial power during the 19th century. Among them are a beam engine from the Smithwick's Brewery in Kilkenny and a pumping engine that once worked in Dublin's Jameson Distillery. Every Sunday, the air is filled with the sound of hissing and gasping engines as they're fired up.

Open Jun–Aug Wed–Sun 2–6pm. **Adm** adults €7.50, seniors/children €5, family €20. **Credit** V, MC. **Amenities** toilets, tearoom, gift shop, walled garden.

Lullymore Heritage Park ★★
ALL AGES

Lullymore, Rathangan, Co Kildare, ☎ 045 870 238; www.lullymore heritagepark.com. 10km NE of Rathangan along N414.

In the heart of Ireland's largest bog, the Bog Allen, in the Lullymore Heritage Park woodland are reconstructions of some of the key events in Irish history, from a Neolithic farmstead through to the Great Famine and the Uprising. Nature walks, falabella miniature horses, a road train, 18-hole crazy golf and fully equipped in- and outdoor play areas offer entertaining alternatives.

Open daily 10am–6pm. **Adm** adults €9, children €9, family (2+2) €24. **Credit** V, MC. **Amenities** tearoom.

Maynooth Castle ★ ALL AGES

Maynooth, Co Kildare, ☎ 01 628 6744; www.heritageireland.ie.

One of the largest keeps of its kind in the country, built in the 12th century, Maynooth belonged to the Fitzgeralds, who emerged as one of the most powerful families in the land. This was their family seat and their showpiece, a reflection of the power and influence that kept the population in its place. An exhibition tells the story, but youngsters will be more interested in just clambering round the ruins in search of dark corners.

Open Jun–Sep Mon–Fri 10am–6pm Sat–Sun and bank holidays 1–6pm, Oct Sun and bank holidays 1–5pm. **Adm** free.

Train at Lullymore Heritage Park

Millennium Maze ★ ALL AGES

*Ballinafagh Farm, Prosperous, Naas,
Co Kildare, ☎ 045 868 151; www.
themillenniummaze.com. 8km W of
Clane on R403.*

The maze, created to mark the
Millennium, is bounded by 2-
metre high hedges to keep you
guessing, and is designed in the
shape of St Brigid's cross. Spread
over 4,000 square metres, it contains more than 2.5km of pathways, so even if children work
out the correct route, it's going
to keep them occupied for quite
a while. And there are attractions
such as crazy golf, a sand pit and
pets corner for when they've
solved the puzzle.

*Open May–Sep daily 12–6pm.
Amenities parking, gift shop,
picnic area, toilets.*

Straffan Butterfly Farm ★★
ALL AGES

*Ovidstown, Straffan, Co Kildare, ☎ 01
627 1109; www.straffanbutterfly
farm.com.*

Ireland's first butterfly farm,
Straffan is a tropical indoor garden
where the butterflies flutter freely
round feeding on the nectar of the
flowers as you wander through.

Children can study the life
cycle from egg, through cater-
pillar to the butterfly, and learn
how to make their own gardens
more 'butterfly friendly'.

Also on show are some less
endearing creepy crawlies such
as tarantulas, scorpions and stick
insects – safely behind glass –
plus Larry the gecko, Iggy the
green iguana and Roger the
Californian king snake.

*Open Jun–Aug daily 12–5.30pm.
Adm adults €7, seniors/children
€4.50, family (2+3) €25. Credit V,
MC. Amenities toilets, picnic area,
disabled access, gift shop.*

Laois

Monicknew Woods ★★
ALL AGES

*Monicknew, Mountrath, Co Laois,
☎ 057 866 0831; www.coillte.ie.*

Among the deep glens that fall
from Slieve Bloom, this woodland park is set around Glen
Bridge, which was built in 1840
in the style of a Roman arch. A
picnic site and pleasant woodland walks make it a good spot
for an afternoon break where
children can let off a bit of
steam. If you persuade them to
wander quietly, they might see
fallow deer, or if you arrive in
the early evening, there's the
chance of spotting a badger.

*Open always. Adm free. Amenities
picnic site, forest trails.*

Stradbally Steam Museum ★
OLDER CHILDREN

*Stradbally, Co Laois, ☎ 057 862
5154; www.irishsteam.ie.*

Although still under development, this museum is worth
seeking out, but ring in advance
to check it's open. Among the
exhibits is a steam locomotive
used at the Guinness Brewery in
Dublin and a homemade steam
tractor. There's an expanding
assortment of steam-powered
fire engines, lorries and road
rollers as well as stationary

HISTORY ›› A Break – with Tradition ‹‹

A holiday in a traditional horse drawn caravan is something youngsters are guaranteed never to forget. After a night on a restored Georgian working farm, you set off along quiet byways soaking up the scenery and sights. Overnight stop-overs are beside country pubs or rural farmhouses (if you want a break from cooking) and pasture for the horse. Children love helping to look after the horse, and do some of the driving.

Kilvahan Horse Drawn Caravans, Tullibards Stud, Coolrain, Co Laois, 📞 *057 873 5178; www.horsedrawncaravans.com. Open May–Sep.*

engines used to provide power on farms and in workshops.

On bank holiday weekends a narrow gauge railway drawn by either veteran steam or diesel locomotives is a popular attraction, but the big event of the year is the annual Steam Rally. Held here for more than 40 years on the first weekend in August, it attracts engines from right across the country.

Open *Apr–Oct daily (please ring in advance –* 📞 *086 125 8813). **Adm** adults €5, students €3, children €2 (under-5s free).*

For Active Families

Cycling

In **Monaghan**, the main centre for **Raleigh Rent-a-Bike** (*www.raleigh.ie*) (see By Bike in Chapter 2, p. 29) is Paddy McQuaid, Emyvale Cycles, Knockafubble, Emyvale, Co Monaghan.

In **Cavan**, the dealer is Fitz Hire, Bridge Street, Belturbet, Co Cavan; 📞 *049 952 2866.*

In **Westmeath**, the agent is Buckley Cycles, Garden Vale, Irishtown, Athlone, Co Westmeath; 📞 *0902 78989.*

FAMILY-FRIENDLY ACCOMMODATION

MODERATE–EXPENSIVE

Cabra Castle ★★★

Kingscourt, Co. Cavan, 📞 *042 966 7030; www.cabracastle.com. Located on R 179 opposite Dún na Rí Forest Park.*

Opposite a forest park with walks, this elegant hotel in a romantic Victorian castle offers high standards, tastefully-decorated rooms and public areas harking back to the 19th century.

The sun terrace looks out over extensive grounds that include a tennis court and golf course, both of which younger guests are welcome to enjoy.

Early dinners for children can be taken in the more informal setting of the bar, so that parents can eat on their own in the restaurant.

Rooms *86.* **Rates** *double €145–236, children over 4 years €20, enquire for special deals.* **Credit** *all major credit cards accepted.* **Amenities** *WiFi in public areas, cots, baby-sitting, bottle service, children's menu and small portions available, fridge available in room on request, relaxation and beauty treatments.* **In room** *room service, tea/coffee-making facilities, safes in* some rooms and at reception, sat TV, Internet facilities in some rooms, laundry service, irons and boards.

MODERATE–EXPENSIVE

Longford Arms Hotel ★★

Main Street, Longford, Co Longford, ☎ 043 46296; www.longfordarms.ie.

In the centre of Longford Town, this renovated hotel makes a great base from which to visit the surrounding area as well as offering the facilities of its leisure centre with its pool, sauna, steam room, Jacuzzi, gym and massage clinic.

Dinner is served in the à la carte restaurant; the carvery and menu in the bar, where children are welcome until 9pm, offer less formal alternatives.

Rooms 60. Rates double €150–250, reductions for children, enquire for special deals. Credit all major credit cards accepted. Amenities guest parking, cots, bottle service, children's menu and small portions available. In room room service, tea/coffee-making facilities, sat TV, laundry service, irons and boards, trouser press.

MODERATE

Viewmount House ★★

Dublin Road, Longford, Co Longford. ☎ 043 41919; www.viewmount house.com.

Built in 1750 for the Earl of Longford's land agent, this beautifully restored country house offers comfortable and individually furnished rooms, which look out over extensive and beautifully tended gardens.

Children are made very welcome and are free to play on the lawn.

The recently completed licensed restaurant is open in the evening to non-residents Wednesday to Saturday, and dinner is served to guests throughout the week by arrangement.

Rooms 13. Rates double €110–160, children over 3 50%. Credit all major credit cards accepted. Amenities cots, bottle service, children's menu and small portions available. In room TV, iron and board on request.

EXPENSIVE

Mullingar Park Hotel ★★★

Dublin Road, Mullingar, Co Westmeath, ☎ 044 44446; www.mullingarparkhotel.com.

Elegant, contemporary, sumptuous and comfortable sum up Mullingar Park – an experience to remember.

There's a children's play garden and pool, sauna, steam room, pool, Jacuzzi and hydrotherapy pool, as well as a fitness suite, aerobics studio, beauty therapies and treatments.

Food is excellent with a wide choice at both lunch in the carvery and evening menus. And if children aren't up to a smaller version of the main menu, there are special options available.

Rooms 95. Rates double €200, children under 2 free, 2–10 €30, 10–14 €35, enquire for special deals. Credit all major credit cards accepted. Amenities safety deposit at reception, cots, baby-sitting service available, bottle service. In room room service, tea/coffee-making facilities, mini bar, TV, WiFi throughout hotel, laundry service, irons and boards.

Viewmount House, Longford

Hodson Bay Hotel ★ ★ ★

Hodson Bay, Athlone, Co Westmeath, ✆ *090 644 2000; www.hodsonbayhotel.com.*

On the shores of Lough Rea, the Hodson Bay offers everything you would expect of a 4-star hotel. There are fully equipped and spacious family rooms, a choice of eating places, and plenty of leisure and health facilities including not just a pool, sauna, steam room, hydro-therapy pool, fitness suite, aerobics studio, spa therapies and treatments, but also children's pool and children's play room.

In addition to the nearby attractions for youngsters such as Athlone Castle, Glendeer Pet Farm and Athlone Leisure World, during the summer they can join the Penguin Activity Kids Camp. Morning and evening sessions offer a packed programme of events and activities, with a video to round off the day.

*Rooms 182. **Rates** double €210, children €30, enquire for special deals. **Credit** all major credit cards accepted. **Amenities** cots, bottle service, children's menu and small portions available. **In room** room service, tea/coffee-making facilities, safe, TV, WiFi, laundry service.*

Enroute Bistro, Bar and Guesthouse ★

Five Alley, Birr, Co Offaly, ✆ *059 713 3976; www.guesthouse.ie.*

A good place to stop for food, but also a very family friendly guesthouse, Enroute has a large family room as well as one that is fully wheelchair accessible. There are both a public and a guests' TV lounge, plus an enclosed rooftop winter garden and patio where children can have some freedom. Décor is modern and rooms are fully equipped, plus there is excellent home-cooked food available all day.

Enroute is central to many attractions in the Midlands area, including Birr Castle (see p. 127), Slieve Bloom, Clonmacnoise and the peat railway (see p. 127).

Rooms 7. **Rates** *double €140, 50% reduction for children.* **Credit** *all major credit cards.* **Amenities** *guest parking, weekend entertainment, baby-sitting service available.* **In room** *room service, tea/coffee-making facilities, TV, iron and board available.*

MODERATE–EXPENSIVE

Tullamore Court Hotel ★★★

Tullamore, Co Offaly, ☎ *057 934 6666; www.tullamorecourthotel.ie.*

This recently extended contemporary hotel is central for exploring the Midland region. Its White Flag leisure centre with sauna, steam room fitness and aerobic suite has a 20 metre pool with a children's area set aside and there are supervised activities offered in Harry the Hedgehog's Kid's Club

in summer, which includes high tea and evening films, plus a crèche for the very young.

Rooms 105. **Rates** *€110–290, children 4–12 years €25, enquire for special deals.* **Credit** *all major credit cards.* **Amenities** *cots, bottle service, children's menu and small portions available. baby-sitting.* **In room** *room service, tea/coffee-making facilities, TV, WiFi access.*

CAFÉS & FAMILY-FRIENDLY DINING

MODERATE

The Pantry Restaurant at Lockes Distillery Museum
★★ **MODERN IRISH**

Kilbeggan, Co Westmeath, ☎ *057 933 2795.*

There's no longer commercial production here but the smell still winds through this converted distillery. Even if you don't visit

Tullamore Court Hotel

the museum, you can enjoy a snack or meal at the adjoining country-style restaurant. Open through the day, it serves everything from a drink and sandwiches to lasagne, beer battered cod, grilled Irish salmon and marinated lamb shank, as well as traditional Irish favourites such as bacon and cabbage.

Open daily Apr–Oct 9am–6pm, Nov–Mar 10am–4pm. **Main courses** €6.95–10.95. **Credit** V, MC. **Amenities** children's menu and small portions, highchairs, bottle warming, baby-changing facilities, car park.

MODERATE

Ilia A Coffee Experience ★
MODERN IRISH

28 Oliver Plunkett Street, Mullingar, Co Westmeath, ☎ 044 934 0300.

This coffee house and informal restaurant serves everything from breakfasts (pancakes or waffle to a full Irish) through coffee and scones or pastries to panini, bagels, wraps, open sandwiches lasagne and homemade burgers.

Open Mon–Sat 9am–6pm. **Main courses** €6.50–10. **Credit** V, MC. **Amenities** children's menu and portions, highchairs, baby-changing facilities, bottle warming.

MODERATE

The Thatch Bar and Restaurant ★★ PUB GRUB

Military Road, Crinkill, Birr, Co Offaly, ☎ 057 9120682; www.thethatch crinkill.com.

Still capped with traditional thatch, this is one of the oldest pubs in the county and has been

run by the same family for more than 200 years in traditional style. The bar is full of nooks and crannies and there's a larger restaurant for family dining to the rear. Portions are huge and it's as packed as a good French road café at lunchtime.

Options usually include a joint, fish dish and vegetarian dish. Alternatively there's soup and sandwiches. They have a longer evening à la carte menu with surprises such as ostrich and kangaroo medallions, and if you arrive between 5 and 7pm, you can take advantage of the early bird menu (not Sun); ensure that you book for evenings and the weekend.

Open daily, lunch 12.30–3.30pm, dinner 5–9pm. **Main courses** lunch €11.50, dinner €24–29. **Credit** V, MC. **Amenities** children's menu, small portions, bottle warming, highchairs, car park.

MODERATE

Enroute Bistro, Bar and Guesthouse. ★★ MODERN IRISH

Five Alley, Birr, Co Offaly, ☎ 059 713 3976; www.guesthouse.ie.

Midway between Birr and Kilcormac on the N52, this modern roadside inn is an open, airy place, serving all day, everything from hearty Irish breakfasts to à la carte in the evening. Local delicacies such as Tullamore ham, Irish sirloins and North Atlantic salmon feature alongside honey roast duckling and pan-fried chicken, with seafood chowder to start, and perhaps fruit pavlova to round it all off. In summer the beer garden with its sun umbrellas is a firm favourite, with regular barbecues and live music at weekends. Booking for evenings in the restaurant is usually necessary, but otherwise, just drop in.

Open breakfast, lunch and bar snack menu during the day, dinner menu from 7–9pm (8pm Sun). **Main courses** *lunch €9.75–19.95, inclusive 3-course dinner €26, children €14.* **Credit** *V, MC.* **Amenities** *children's menu, small portions, bottle warming, highchairs, baby-changing facilities, car park.*

MODERATE–EXPENSIVE

Ballymore Inn ★ ★ ★
MODERN IRISH/FISH

Main Street, Ballymore, Eustace, Co Kildare, ☎ *0045 864 585; www.ballymoreinn.com.*

This renovated family pub offers food in the back bar, popular with locals and families, or the more swish front of house restaurant. It's all good, from the back bar sandwiches, pizzas, salads and home-cooked meals to the restaurant options of Clare Island organic salmon with pickled cucumber and ginger salad, or rack of Slaney lamb with sweet and sour courgette and carrot drizzled with a caper dressing. It also does a decent coffee and pastry and they also cook pizzas for take-away.

Open daily, restaurant lunch 12.30–3pm, dinner 6–9pm, bar food until 9pm. **Main courses** *restaurant €10.50 (lunch), €33.50 (dinner), bar €9.50–17.50.* **Credit** *V, MC.* **Amenities** *children's menu, small portions, bottle warming, highchairs, baby-changing facilities (in both male and female toilets), car park.*

INEXPENSIVE–MODERATE

Aubergine ★ ★ PIZZA AND PASTA

17 Ballymahon Street, Longford, Co Longford, ☎ *043 48633.*

Nothing is too much trouble in this upstairs bistro-style restaurant on the town's main street, which really cares about food. Aubergine's modern décor and background jazz create a relaxed atmosphere and even children will appreciate the emphasis on quality, with a range of ever-changing dishes on the menu, from penne pasta with smoked bacon and mushroom to shepherd's pie with root vegetable mash. Desserts are just as appealing and might include passion fruit cheesecake or rhubarb and strawberry crumble. Although there's no specific children's menu, they're happy to deal with youngster's fussiness, adjusting dishes to suit.

Open Tue 2–5pm, Wed–Thu 12–5pm and 6–8pm, Fri–Sat 12–4pm and Sun 2–8pm. **Main courses** *lunch €8.50–9.95, dinner €15–19.* **Credit** *V, MC.* **Amenities** *small portions, bottle warming, highchairs, baby-changing facilities.*

7 The South-west: Limerick, Kerry & Cork

SOUTH-WEST IRELAND

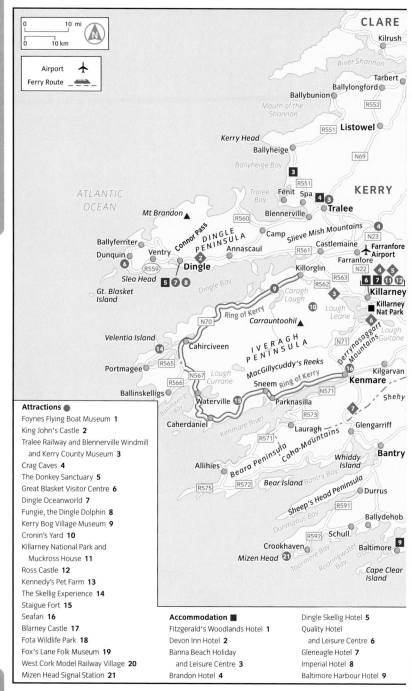

Map legend and labels:

- Scale: 0 — 10 mi / 0 — 10 km
- N (compass)
- Airport ✈
- Ferry Route

CLARE

Kilrush
River Shannon
Tarbert
Ballylongford
Ballybunion
Mouth of the Shannon
R552
R551 Listowel
Kerry Head
Ballyheige
N69
Ballyheige Bay
3
R551
ATLANTIC OCEAN
Tralee Bay
Fenit Spa
KERRY
Mt Brandon
R560
Blennerville
4 3
Tralee
DINGLE PENINSULA
Connor Pass
Camp
Slieve Mish Mountains
4
Ballyferriter
Annascaul
Castlemaine
N23
Dunquin
Ventry
R561
Farranfore Airport
6
R559
2
Dingle
Killorglin
Farranfore
N22
Slea Head
5 7 8
Dingle Bay
R563
4 5
Gt. Blasket Island
9
R562
6 7 11 12
Caragh Lough
3
Killarney
Ring of Kerry
10
Lough Leane
Killarney Nat Park
Carrauntoohil
N70
Killarney Nat Park
6
Velentia Island
IVERAGH PENINSULA
N71
Lough Guitane
14
Cahirciveen
Derrynasaggart Mountains
Portmagee
R565
MacGillycuddy's Reeks
Kilgarvan
N567
Sneem
Ring of Kerry
16
Ballinskelligs
R566
Lough Currane
Parknasilla
Kenmare
Waterville
15
N571
Shehy
Caherdaniel
R573
7
Lauragh
Glengarriff
Ballinskelligs Bay
Kenmare River
R571
Coha Mountains
Bantry
Allihies
Beara Peninsula
Whiddy Island
R575
R572
Bear Island
Bantry Bay
Durrus
Sheep's Head Peninsula
R591
Dunmanus Bay
Ballydehob
R592
Schull
9
Crookhaven
Baltimore
Mizen Head
21
Toormore Bay
Roaringwater Bay
Cape Clear Island

Attractions ●

Foynes Flying Boat Museum **1**
King John's Castle **2**
Tralee Railway and Blennerville Windmill and Kerry County Museum **3**
Crag Caves **4**
The Donkey Sanctuary **5**
Great Blasket Visitor Centre **6**
Dingle Oceanworld **7**
Fungie, the Dingle Dolphin **8**
Kerry Bog Village Museum **9**
Cronin's Yard **10**
Killarney National Park and Muckross House **11**
Ross Castle **12**
Kennedy's Pet Farm **13**
The Skellig Experience **14**
Staigue Fort **15**
Seafari **16**
Blarney Castle **17**
Fota Wildlife Park **18**
Fox's Lane Folk Museum **19**
West Cork Model Railway Village **20**
Mizen Head Signal Station **21**

Accommodation ■

Fitzgerald's Woodlands Hotel **1**
Devon Inn Hotel **2**
Banna Beach Holiday and Leisure Centre **3**
Brandon Hotel **4**

Dingle Skellig Hotel **5**
Quality Hotel and Leisure Centre **6**
Gleneagle Hotel **7**
Imperial Hotel **8**
Baltimore Harbour Hotel **9**

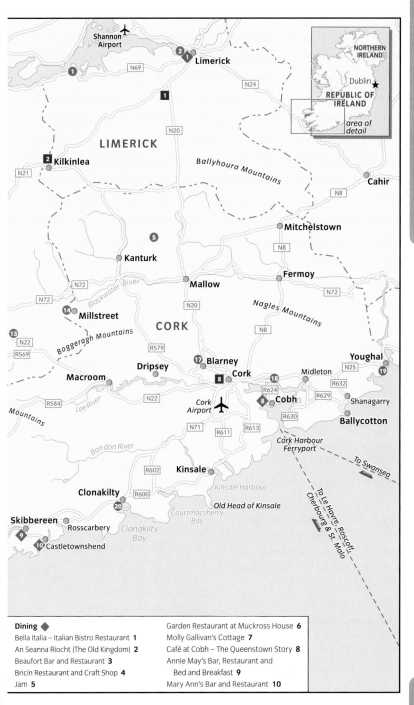

Dining ◆

Bella Italia – Italian Bistro Restaurant **1**
An Seanna Riocht (The Old Kingdom) **2**
Beaufort Bar and Restaurant **3**
Bricin Restaurant and Craft Shop **4**
Jam **5**

Garden Restaurant at Muckross House **6**
Molly Gallivan's Cottage **7**
Café at Cobh – The Queenstown Story **8**
Annie May's Bar, Restaurant and
   Bed and Breakfast **9**
Mary Ann's Bar and Restaurant **10**

The far south-west of Ireland is a remote and beautiful corner where the land shreds in great ragged tatters into the Atlantic Ocean. A succession of long rugged bays bite deep into the land, producing a spectacularly convoluted coastline that twists back and forth around peninsulas and inlets for 1,000km. Inland is no less dramatic, puckered in ridges of cragged mountains and upland bog, sliced by lonely glens, fast-flowing streams and placid lakes.

But a holiday here is not all about landscape. The glorious coastline has multiple Blue Flag beaches, notably Inch Strand, where youngsters can play with buckets and spades, hunt for crabs, catch shrimps in the rock pools or bury dad in the sand. For older children there's dinghy sailing and kayaking. Cork and Limerick have plenty of family entertainment, shopping and eating places, and throughout the whole area there's a cultural legacy stretching back more than 9,000 years with monuments, castles, houses and gardens.

Highlights are the cruises to the Skellig and Blasket Islands, places steeped in history and great for watching wildlife. Our trip was punctuated by the overwhelming excitement of spotting dolphins, and shrieks of laughter every time the boat bashed into a wave and drenched everyone daft enough to stand in the way.

Mostly though, alongside typical warmth and hospitality, this is laid back Ireland – to the point of falling over. So even in high season when there are throngs of holidaymakers, you don't have to wander far from the beaten path to find a quiet corner – for example, walking, cycling and riding the peaceful countryside, and exploring its countless attractive villages.

ESSENTIALS

Getting There

By Air The area is served by three airports:

Shannon International (☎ 061 712 000; *www.shannonairport.com*) is just across the border in Co Clare and only 15 minutes drive from Limerick City.

Cork International (☎ 021 431 3131; *www.corkairport.com*) is 6.5km south of Cork City. Both terminals receive direct flights from all the main UK airports.

Kerry regional airport (☎ 066 976 4644; *www.kerryairport.ie*) is at Farranfore, around 20 minutes drive from Tralee or Killarney. Although there are direct connections with both London and Manchester airports, passengers from other parts of Britain have to fly via Dublin. There are car rental facilities at all the airports, but during the high season or if you want a child safety seat, it's advisable to book in advance.

By Sea Cork ferry port is at Ringaskiddy, 16km southeast of Cork. Swansea Cork Ferries

(☎ (UK) *01792 456116*; *www.wan seacorkferries.com*) operate a seasonal service from Swansea in Wales with up to six sailings a week depending on time of year. For more flexibility in sailings, drive across country from Rosslare or Dublin.

VISITOR INFORMATION

The main website for the whole region is the Discover Ireland site *www.ireland.ie*. More specifically, Cork and Kerry are covered by *www.corkkerry.ie*, whereas Limerick falls within *www. shannonregiontourism.ie*.

For further information on the individual counties, *www. eastcorktourism.com*, *www.west cork.ie* and *www.visitlimerick.com* are all useful sources of information to check out.

The main Tourist Information Offices in each of the counties are as follows:

Limerick

Limerick City Tourist Office, Arthurs Quay, Limerick City, Co Limerick. ☎ *061 317 522*.

Adare Tourist Office (seasonal), Adare Heritage Centre, Main Street, Adare, Co Limerick. ☎ *061 396 255*.

Kerry

Killarney Tourist Office, Áras Fáilte, Beech Road, Killarney, Co Kerry. ☎ *064 31633*.

Dingle Tourist Office, The Quay, Dingle, Co Kerry. ☎ *066 915 1188*.

Tralee Tourist Office, Ashe Memorial Hall, Tralee, Co Kerry. ☎ *066 712 1288*.

Cahersiveen Tourist Office (seasonal), Cahersiveen, Co Kerry. ☎ *066 947 2589*.

Kenmare Tourist Office (Seasonal), Kenmare Heritage Centre, Kenmare, Co Kerry. ☎ *064 41233*.

Listowel Tourist Office (seasonal), St John's Church, Listowel, Co Kerry. ☎ *068 22590*.

Waterville Tourist Office (seasonal), Waterville, Co Kerry. ☎ *066 947 4646*.

Cork

Cork City Tourist Information Office, Áras Fáilte, Grand Parade, Cork City, Co Cork. ☎ *021 425 5100*.

Blarney Tourist Information Office, Blarney, Co Cork. ☎ *021 438 1624*.

Clonakilty Tourist Information Office, Ashe Street, Clonakilty, Co Cork. ☎ *023 33226*.

Kinsale Tourist Information Office, Pier Road, Kinsale, Co Cork. ☎ *021 477 2234*.

Skibbereen Tourist Information Office, Oifig Fáilte, Town Hall, Skibbereen, Co Cork. ☎ *028 21766*.

Bantry Tourist Office (seasonal), Old Courthouse, Bantry, Co Cork. ℓ 027 50229.

Glengarriff Tourist Office (seasonal), Glengarriff, Co Cork. ℓ 027 63084.

Macroom Tourist Office (seasonal), Castle Gates, The Square, Macroom, Co Cork. ℓ 026 43280.

Midleton Tourist Office (seasonal), Jameson Heritage Centre, Midleton, Co Cork. ℓ 021 461 3702.

ORIENTATION

Limerick is 195km (121 miles) SW of Dublin, 197km (122 miles) NW of Rosslare and 361km (224 miles) SW of Belfast.

Killarney is 303km (188 miles) SW of Dublin, 264km (164 miles) W of Rosslare and 469km (291 miles) SW of Belfast.

Cork is 254km (158 miles) SW of Dublin, 203km (126 miles) W of Rosslare and 420km (261 miles) SW of Belfast.

Getting Around

The main roads of the region link the principal cities and towns in a great triangle and are the most direct routes between the three counties.

Drivers from Dublin can follow the N7 all the way to Limerick, continuing along the N21 if they are then heading towards Killarney or Tralee. For Cork, it's best to turn off at Portlaoise on the N8 to go through Cashel.

Visitors entering the country at Rosslare need first to head for Waterford and then stick with the N25 to Cork. If you're visiting the city itself, consider using the park and ride, just north of the Kinsale Interchange (on the N22, 3km S of the city). Open Monday–Saturday 7.30am–7.15pm, the €5 charge includes parking and return bus fare.

If you are heading for Killarney you can bypass Cork (which can be a bottleneck) by turning off before Dungarvan on the N72 through Mallow.

For Limerick, follow the N24 from Waterford along the Suir Valley, continuing via Cahir and Tipperary.

Bus Éireann (ℓ 01 836 6111; www.buseireann.ie) runs services linking the main towns and there are additionally a number of local services.

The rail network from Dublin reaches to Cork, Tralee and Ennis, with stations in the principal towns (ℓ 01 836 6222; www.irishrail.ie).

For those without their own transport, there are coach excursions from Killarney and Cork that will enable you to enjoy some of the more popular tourist destinations and scenic drives within the region. Check out **Dero's Tours**, Killarney (ℓ 064 31251; www.derostours.com), **Buckley's Tours**, Killarney (ℓ 064 31945; www.buckleytours.com) and **Easy Tours**, Grange, Cork (ℓ 021 4362484; www.easytourscork.com).

However, as elsewhere in Ireland, the only way to get to many of the places is by car.

Car rental is available at airports and in large towns. In high season or if you require child seats it's best to book in advance.

Discover the Counties

Limerick

Everyone has heard of Limerick, if only for the often-ribald rhymes to which it lends its name. Ancient Limerick City is strategically set at the lowest bridging point of the River Shannon and is a focus for the whole region. Recent investment has brought a revival and the place is earning an enviable reputation for entertainment, shopping and good food, as well as for cultural and sporting attractions.

It's surrounded by unspoiled countryside, which though lacking the scenic impact of neighbouring Kerry, is still charming. To the southeast, the county follows the sweep of the Golden Vale, a fertile, undulating landscape speckled with attractive farms and villages, while in the south, the land rises to a more untamed fringe of bordering hills that are good walking country.

Among the places to visit is the prehistoric farming settlement on the shores of Lough Gur, the village of Adare, often considered the prettiest in the country, and the Foynes Flying Boat Museum (see p. 147), where, it's said, Irish Coffee was invented.

Kerry

Kerry's dramatic peninsula scenery makes it the most visited county in the whole of Ireland, and in the height of the season, crowded hotspots and tacky commercialism can occasionally dull the magic. But don't let that put you off because there are plenty of beaches to lose yourself on, including 13 Blue Flag ones.

For the most dramatic views travel counter-clockwise on the coastal drive of the Ring of Kerry around the Iveragh Peninsula.

The Dingle Peninsula is equally beautiful, especially around the extremity of Ceann Sléibhe (Slea Head), which lies in one of the Gaeltacht (Irish speaking) areas of the country. From An Daingean (Dingle), you can take a boat into the bay and with luck you'll get close to Fungie the dolphin (see p. 150), who has taken up residence there and apparently takes delight in entertaining human visitors.

Most of the Killarney National Park (see p. 152) is car-free and a great place to explore by bike or in a horse-drawn *jarvey* or jaunting car. The whole area has a rich and mysterious distant history, revealed in such things as footprints pre-dating the dinosaurs, the Kenmare stone circle, a 2,500 year-old fort, and curious villages of stone beehive-shaped huts.

There are plenty of castles to explore too, or you can take a train ride to see the restored Blennerville Windmill (see p. 154).

Slea Head, Dingle Peninsula

Older active children can try activities from sailing to riding and there's walking, from easy strolls through quiet glens to rugged clifftop and mountain paths. The gentle walk into Hag's Glen to the lakes nestling at the foot of the mountain is something not to be missed.

Cork

Second in size only to Dublin, lively Cork City is every bit its equal as a family holiday destination. The heart of the city is an island in the River Lee and its many bridges and riverside walks and parks make it a delight to stroll. An attraction with potential child appeal is the City Gaol, and while few youngsters relish being dragged round the shops, they will be keen to help choose picnic food at the 18th-century English Market selling delicacies from around the world.

Outside the city, the countryside goes from a fertile rolling agricultural landscape to lonely upland terrain and forest park. The coast is outstanding, with precipitous jagged cliffs, unbroken stretches of soft sand and secluded coves.

Cork's ragged coast culminates in Mizen Head (see p. 157), Ireland's most southwesterly point, where a visit to the lighthouse is a thrilling experience, and a great place to watch for dolphins and whales or take an offshore cruise. And, with no less than 10 Blue Flag beaches, there's no shortage of spots to spend a day by the sea.

Inland various museums and heritage centres recall different aspects of the area's history. At Skibbereen children can learn about the terrible disaster of the potato famine, while Cobh tells the story of the massive emigration that followed and the convict ships that delivered their banished human cargoes to the Antipodes.

Natural wonders include the Mitchelstown Cave, one of the finest in Europe, and the forest park of Gougane Barra, where Cork's patron saint St Finn Barre founded a monastic community on the lake island in the 6th century – another great place for family walks and picnics.

And of course there's the Blarney Stone (see p. 155), though if you think your children chatter enough as it is, you may not want them to kiss it.

Children-friendly Events & Entertainment

The region hosts several international festivals as well as numerous smaller events organised by villages and towns, especially in the summer months, often a great opportunity to enjoy traditional Irish music and dance.

The Irish have a passion for their national sports too, and if you come across a game of Gaelic football or hurling during your visit, you shouldn't miss it, the atmosphere is great.

Limerick

Ballylanders Pattern Festival
Ballylanders, Co Limerick, 062 46751.

This is held over a couple of days to celebrate the feast day of Our Lady on 15th August and sees visitors from far and wide. There are sports and amusements for children, and football

and soccer matches for adults, a vintage car rally, and traditional country craft demonstrations such as butter making, wood turning, wattle fence making and sheep shearing.

Kilmallock Medieval Festival
Kilmallock, Co Limerick, 063 98727.

As well as musical concerts, the annual festival in August features a medieval fun day with a re-enactment, parades, competitions and more.

Riverfest Limerick
Limerick City, Co Limerick. 061 209 173.

Riverfest is Limerick's biggest annual event, held each May Bank Holiday. From humble beginnings this celebration of Limerick City has quickly grown and there's street theatre and entertainment, arts open days, fireworks and shows in venues around the city.

Kerry

Killarney Summerfest
(June/July)
Killarney, Co Kerry, 064 71560, *www.killarneysummerfest.com*.

A growing event that has become one of Ireland's leading family festivals, this offers activities for all ages and tastes with outdoor theatre, concerts, parades, marching bands, cycle races, hot air balloons, a fun run and art exhibitions.

Very popular are the street entertainers from acrobats to

mime artists and musicians to stilt walkers who come from around the world. There's also a programme of children's workshops where they can try a new craft or learn to dance.

National Folk Theatre of Ireland

Siamsa Tíre, Theatre and Arts Centre, Town Park, Tralee, Co Kerry, 📞 *066 712 3055; www.siamsatire.com.*

A programme of colourful shows, incorporating Irish music, song and dance traditions, takes place every summer in the National Folk Theatre. Performances: Apr–Oct at 8.30pm.

Puck Fair

Killorglin, Co Kerry, 📞 *066 976 2366; www.puckfair.ie.*

It's unthinkable to be in Co Kerry in August and not go to Puck Fair. One of Ireland's oldest fairs, this annual event includes traditional cattle and horse fairs, and culminates in the coronation of King Puck, a mountain goat. There are parades, fireworks, street entertainment, children's competitions, dancing and concerts.

Rose of Tralee International Festival

Tralee, Co Kerry, 📞 *066 712 1322; www.roseoftralee.ie.*

Taking place in August, this is one of Ireland's premier festivals. Central to it is the crowning of the new Rose of Tralee and no one should miss the excitement of the Rose Parade with its decorative floats, jugglers, magicians, and acrobats but there is also a spectacular firework display, fun fair and circus.

The Rose of Tralee

Mary O'Connor, the daughter of a shoemaker and a dairymaid, lived in Brogue Lane in the middle of Tralee. At 17 she left the family home to earn a living as maid to the Mulchinocks, a wealthy merchant family who owned a wool and linen draper's shop. One of the sons, William, was immediately spellbound by her beauty. The couple fell in love and one moonlit night, William proposed to Mary, but she knew his family disapproved and turned him down. The next evening, William was wrongly accused of murder and fled to India and six years passed before he could return as a free man. Stopping off at the Kings Arms before he went to visit Mary, he learned of a funeral and on enquiring whose it was, discovered tragically that it was that of his true love. William was broken hearted. He expressed his love for her in a poem and on his death requested that he be buried next to his Rose of Tralee.

She was lovely and fair as the rose of the summer,
Yet 'twas not her beauty alone that won me.
Oh no, 'twas the truth in her eyes ever dawning
That made me love Mary, the Rose of Tralee.

Cork

Cork Midsummer Festival

Cork City, Co Cork, 📞 *021 421 5131;*
www.corkfestival.com.

Two weeks in June of theatre,
dance and music, each year this
event builds on its previous suc-
cesses, becoming even more
exciting and including some
shows specifically for children
and families.

WHAT TO SEE & DO

Children's Top 10 Attractions

❶ **Pilot a B314 flying boat** at
Foynes Flying Boat Museum.
See below.

❷ **Touch strange creatures**
from the deep at Dingle
Oceanworld. See p. 150.

❸ **Thrill to the sight** of Fungie
the Dingle dolphin swimming
alongside the boat. See p. 150.

❹ **Walk** through breathtaking
scenery in the Killarney National
Park. See p. 152.

❺ **Receive the 'gift of the gab'**
at Blarney Castle. See p. 155.

❻ **Learn** about Ireland's emi-
grants and the sinking of the
Lusitania at Cobh, the
Queenstown Story. See p. 166.

❼ **Wonder** at the amazing animals at Fota Wildlife Park. See
p. 155.

❽ **Be beside the seaside** at one
of 23 Blue Flag beaches. Check
out Inch and Ventry on the

Dingle Peninsula and Garryvoe
between Cork and Youghal.

❾ **Lookout for seals**, dolphins
and whales on the Seafari. See
p. 153.

❿ **Ride the Blennerville
Railway** to Ireland's tallest
working windmill. See p. 154.

Children-friendly Attractions

Limerick

Foynes Flying Boat Museum ★ ★ ★ ALL AGES

Foynes, Co Limerick, 📞 *069 65416;*
www.flyingboatmuseum.com.
37km W of Limerick on N69.

Here children can board a full-
scale replica of a B314 Flying
Boat and climb up to the cock-
pit. Older children can actually
try their hand at taking off and
landing in a flight simulator and
for the little ones there's a mock
flight deck to sit in, and a
weekly competition for the best
drawing of the seaplane.

On 9th July 1939, the
'Yankee Clipper' flying boat
landed at Foynes, the first commercial passenger flight direct
from the USA to Europe. Foynes
became the centre for the
transatlantic passenger service,
but the era of flying boats was
short and in 1945 the last sea
plane flew out of Foynes to New
York and Atlantic air travel
moved to land-based aircraft
operating out of Shannon.

The museum, housed in the
original terminal building,
vividly recalls the era with
exhibits that include the wireless

Foynes Flying Boat Museum

transmitters, receivers and Morse equipment from the radio and weather rooms and a host of memorabilia, posters, cuttings and displays that tell the story of this pioneering achievement. A 1940s cinema presentation shows the inaugural flights.

Sheridan, the inventor of Irish coffee – see box below – went on to work in San Francisco, but mums and dads can still get the real thing here today in the coffee shop, which also sells a range of other beverages, biscuits, muffins and ice creams.

Open Mar–Sep daily 10am–6pm, Oct–Nov daily 10am–4pm. *Adm* adults €8, children (5–13) €5, family (2+4) €25. *Credit* V, MC. *Amenities* toilets, baby-changing facilities, full disabled access, gift shop.

King John's Castle ★
AGES 4 AND UP

Nicholas Street, King's Island, Limerick City, Co Limerick, 061 361020.

The castle is impressively set overlooking the River Shannon in what was the heart of medieval Limerick City. An imaginative exhibition tells the story of the castle, complete with medieval weaponry, and you can climb up to the battlements, from which there are fine views.

Open daily Apr–Oct 10.30am–5.30pm, Nov–Mar 10.30am–4.30pm. *Adm* adults €9, seniors/students €6.65, children €5.25 (under-6s free), family (2+2) €20.60. *Credit* V, MC. *Amenities* souvenir shop.

Kerry

Blasket Island (Ionad an Bhlascaoid Mhóir) The Great Blasket Visitor Centre ★
AGES 5 AND UP

Dún Chaoin (Dunquin), Co Kerry, 066 915 6444 / 915 6371; www. heritageireland.ie. On the tip of Dingle Peninsula, 16km from Dingle.

Ferries and excursions to the islands ★★★

From Dingle and Dunquin, bookings 086 895 5020, www.blasket islands.ie and www.dinglebay charters.com.

DID YOU KNOW? **Irish Coffee**

Irish Coffee was invented in Limerick back in 1942. Joe Sheridan, a restaurant chef took pity on a group of cold and rain swept passengers waiting for their flight and concocted something special to really warm them up, rich coffee and thickly whipped cream with a generous dash of Powers Irish Whiskey.

Until 1953, a small community lived on Great Blasket, the largest of an island group lying 5km off the Dingle Peninsula and the most westerly point in Europe. A trip around the islands is a truly memorable experience, giving spectacular views of the Dingle coastline as well as the offshore rocks, reefs and stacks. The island cliffs are teeming with birds while seals, dolphins, sharks and whales are often seen in the water.

If you have the time, spend an hour or even the full day on Great Blasket to walk through the deserted village, explore the green lanes and cliff paths or just idle on the superb sandy beach.

Both excursions and ferries leave from Dingle and Dún Chaoin, where there's a Visitor Centre in which an exhibition, scale model of the village and video presentation explore the island's way of life and the heritage of native Gaelic literature that developed there.

INSIDER TIP
There are toilets but no other facilities on Great Blasket, so take a picnic and appropriate clothing in case the weather changes.

Ferries 9.30am–5.30pm. *Fare (ferries)* adults from €30, children €15; (excursions) adults from €40, children €20; (Dingle Peninsula trips) adults €30, children €15; (fishing trips) adults from €25, children from €15. Pre-booking for excursions necessary. All dependent upon weather.

Open (Visitor Centre) daily Easter–Jun 10am–6pm (Jul and Aug 7pm, Sep and Oct 6pm). *Adm* adults

€3.70, children €1.30, family €8.70, OPW Heritage Card. *Credit* V, MC.

Crag Caves ★★ ALL AGES

Castleisland, Co Kerry, ☎ 066 714 1244; www.cragcave.com. 20km E of Tralee.

Discovered in 1983, Crag Caves are one of the largest cave systems in Ireland. The showcase cave, which was first opened to the public in 1989, is a wonderland of stalagmites and stalactites in the Big Chamber, the Cathedral, the Kitchen and the Crystal Gallery. And for under-12s there's the Crazy Cave indoor play area (separate charge).

Open mid-Mar–Oct daily 10am–6pm. *Adm* adults €12, seniors/students €8, children €5 (under-5s free), family (2+2) €30; (Crazy Cave) €7 for 90 minutes play; (combined cave and play area) €10. *Credit* V, MC. *Amenities* coffee shop serving fresh home cooked lunches and snacks, gift shop.

Cronin's Yard ★★ ALL AGES

Mealis, Beaufort, Killarney, Co Kerry, ☎ 087 679 2341; www.cronins yard.com. Off N72 between Killorglin and Killarney, 8km SW of Beaufort Bridge.

There's an unforgettable view up the glen to Carrauntoohil, Ireland's highest peak, and for experienced walkers, the ascent of the mountain is not to be missed. The panorama from the summit on a fine day takes in the long line of Macgillycuddy's Reeks and the Iveragh Peninsula to the inlets and off-shore islands. The valley is also a great place for picnics and shorter family walks, following the stream through the stunning scenery of Hag's Glen, easy as far as a couple of lakes at its head.

Five generations of Cronins have offered hospitality to walkers embarking on the ascent and we can vouch for the Cronin's generosity, having succumbed to Eileen's bottomless teapot for many years.

The farmyard now boasts superb modern facilities that include toilets, hot showers and an inviting coffee shop warmed by an open peat fire. There's a range of drinks, soup and home-baked cakes and snacks, and you can also buy local maps and walking books. And if you can't drag yourself away at the end of the day, there's always the camping field in which to put up your tent.

Open daily during summer. **Adm** €2 per car. **Amenities** parking, coffee shop, toilets, showers.

Dingle Oceanworld ★ ★ ★
ALL AGES

The Wood, Dingle, Co Kerry, ☎ 066 915 2111; www.dingle-oceanworld. ie. Overlooking the harbour in Dingle.

This is one of Ireland's premier aquariums – educational as well as fun. There's an ocean tunnel where the sharks, big rays and leatherback turtle are always a big hit. In the deep-water tank, you come face to face with conger eels and wreck fish and many species native to the Irish coast.

In the Amazonian and exotic sections there are tropical freshwater species such as piranha, as well as vividly coloured fish from coral seas. There's also a touch pool with an assortment of crabs, sea urchins, starfish and graceful rays – and staff to tell you about the fish and their different habitats.

Open daily 10am–5pm. **Adm** adults €11, seniors/students €8.50, children €6.50, family (2+4) €30. **Credit** most cards accepted. **Amenities** disabled access, toilets, baby-changing facilities, gift shop, café.

Fungie, the Dingle Dolphin ★ ★ ★
ALL AGES—SWIMMING FOR 8 AND OVER

Dingle Boatmen's Association, Dingle Pier, Dingle, Co Kerry, ☎ 066 915 1967.

Ever since he took up residence in Dingle Bay in 1983, Fungie has been enthralling visitors of all ages. He thrives on human company and makes a beeline for boats sailing in the harbour. The Dingle boatmen are more than happy to participate in his playful antics and offer one-hour boat trips to see him.

Coursing alongside the boat, leaping clean out of the water and generally having a good time, he makes an unforgettable highlight to any holiday in Dingle. But there's one thing that tops even that: the chance to swim alongside him. With wetsuits provided, you can take an early morning trip and really get up close to this wonderful creature in his own environment – a truly magical experience. In fact, you don't even have to be the best of swimmers: the wetsuits have built-in buoyancy and are suitable for all from about the age of 8 or 9 years.

The trips operate throughout the year and if Fungie doesn't show, you're not charged.

Sailings *daily weather permitting.* **Fare** *adults €16, children (under-12s) €8, early morning trip €25, wetsuit hire €25. Cash only.*

Kennedy's Pet Farm ★★
ALL AGES

Glenflesk, Killarney, Co Kerry, 📞 *064 54054;* **www.killarneypetfarm.com.** *SE of Killarney on the N22.*

Kennedy's is an all-weather pet farm with in- and outdoor playgrounds. Spring and early summer are a great time to visit when there are plenty of baby animals: deer and fawn, donkeys and foals, goats and kids, sheep and lambs, calves, geese and goslings, ducks and ducklings, rabbits and guinea pigs. Many animals wander freely and children will love being able to cuddle and feed them. Pony rides are available too.

Open *mid-Feb–Sep daily 10am–6pm.* **Adm** *€7 adults and children.* **Credit** *V, MC.* **Amenities** *hot and cold drinks, and basic snacks, indoor and outdoor picnic areas, toilets, baby-changing.*

Kerry Bog Village Museum ★
ALL AGES

Ballincleave, Glenbeigh, Co Kerry, 📞 *066 976 9184;* **www.kerrybog village.ie.** *SW of Killorglin towards Glenbeigh.*

The museum recreates the famine cottages of rural Ireland in the 19th century, along with other buildings such as an old forge, a stable, a turf cutter's house, dairy house, a vegetable garden and a bog, plus the rare Kerry Bog Ponies, which almost became extinct. There's a play area too.

Open *8:30am–7pm daily.* **Adm** *adults €6, seniors/students €4, children €2.50.* **Credit** *V, MC, traveller's cheques.* **Amenities** *wheelchair*

Deer in Kennedy's Pet Farm

accessible, toilets, live traditional music on Wednesday evenings, gift shop, food and drinks available at adjacent Red Fox Inn.

Killarney National Park ★★★
ALL AGES

Muckross, Co Kerry, ☎ 064 31440; www.heritageireland.ie. 6km S of Killarney on N71.

Splendid mountain scenery, woodland, the dramatic 60-feet high **Torc Waterfall**, and the three Lakes of Killarney make the 10,100-hectare national park a highlight of the area. There are nature trails for families to stretch their legs and a great way to explore the park is by bike. Among those offering bike hire is **O'Sullivan's Cycles and Outdoor Leisure** in Killarney (☎ 064 31282).

A jaunting car ride (pony and trap) through the vast estate can be organised at several locations including Kenmare Place in Killarney town, the entrances to Killarney National Park and at Kate Kearney's Cottage.

Open *pedestrian access always.* **Adm** *no charge to Visitor Centre, gardens or park.* **Amenities** *restaurants at Muckross House, Dinis Cottage and Deenagh Lodge, audio-visual presentation, disabled access to Visitor Centre.*

Killarney Scenic Lake Cruises ★ ALL AGES

MV Lily of Killarney, ☎ 064 31068; www.killarneydaytour.com and My Pride of the Lakes, ☎ 064 32638, both operate daily cruises departing from the pier at Ross Castle.

Take a leisurely view of the park from a different perspective with a cruise on the stunningly beautiful Lakes of Killarney. An entertaining and informative commentary tells of the history of the area and wildlife.

Open *Mar–Oct 10.30am–4.30pm.* **Fare** *adults €8, children €4, family (2+2) €20.* **Credit** *V, MC.*

Muckross House, Gardens and Traditional Farms ★★★
AGES 3 AND UP

Killarney National Park, Killarney, Co Kerry, ☎ 064 31440; www.muckross-house.ie.

Killarney National Park

Within the Killarney National Park, this fine Victorian mansion and beautiful gardens were laid out in the 1850s in preparation for a visit by Queen Victoria. Visitors can visit both above and below stairs and at a craft centre there are a potter, blacksmith, bookbinder and weaver at work. However, the high point will be the three working farms, which take you back to rural life in the 19th and early 20th century before electricity was common-place. There are plenty of animals and a range of horse-drawn machinery, plus a typical labourer's cottage.

Open (house) daily 9am–5.30pm (Jul and Aug 7pm); (farms) Mar–Apr and Oct Sat, Sun and bank holidays 1–6pm, May daily 1–6pm, Jun–Sep daily 10am–6pm. Adm (house or traditional farms) adults €5.75, seniors €4.50, children €2.35, family €14.50; (joint ticket) adults €9.50, seniors €7.50, children €4, family €25, OPW Heritage Card. Credit most cards accepted. Amenities toilets, restaurant, gift shops, audio-visual presentation.

INSIDER TIP ▸

Get your Joint Ticket from Muckross House and have the option to visit the farms on the following day.

Seafari ★ ★ ★ AGES 3 AND UP

3 The Pier, Kenmare, Co Kerry, ☎ 064 42059; www.seafariireland.com.

Seafari run fun and informative two-hour eco cruises around Kenmare Bay and its islands, departing from the idyllic Kenmare harbour. The scenery is wonderful and wildlife includes common seals, a great attraction particularly when the pups are born around July and you can often see up to 100 seals sunning themselves on the rocks.

Passengers have free use of binoculars, complimentary hot drinks are provided, and there's sometimes live traditional music on board too. Booking is advised in July and August.

Availability Apr–Oct, up to four cruises per day dependent upon demand and weather. Fare adults €20, children (12–18) €15, under-12s 12.50, family (2+2) €60–65. Credit V, MC. Amenities parking, toilets.

The Skellig Experience ★
AGES 7 AND UP

Valentia Island, Co Kerry, ☎ 066 947 6306; www.skelligexperience.com. Off N70, 50km W of Killorglin.

This is the place to find out about the Skellig Rocks through an entertaining audio-visual show, and models and recreations of Skellig Michael's important early Christian monastery, lighthouse and keepers, and its seabirds and marine life.

Valentia Island can be reached either by road bridge, leaving the Ring of Kerry between Cahersiveen and Waterville, or by ferry from Renard between April and October (**Valentia Island Ferries** Co Kerry, ☎ 066 9476141).

Open daily Mar–Apr and Oct–Nov 10am–5pm, May, Jun and Sep 10am–6pm, Jul and Aug 10am–7pm. Adm (exhibition only) adults €5, children €3, family (2+2) €14; (exhibition and round-Skellig Cruise) adults €27.50, children €14.50, family (2+2) €71.50. Credit most major cards accepted.

Skellig Cruises ★★★
AGES 4 AND UP

Subject to the weather, daily boat trips are run to the UNESCO World Heritage Site of Skellig Michael. On a two-hour trip passengers pass close to Small Skellig, where 20,000-plus pairs of gannets make it the second largest colony in the world. Next is Skellig Michael where you have a couple of hours to explore the settlement, and enjoy the puffins, razorbills, guillemots, fulmars and kittiwakes. Information about the various boat operators is available at *www.skelligexperience.com*. Among them are Casey's Boat Trips, ☏ *087 239 5470*, Murphy Sea Cruise, ☏ *066 947 7156* and Joe Roddy & Sons, ☏ *087 120 9924* who depart from Portmagee and Lavelles Skellig Trips, ☏ *066 947 6124*, which leave from Valentia Island.

Staigue Fort ★ **AGES 7 AND UP**

Castlecove, Co Kerry. SW tip of Iveragh Peninsula, 74km SW of Killarney.

There are numerous ancient monuments in County Kerry including several earthen and stone ring-forts, but one of the largest and finest is the stone fort at Castlecove, thought to be some 2,500 years old. Its dry-stone wall, with a diameter of 27 metres and standing 5.4 metres at its highest and nearly 4 metres thick at its base, is certainly an impressive sight. Stairways run inside the wall, giving access to narrow platforms on which the occupants stood to defend the fort. The forts were also used for penning livestock at night.

Open (exhibition centre) Easter–Sep 10am–9pm.

Tralee to Blennerville Railway and Blennerville Windmill ★★
ALL AGES

Steam Train: Tralee, Co Kerry, ☏ 066 712 1064. Windmill: Blennerville, Windmill Street, Tralee, Co Kerry, ☏ 066 712 1064; www.kerrygems. com/blennervillewindmill.

Trains chug along a restored section of the Dingle–Tralee line, the most westerly in Europe. A light narrow gauge railway opened here in 1891 and was in operation until 1953.

An historic diesel leaves Ballyard Station near the Aquadome in Tralee, transporting passengers in traditional carriages to Blennerville.

Alighting there you can visit the famous windmill, which has a spectacular setting overlooking Tralee Bay. Built in the 18th century, it put the town on the map as a major grain exporter to England. Standing at a height of almost 21 metres, it's the tallest in Europe and is Ireland's only fully operating windmill. Inside you can see exactly how grains of wheat become flour.

In the adjoining buildings an interesting video relates the history of the town with an exhibition on the history of milling and a look at the 19th-century emigration from Kerry.

Open (railway) May–Sep daily, trains on the hour from 11am–5pm (closed on second Mon and Tue of each month for maintenance); (windmill) daily Apr–May and Sep–Oct 9.30am–5.30pm, Jun–Aug 9am–6pm. **Fare** (railway) adults €5, seniors/students/children €3. **Adm** (windmill) adults €5, seniors/students/children €3, family (2+3) €15. **Credit** no credit cards. **Amenities** restaurant, craft shops at windmill.

Cork

Blarney Castle ★ ★ ★ ALL AGES

Blarney, Co Cork, 📞 *021 438 5252; www.blarneycastle.ie.*

Here you'll find the famous Blarney Stone – the Stone of Eloquence – said to bestow the 'gift of the gab' on all those that kiss it. Among the illustrious who have benefited from its powers are Sir Walter Scott, Winston Churchill and even Laurel and Hardy.

The stone is set below the battlements and it's rather disappointing, for onlookers at any rate, that pilgrims no longer dangle over the wall backwards by their ankles until their lips touch.

But the Stone is not the only reason to come here: the castle itself is impressive, built 600 years ago for the King of Munster, Cormac McCarthy. The labyrinthine passages of the dungeon will appeal to some children, as will Badger's Cave, through which the besieged garrison fled with the castle's gold after Cromwell's forces destroyed the walls.

Go down the Wishing Steps into Rock Close to find the Witch's Kitchen, the Witch's Stone, the Druid Circle and the Sacrificial Altar.

Open Mon–Sat May and Sep 9am–6.30pm, Jun–Aug 9am–7pm and Oct–Apr 9am–sundown, Sun 9.30am–5.30pm (summer) 9.30am–sundown (winter). **Adm** adults €8, children (8–14) €2.50, family (2+2) €18.50. **Credit** most major cards accepted. **Amenities** toilets, picnic area, light refreshments.

The Donkey Sanctuary ★
ALL AGES

Liscarroll, Mallow, Co Cork, 📞 *022 48398; www.thedonkeysanctuary. ie. 50km N of Cork, off N20.*

Set in rolling landscape, this is part of a charity founded in 1969, which has taken more than 2,200 donkeys into care, many from a life of neglect. Here, they enjoy the company of others and receive kindness and attention.

Open Mon–Fri 9am–4.30pm, Sat–Sun and bank holidays 10am–5pm. **Adm** free (donations welcome). **Amenities** visitor information, drinks machine, picnic area, toilets.

Fota Wildlife Park ★ ★ ★
ALL AGES

Carrigtwohill, Co Cork, 📞 *021 481 2678; www.fotawildlife.ie. E of Cork on R624 towards Cobh.*

Open, natural surroundings here are home to more than 90 species including giraffes, antelope, bison, zebra, kangaroos and ostrich. Ring-tailed lemurs and monkeys swing through the trees and get up to mischief on lake islands, and there are even penguins and seals.

INSIDER TIP ▶
Early morning and late afternoon is a good time to be around to watch the animals being fed.

Blarney Castle

Fox's Lane Folk Museum ★
AGES 4 AND UP

Youghal, Co Cork, ☎ *024 91145.*

Best of all is the cheetah run, when around 4pm you can watch the big cats sprinting after their food. There's a tour train, playground and picnic area and children's events are organised during the summer.

The adjacent **Fota House, arboretum and gardens** are also open (separate charge).

Open *Mon–Sat 10am–4.30pm, Sun 11am–4.30pm.* **Adm** *adults €12.50,*

Displaying more than 600 domestic gadgets and appliances, from the 1850s through to the 1950s, there's a fascinating collection of laundry equipment, vacuum cleaners, sewing machines, early gramophones, typewriters, telephones and an assortment of food preparation and cooking equipment. Try guessing the use of items such as buttonhooks, glove stretchers, curling tongs, sugar crushers and hat irons. You will also see what a traditional Irish kitchen of 100 years ago was like.

Open *Jul–Sep Tue–Sat 10am–1pm and 2–6pm.* **Adm** *adults €4, children (6–15) €2, family €10.* **Credit** *most cards.* **Amenities** *wheelchair friendly.*

The Blarney Stone

One legend relates that the Blarney Stone is Jacob's Pillow, brought to Ireland by the prophet Jeremiah. Others have suggested that it was given by Robert the Bruce to Cormac McCarthy in return for help at the battle of Bannockburn in 1314. The story goes that the grateful king gave half the Stone of Scone to McCarthy and the great Irish chieftain incorporated it into the battlements of his castle. Yet another theory is that the Crusaders carried the stone back, and it's the rock behind which David hid from his enemy, Saul. Whatever its origin, it is said that a witch, saved from drowning, revealed to the McCarthys its power of bestowing eloquence on all who kiss it.

Mizen Head Signal Station

★ ★ ★ **AGES 4 AND UP**

Mizen Head Visitor Centre, Mizen Head, Co Cork; 📞 *028 35115/35225,* www.mizenhead.net*. 40km SW of Bantry.*

At the southwest tip of Ireland, this place truly feels at the end of the world. Beginning in the Fastnet Hall, children can discover how ships find their way at sea with the Navigational Aids Simulator, discover about the weather, and see a scale model of the Fastnet Lighthouse out at sea.

Then it's off to the **Mizen Light,** passing the cutter that was used to take provisions out to the lighthouses. The light itself is on an island, reached by a dramatic arched bridge spanning the surging waves far below. You can see the keeper's kitchen, bedroom and the engine room, which provided emergency power to the light. There are displays recounting the building of the Fastnet Light and tales of some of the ships wrecked off the coast. There's also information about the bird and sea life surrounding the point and going back, you might spot dolphins and perhaps even a whale. The final test comes in climbing the 99 steps back up from the bridge, but the café will provide well-earned refreshment at the top.

Open mid-Mar–Apr, May and Oct daily 10.30am–5pm, Jun–Sep daily 10am–6pm, Nov–mid-Mar Sat–Sun 11am–4pm. Admission adults €6, seniors/students €4.50, children (5–11) €3.50, family (2+3) €18. Credit V, MC. Amenities toilets, gift shop.

West Cork Model Railway Village ★ ★ ALL AGES

Inchydoney Road, Clonakilty, Co Cork, 📞 *023 33224;* www.model village.ie*. 41km SW of Cork along N71.*

This superb model railway layout is entered through a life-size reconstruction of Clonakilty Station. Accurately hand-crafted at 1:24 scale, it depicts sections of the now defunct West Cork Railway as it was in the 1940s. Everything is here in exquisite detail and it's not just trains; the terminus at Cork, Clonakilty Station and the town on market day are just some of the scenes illustrated. To give some idea of the painstaking attention to detail, the model of Clonakilty's church took four and a half months to complete and is estimated to have cost almost half as much as the real one.

There's also the Tschu Tschu – Irish for Choo Choo – a bright red and green road train that tours the sights of the town, plus a children's playroom, full of colourful climbing frames, ball pools and rollers.

Open Feb–Oct daily 11am–5pm (Jul–Aug 10am–6pm). Adm (model railway and village only) adults €7, seniors/students €6, children €4.25, infants (under 5) €2.25, family €22.50; (combined ticket with train ride) adults €11, seniors/students €9, children €6.25, infants €3.25, family €33.50; (play room) children €4. Credit most cards accepted. Amenities light refreshments, shop selling pocket money gifts, toilets, baby-changing facilities, wheelchair access, picnic tables.

Mizen Head

Whale of a Time ★★

AGES 4 AND UP

Cork, Youghal and Kinsale, ☏ *086 328 3250 or 087 120 3463 (Castletownsend); www.whaleof atime.ie.*

Seeing whales and dolphins swimming in their natural habitat is a real thrill, and here along the southwest coast of Ireland is one of the best places for it.

Experienced skippers take you along the coast in search of these magnificent mammals, and while you're not guaranteed to see them, they only sail when conditions are judged favourable.

Other trips explore Cork Harbour, or head out to the nature reserve of Capel Island, home to cormorants, fulmars and gulls and often with seals basking on the shore rocks. Another excursion follows the River Blackwater upstream through the beautiful Irish countryside, passing the ruined Molana Abbey and Strancally Castle.

Boats operate from Cork Harbour, Youghal, Kinsale and Castletownsend, for which pre-booking is necessary.

Open *daily throughout most of the year, dependent upon weather conditions.* **Fare** *from €25 per person.* **Credit** *V, MC.*

FAMILY-FRIENDLY ACCOMMODATION

MODERATE

Devon Inn Hotel ★★

Templeglantine, Co Limerick, ☏ *069 84122; www.devoninnhotel.com.*

The Devon Inn Hotel offers comfortable rooms, friendly service and a relaxing atmosphere. It also makes children welcome and in summer the patio and garden area is great for informal meals from the bar. Dishes on the restaurant evening menu include steaks, a choice of fish and rack of lamb, and children can order small portions or choose from their own menu. Midway between Limerick and Killarney, this makes a great base for exploring the region.

Rooms 52. *Rates* double €120–150, child sharing (6–15) meals only, enquire for special deals. *Credit* all major credit cards accepted. *Amenities* guest parking, cots, bottle service, highchairs, baby-sitting arranged. *In room* room service, tea/coffee-making facilities, safes in some rooms, sat TV, laundry service on request.

Fitzgerald's Woodlands Hotel ★★

Knocknanes, Adare, Co Limerick, ☎ 061 605 100; www.woodlands-hotel.ie.

Not far from Adare, reckoned to be Ireland's prettiest village, this hotel runs Woody's Fun Club that offers in- and outdoor activities for children during the holidays. There's also a pool, spa and gym plus pool table, and children get high tea, so parents can enjoy the Brennan Room restaurant in the evening.

Rooms 94. *Rates* double €145–€155, child sharing (4–16) €20, enquire for special deals. *Credit* all major credit cards accepted. *Amenities* cots, bottle service, children's menus and small portions available, highchairs, baby-sitting arranged. *In room* room service, tea/coffee-making facilities, safe deposit at reception, sat TV, WiFi available in some rooms, laundry service, irons and boards.

Dingle Skellig Hotel ★★★
FIND

Dingle, Co Kerry; ☎ 066 915 0200; www.dingleskellig.com.

Originally built to house the cast and crew for the 1970 film *Ryan's Daughter*, this splendid hotel enjoys superb views across Dingle Bay where you might even see dolphins. There's a children's games room and play area and while youngsters are entertained in the Fungi club, parents can try out The Peninsula Spa and Relaxation Suite or the gym. The pool has a good-sized children's area and there's also sauna, Jacuzzi and eucalyptus pool.

Rooms 111. *Rates* double €120–€240, child sharing (4–7) €40, (7–12) €50, enquire for special deals. *Credit* all major credit cards accepted. *Amenities* cots, bottle service, children's menus and small portions available, highchairs, baby-sitting, laundry room with tumble driers and irons, kitchen with fridge and sterilising equipment, WiFi. *In room* room service, tea/coffee-making facilities, safe deposit at reception, sat TV, CD and DVD players in superior rooms, phone, laundry service.

Brandon Hotel ★★★

Princes Street, Tralee, Co. Kerry, ☎ 066 712 3333; www.brandon hotel.ie.

This 3-star hotel prides itself in offering a 5-star service. The restaurant combines classical cuisine with contemporary influences or there's the more informal environment of the bar

with a separate children's menu.
Other amenities include a spa,
fitness centre and pool, and
across the road is the excellent
town park where the children can
run about to their heart's content.

Rooms 185. *Rates* double
€140–350, child sharing (over 12)
50%, enquire for special deals.
Credit all major credit cards
accepted. *Amenities* cots, bottle
service, children's menus and small
portions available, highchairs, baby-
sitting arranged. *In room* room service, tea/coffee-making facilities, safe
deposit at reception, sat TV, WiFi
throughout hotel, laundry service.

MODERATE–EXPENSIVE

Banna Beach Holiday and Leisure Centre ★★

Ardfert, Co Kerry, 📞 066 713 4103;
www.bannabeachhotel.net.

Although the hotel is currently
undergoing refurbishment, the
Leisure Village holiday homes
offer ideal self-catering accommodation for families, right by the
Blue Flag Banna Beach and with
full use of the leisure centre facilities. These include a 20-metre
pool incorporating a children's
section and separate infant's pool,
bubble sprays, sauna, Jacuzzi, and
fitness centre.

There's also a well-equipped
outdoor play area and an indoor
soft play area, which has special
sessions for the very young,
while for older children the
supervised games room has pool
tables and video games.

Magician, karaoke competition, discos and sports events are
among the organised entertainment for youngsters, and each

evening during the season there's
a family show in O'Shea's Pub.

If parents want a quiet drink
on their own, there's the B Bar
(over 18s only). And on site
there's a small supermarket,
Chinese restaurant and fast food
diner.

Accommodation 80 holiday homes.
Rates €349–1049 per week; *Credit*
all major credit cards. *In rooms*
open-plan living area, fully fitted
kitchen, fridge-freezer, washing
machine, TV, video or DVD and audio
system, cot, highchair.

MODERATE

Quality Hotel and Leisure Centre ★★ FIND

Cork Road, Killarney, Co Kerry, 📞 064
31555; *www.qualityhotelkillarney*.

Stay in the resort hotel or rent a
fully contained self-catering cottage; either way there's so much
to do you could spend your
whole holiday here.

Entertainment for children is
offered at four different levels
from tiny tots to young teens. The
crèche is staffed by qualified carers
and is equipped with everything
you need to feed babies. Teens on
the other hand can use pool and
snooker tables, air hockey and
even DJ for the day on the hotel's
own radio station. There's a pool,
spa and fitness suite, and outside
18-hole mini golf, KMX carting
and aqua gliding as well as a
sports pitch.

Rooms range of hotel rooms, suites,
family apartments and holiday
homes. *Rates* double €120–180,
child sharing €20–30 dependent on
age, enquire for special deals. *Credit*

all major credit cards accepted.
Amenities cots, bottle service, children's menus and small portions available, highchairs, baby-sitting arranged. **In room** room service, tea/coffee-making facilities, sat TV, WiFi throughout hotel, laundry service, irons and boards on request.

MODERATE

Gleneagle Hotel ★★

Muckross Road, Killarney, Co Kerry, 064 36000; www.gleneagle hotel.com.

Ireland's National Event Centre, part of the Gleneagle Hotel complex, hosts top acts, cabaret and major shows throughout the year. The hotel also offers a children's club with three age groups including a crèche, plus facilities such as pitch-and-putt and tennis courts, and an aqua leisure centre, fitness suite, and cabaret. There are also three restaurants, from the formal Flesk to the casual Argyll Bistro.

The hotel is well placed for visiting some of the area's finest beauty spots, with Killarney National Park on the doorstep.

Look out for the vintage car in one of the hotel entrances.

Rooms hotel rooms, family apartments. **Rates** double €150–190: enquire for special deals. **Credit** all major credit cards accepted.
Amenities WiFi in public areas, cots, bottle service, children's menus and small portions available, highchairs, baby-sitting arranged, shuttle bus into town. **In room** room service, tea/coffee-making facilities, sat TV, laundry service, irons and boards on request.

MODERATE–EXPENSIVE

Baltimore Harbour Hotel
★★★ FIND

Baltimore, West Cork. 028 20362; www.baltimoreharbourhotel.ie.

Although most rooms here boast a stunning view out to sea, this is not just a really attractive and comfortable hotel, but also one that welcomes youngsters with a summer holiday Sammy the Seal Children's Club. The club organises supervised games and activities such as swimming competitions, painting, outdoor games, videos and Playstation.

If it rains you can spend time in the swimming pool with the children's bubble pool, and for parents and older teens, there's a fully equipped fitness centre, and relaxation and beauty therapies can be arranged.

For informal eating there's the chartroom bar or barbecues, arranged two or three times a week. Specialities at the Clipper Restaurant highlight Atlantic fish as well as Irish meat. Many dishes lend themselves to smaller portions, but children can choose from their own menu too.

The hotel is ideally placed for exploring this spectacular coastline and sea-based activities as well as the Schull Planetarium at Mizen Head.

Rooms 82, some interconnecting rooms and 3 bedroom suites. **Rates** double €120–168, children (aged 4–12) €20–30, (aged 13–16) €25–35:

enquire for special deals. **Credit** all major credit cards accepted. **Amenities** WiFi in public areas, cots, bottle service, highchairs, baby-sitting arranged. **In room** room service, tea/coffee-making facilities, reception safe deposit, sat TV, laundry service can be arranged, irons and boards on request.

Imperial Hotel ★★★

South Mall, Cork City, Co Cork,
📞 *021 427 4040; www.flynnhotels. com.*

Book in here and you may spend the night in the room where 'the Big Fella', Michael Collins spent his last night before being killed in an ambush on 22nd August 1922 at Bealnablath. Built in 1813, this hotel combines period elegance and charm with modern comforts and prides itself on being one of the best places to stay in the city, conveniently within walking distance of the shopping centre.

Food is served in three separate venues: Lafayette's is open from first thing in the morning into the evening, serving breakfasts, sandwiches, wraps and a selection of light dishes plus and coffee; light snacks are available during the day in the Food Hall; and for fine dining there's the Pembroke Restaurant, which serves lunch and dinner, including an early bird menu between 6 and 7pm Sunday to Thursday. Although there's no separate children's menu, many dishes are available in smaller portions and they're well used to adapting dishes to suit.

Rooms 126. **Rates** double €145–245, children €35, enquire for special deals. **Credit** all major credit cards accepted. **Amenities** discount parking, cots, bottle service, small portions available, highchairs, baby-sitting arranged, beauty and treatment spa. **In room** room service, tea/coffee-making facilities, reception safe deposit, sat TV, laundry and dry cleaning service, irons and boards on request, computers in rooms.

CAFÉS & FAMILY-FRIENDLY DINING

Bella Italia – Italian Bistro Restaurant ★★ ITALIAN

43a Thomas Street, off O'Connell Street, Limerick City, Co Limerick,
📞 *061 418 872.*

Just off the main shopping street, in a developing area of town, this no frills Italian licensed restaurant offers everything from snacks to full evening meals with fresh pasta and homemade sauces. Children can create their own pizza and there's a host of salads and house specials every day. Snacks include soups, open sandwiches, baked potatoes and toasted baps.

Eat inside or watch the world go by from the pavement tables. And if you're on the move, the bistro also offers an extensive take away menu.

Open daily, 10am–9.30pm. **Main courses** €9–22.50. **Credit** V, MC. **Amenities** small portions, bottle warming, highchairs, disabled toilets and baby-changing facilities, licensed.

Beaufort Bar and Restaurant ★★ SEAFOOD & IRISH

Beaufort, Killarney, Co Kerry, 📞 *064 44149; www.beaufortbar.com.*

Run by successive generations of the O'Sullivan family since it opened in 1841, the Beaufort offers real personal attention, with one of the brothers usually on hand.

The inn achieved fame in the early 1900s when it became an American film company's base. The village and its inhabitants featured alongside stars of the early silver screen in more than 70 films and the many stills on the walls are one of the endearing features of this welcoming country inn.

Today, the place is known for its splendid food, made with fresh local produce. During the week, informal meals are served in the bar, and a more extensive menu is offered at weekends in the restaurant, where children are more than welcome at the 7pm sitting – booking advisable. Starters include a delicious chowder, seafood salad and black puddings, while main courses feature herb-crusted salmon, scampi and racks of Kerry lamb.

Open *bar menu Tue–Thu 6–9pm, restaurant Fri–Sat 6.30–9.30pm (children at first sitting only), Sun lunch 1–2.30pm.* **Main courses** *bar menu €7–15, restaurant €16–29;* **Credit** *V, MC.* **Amenities** *car park, children's menus, small portions, bottle warming, highchairs, baby-changing facilities.*

Molly Gallivan's Cottage ★★ SNACKS, CAKES AND LIGHT LUNCHES

Releigh, Bonane, Kenmare, Co Kerry, 📞 *064 40714; www.mollygallivans.com.*

Widowed with seven children to bring up, Molly Gallivan became something of a local character, supplementing the meagre income from her small farm by selling a drop of *poitín* (illegal whiskey) to passing travellers and early tourists heading up to Killarney. Her 200-year-old cottage now houses a small museum, tea room and craft shop, retaining its character with a mismatch of tables and chairs in the old parlour.

Serving soup, open sandwiches, home-baked cakes (try the Guinness one), fruit crumbles and delicious pies, it's ideal for a light lunch or snack.

A short farm trail winds past the vegetable garden and duck pond to a tiny famine cottage, torched to prevent the family returning after eviction. There's a prehistoric calendar, a couple of donkeys wandering about, and old farm machinery as well as the ancient still where 'Molly's Mountain Dew' was made.

Open *Apr–Oct daily 10am–6pm.* **Main courses** *from €9.50.* **Amenities** *car park, small portions, bottle warming, highchairs.*

An Seanna Ríocht (The Old Kingdom) ★★ TEA ROOM

Emlagh, Lispole, Co Kerry, ☎ 066 915 1750.

On the Lispole to Dingle Road some 5km out of Dingle is this spacious modern country-style tearoom with plenty of inside seating as well as a terrace with great views across a lough.

There's background Irish music and an emphasis on traditional cooking using local and organic produce where possible. Pop in for coffee and cake, a light lunch of soup and sandwiches or toasties, or try Irish lamb stew or bacon and cabbage.

A gift shop sells local crafts, or follow the heritage and nature trail that's being developed around the lake.

Open daily 10am–5pm. **Main courses** *from €8.50.* **Amenities** *car park, children's menu, small portions, bottle warming, highchairs, baby-changing facilities.*

Jam ★ LIGHT LUNCHES

77 High Street, Killarney, Co Kerry, ☎ 064 31441; www.jam.ie.

This is a busy high street bakery and café, and deservedly so with a delicious array of sweet and savoury goodies on the counter for the children to ogle. There's also soup, baked potatoes, and more substantial offerings such as beef lasagne, shepherd's pie, and vegetarian dishes, all freshly prepared. The dozen or so accompanying salads are interesting too. The branch in Kenmare serves the same home-baked assortment.

Open daily 8am–6pm. **Main courses** *€5–9.65.* **Amenities** *children's menu, small portions, bottle warming, highchairs.*

Bricín Restaurant and Craft Shop ★★ MODERN IRISH

26 High Street, Killarney, Co Kerry, ☎ 064 34902; www.bricin.com.

Molly Gallivan's Cottage

Above an enticing shop selling crafts including wooden toys and puppets, artwork, and books for adults and children, is this impressive restaurant serving a mouth-watering range of freshly home-cooked food. There are paninis stuffed with cajun chicken and pineapple, or fisherman's pie with salad and chips on the side, followed by pear and almond or chocolate and strawberry tart. The evening menu is equally appetising with dishes such as Thai red chicken curry and salmon stuffed with crabmeat and mushrooms under a mozzarella topping. The house speciality is boxty, traditional Irish potato pancake cooked on a griddle and filled with fish, chicken, meat or vegetables.

Open Mon–Sat Mar–Dec lunch 12–3pm, dinner 6–9.30pm. **Main courses** lunch €8.30–9.40, dinner €18.50–25. **Credit** V. MC. **Amenities** children's options, small portions, bottle warming, highchairs, licensed.

MODERATE

Garden Restaurant at Muckross House ★
MODERN IRISH

Killarney National Park, Killarney, Co Kerry, ☎ 064 31440; www. muckross-house.ie.

Convenient for visiting Muckross House, the Traditional Farms, or exploring the National Park, this large, modern self-service cafeteria offers a wide selection of freshly prepared sandwiches, salads, pastries, cakes and scones as well as main courses. Options from the hot buffet include braised beef in red wine and mushroom sauce or Cajun chicken with barbecue sauce. There's split level indoor seating as well as outside tables overlooking the gardens.

Open daily 9am–5pm, lunch 12–3pm. **Main courses** around €9.50. **Credit** V, MC. **Amenities** children's options, small portions, highchairs, baby-changing facilities.

MODERATE

Annie May's Bar, Restaurant and Bed and Breakfast ★
BAR FOOD

11 Bridge Street, Skibbereen, Co Cork, ☎ 028 22930.

On the main street, this traditional family-run bar and restaurant serves through the day to 9.30pm and offers bed and breakfast. Children with hearty appetites are welcome and the emphasis is on traditional home-cooked Irish food, but there's an assortment of sandwiches, toasties and light snacks as well. Main courses include a Roast of the Day with fresh-cooked vegetables and the house speciality, Irish stew and potatoes.

The evening menu is longer with, for example, leg of lamb with mint sauce and rosemary and chicken stuffed with herbs and wrapped in bacon.

Open daily, food from 8.30am–9.30pm. **Main courses** €8.95–16. **Credit** V, MC. **Amenities** children's options, small portions, bottle warming, highchairs.

Café at Cobh – The Queenstown Story ★ SNACKS

Old Railway Station, Cobh, Co Cork, 📞 *021 481 3591.*

You don't have to visit the water-front Cobh heritage centre to eat at this café in the old railway station, and it deserves a visit with a menu that caters for everyone: cakes, biscuits and tarts with tea or coffee; sandwiches, panini and toasties; quiche, pasties and salads; lasagne and shepherd's pie. For children there's a special 'lunch box'.

Open *daily, food from 8.30am–4.30pm.* **Main courses** *from €8.50.* **Credit** *V, MC.* **Amenities** *children's option, small portions, bottle warming, highchairs, baby-changing facilities.*

MODERATE–EXPENSIVE

Mary Ann's Bar and Restaurant ★★★
SEAFOOD AND MODERN IRISH

Castletownshend, Co Cork, 📞 *028 36146; www.westcorkweek.com\maryanns.*

At this traditional pub in an attractive town, Fergus the owner is passionate about fine food and good service – including for children who are considered part of everyday life here.

Fergus' enthusiasm bubbles over into everything about the place. He uses local producers and suppliers for the best of Irish ingredients, and travels the world in search of superb wines, many of which are available by the glass. Despite this, his prices aren't through the roof and you'll find some blinding bargains in the house wines.

Fish is much in evidence, from seared scallops to pan-fried John Dory. Meat might include roast breast of duck, red wine and vanilla jus, or Irish fillet steak with gratin dauphinois and wild mushroom sauce. There's also a changing blackboard of daily specials. Booking is necessary for the restaurant, but the same menus are also available in the bar.

Open *daily (Nov–Mar, not Mon), meals 12–2.30pm and 6–9pm.* **Main courses** *€9.50–25.* **Credit** *most major cards.* **Amenities** *children's options, small portions, bottle warming, highchairs, baby-changing facilities.*

The Way to a Man's Heart

Irish girls need more than a pretty face to get themselves a husband, the way to a man's heart is through his stomach as this little ditty explains:
Boxty on the griddle
Boxty in the pan.
If you can't make Boxty,
You'll never get a man.

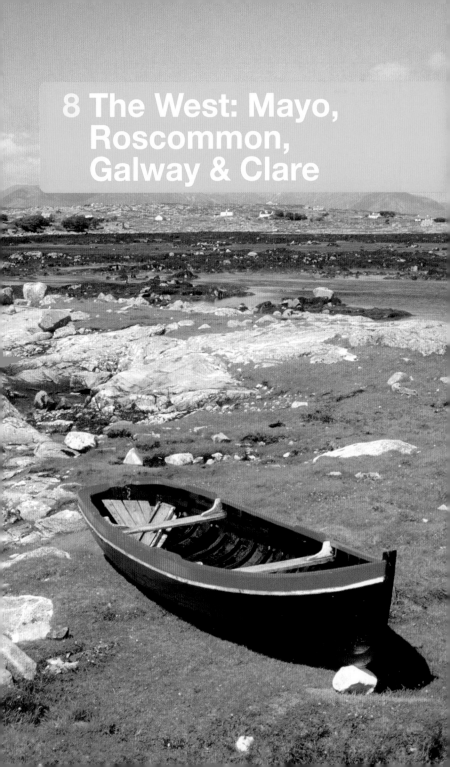

8 The West: Mayo, Roscommon, Galway & Clare

WEST IRELAND

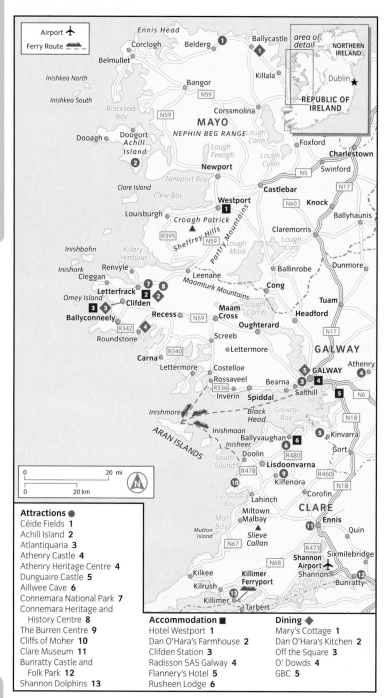

area of detail NORTHERN IRELAND

REPUBLIC OF IRELAND

Dublin ★

Ennis Head
Corclogh
Belderg
Ballycastle
Belmullet
Killala
Inishkea North
Bangor
Inishkea South
Corssmolina
Blacksod Bay
MAYO
Dooagh
Doogort
NEPHIN BEG RANGE
Lough Conn
Foxford
Charlestown
Achill Island
Lough Feeagh
Lough Cullin
Swinford
Newport
N5
Clare Island
Newport Bay
Castlebar
Knock
Louisburgh
Clew Bay
Westport
N60
Croagh Patrick
Sheffrey Hills
Ballyhaunis
Inishbofin
Killary Harbour
R395
Claremorris
Inishark
Renvyle
Leenane
Lough Mask
Ballinrobe
Dunmore
Cleggan
Letterfrack
Maamturk Mountains
Cong
Omey Island
Clifden
Recess
Maam Cross
Tuam
Ballyconneely
R342
Headford
Roundstone
R340
Oughterard
Carna
Lettermore
Screeb
GALWAY
Lettermore
Costelloe
Rossaveel
GALWAY
Athenry
Inver
Bearna
Salthill
N6
ARAN ISLANDS
Inishmore
Spiddal
Black Head
Galway Bay
N18
Inishmaan
Ballyvaughan
Kinvarra
Inisheer
Doolin
Gort
South Sound
Lisdoonvarna
R480
Liscannor Bay
R478
Kilfenora
N18
Mal Bay
Lahinch
Corofin
Mutton Island
Miltown Malbay
CLARE
Ennis
Quin
Slieve Callan
N67
Sixmilebridge
Kilkee
Shannon Airport
R473
Kilrush
Killimer Ferryport
Shannon
Bunratty
Killimer
River Shannon
Tarbert

0   20 mi
0   20 km

Attractions ●
Céide Fields **1**
Achill Island **2**
Atlantiquaria **3**
Athenry Castle **4**
Athenry Heritage Centre **4**
Dunguaire Castle **5**
Aillwee Cave **6**
Connemara National Park **7**
Connemara Heritage and
   History Centre **8**
The Burren Centre **9**
Cliffs of Moher **10**
Clare Museum **11**
Bunratty Castle and
   Folk Park **12**
Shannon Dolphins **13**

Accommodation ■
Hotel Westport **1**
Dan O'Hara's Farmhouse **2**
Clifden Station **3**
Radisson SAS Galway **4**
Flannery's Hotel **5**
Rusheen Lodge **6**

Dining ◆
Mary's Cottage **1**
Dan O'Hara's Kitchen **2**
Off the Square **3**
O' Dowds **4**
GBC **5**

There is a breathtaking quality to the counties of the west of Ireland. All but Roscommon have fine Atlantic seaboards, all are achingly beautiful, and all excellent for families who love the outdoors. The area is also in part the Connacht, the westernmost province of Ireland, which is seeing a steady rebuilding of communities around the region's traditions, folklore and characteristic old-Irish standards of hospitality.

Given the size of the area it helps to make first for the various county towns – Castlebar, Roscommon, Galway and Ennis.

Galway is the big draw, focused on the bustling city of Galway and modern beach destination Salthill on Galway Bay, with its cafés, restaurants, swimming pool, gym and the popular Atlantaquaria. Galway also gives access to the untamed landscapes of Connemara and its raised bog, heathered hills and moorland mountains.

Threaded by the Shannon river, tidy farm fields and heather expanses overlay much of Roscommon and Galway, dotted with lakes that reflect the sky so intensely you feel the light is rising from the earth.

But Co Clare, with the renowned limestone landscapes of The Burren and strong musical tradition also has much to offer. Its coastline south of Galway Bay features fine, but not always sandy, beaches and coastal villages, while inland are farming areas ideal for exploring by bike.

Like much of western Ireland, the beaches are outstanding, with numerous Blue Flags including one on the freshwater lake at Loughrea, and as with the northwest, these western counties have a clutch of in-shore islands that are a delight to explore including the Aran Islands off Clare. Even if you have only a few days make sure that you fit them in – the 30-minute trip to Aran is as much a draw as the island itself, and Achill is a delight to wander. But be sure that everyone can cope with the sometimes bumpy conditions – you are, after all, heading out into the Atlantic.

ESSENTIALS

Getting There

By Air Galway: The airport at Galway (Carnmore, Co. Galway. 091 755 569; *www.galwayairport. com*) is 6km east of the city, and has Aer Arann (*www.aerarann. com*) flights linking it with Dublin, Cork, London Luton, Manchester, Edinburgh, Leeds-Bradford and Cardiff. FlyBe (*www.flybe.com*) has flights to Galway from Belfast, Birmingham and Southampton. There is an infrequent bus service into Galway from the airport, and Aer Arann operates its own shuttle; taxis cost around €25 into Galway.

Car hire is available at Galway Airport through Budget Car Rental (090 662 7711; *www. budget.ie*).

Mayo: Mayo has an international airport at Knock (Ireland West Airport), near Charlestown (☎ 094 9368100; www.knockairport. com). Aer Arann has once daily flights to Knock from Dublin; Bmibaby (www.bmibaby.com) flies from Manchester and Birmingham each day, and Ryanair (www.ryanair.com) flies daily from London Luton, London Stansted and Tuesdays, Thursday and weekends from Nottingham (East Midlands). The Ireland West Airport in conjunction with Bus Éireann offers a shuttle bus service between the airport and Charlestown, which links with the national Bus Éireann network.

Car hire is available at Knock Airport from **Budget** (☎ 087 269 5461 or ☎ 090 662 4668; www. budget.ie); **Hertz** (☎ 094 936 7333 or ☎ 071 916 0111; www.hertz. com); **Murrays/Europcar** (☎ 094 936 7221; www.europcar.ie); **Caseys** (☎ 094 902 1411; www. caseycar.com); **Diplomat/ National/Alamo** (☎ 094 936 7252; www.carhire.ie), and **Avis** (☎ 094 936 7707 or ☎ 071 916 8386; www.avis.ie).

Clare: Shannon Airport (☎ 061 712 400; www.aer-rianta.ie) is 21km from Ennis, the county town of Clare. Shannon is an important international airport with flights to and from worldwide destinations. UK destinations are Bournemouth, Bristol, Edinburgh, Glasgow, Liverpool, London (Gatwick, Heathrow and Stansted), Manchester and Nottingham (East Midlands),

with services operated by Ryanair and Aer Lingus.

By Rail Trains to Galway operate from Dublin Heuston. Services to Mayo are infrequent are operate three times daily to Westport, Castlebar and Ballina. Roscommon Town is on the Dublin Heuston–Ballina line, while Ennis in Co Clare is along the Limerick line with direct links to Dublin.

By Bus Bus Éireann (see p. 24) runs services from Dublin and other towns to Galway, Ennis, Ballina, Westport and Castlebar and Roscommon.

VISITOR INFORMATION

Co Galway

Ireland West Region Áras Fáilte, Forster Street, Galway. ☎ 091 537 700; www.irelandwest.ie or www.visitgalway.com.

Aran Tourist Office, Aran Heritage Centre, Cill Ronain, Inis Mor, Arainn. ☎ 099 61263; www.visitaranislands.com.

Oranmore Tourist Office ☎ 091 790 811

Oughterard Tourist Office ☎ 091 552 808.

There are seasonal tourist offices at:

Ballinasloe ☎ 090 964 26040

Clifden ☎ 090 095 21163

Salthill ☎ 091 520 500

Thoor Ballylee, Gort
📞 *091 631 436*

Tuam 📞 *093-25486/24463*

Co Mayo

Your first call for information should be the following general websites:
www.visitmayo.com and *www.irelandwest.ie*.

Achill Tourism, Cashel, Achill Island. 📞 *098 47353*; *www.achilltourism.com*.

Westport Tourist Office, James Street, Westport. 📞 *098 25711*.

There are seasonal tourist offices at:

Ballina 📞 *096 70848*

Ballinrobe 📞 *094 954 2150*

Castlebar 📞 *094 902 1207*

Cong 📞 *094 954 6542*

Knock Village 📞 *094 938 8193*

Co Roscommon

Start at this website: *www.irelandwest.ie*.

There are seasonal tourist offices at:

Boyle 📞 *071 966 2145*

Roscommon 📞 *090 662 6342*

Co Clare

The general area website is: *www.shannonregiontourism.ie*.

Ennis Tourist Information Office, Arthur's Row, off

O'Connel Square, Ennis. 📞 *065 682 8366*

Shannon Airport, Arrivals Hall, Shannon. 📞 *061 471 664*.

There are seasonal tourist offices at:

Kilrush 📞 *065 905 1577*

Kilkee 📞 *065 905 6112*

Cliffs of Moher 📞 *065 708 1171*

Killaloe 📞 *061 376 866*

ORIENTATION

Dublin to Castlebar is 237km (148 miles), to Roscommon Town 144km (90 miles), to Galway 215km (135 miles) and to Ennis 232km (145 miles)

Getting Around

Although well served by railways and bus services, the best way of exploring the west region is by car or, locally, by bicycle.

Information about bus timetables is available at the various tourist information offices, and a little ingenuity (and careful planning) can produce a memorable family day exploring the different counties.

Discovering the Counties

Galway

The largest county in the province of Connacht, Galway lies in the centre of the western seaboard of Ireland, and encompasses nearly 6,000 square kilometres, divided by Lough Corrib, Ireland's second largest lake. There are two distinct landscapes: the vast mountain and wildly beautiful land of Connemara to the west of Lough Corrib, where the walking is good for all but the very young, and the rolling, rich limestone farmland plains of Galway East, bounded by the rivers Suck and Shannon, a land for leisurely exploration. The county town is Galway, a modern, bustling centre with all mainstream services and facilities including an excellent shopping centre and numerous eateries.

Mayo

Mayo, with an area of 5,400 square kilometres, is the third largest county in Ireland, and stretches from Lough Corrib and the long fjord of Killary Harbour in the south, to Kilalla Bay and Erris in the north, and from Achill Island, Clew Bay and the Mullet peninsula in the west to the counties of Sligo and Roscommon in the east. The county town of Castlebar is known for both walking and angling, but also offers swimming, bowling, horse riding and tennis.

The landscape varies from mainly flat terrain in East Mayo, through the island-adorned lakes of Lough Conn, Lough Cullin, Lough Carra, Lough Mask, to the quartzite peaks along the indented Atlantic coast, where sea cliffs alternate with gold-sand beaches. In the north, widespread swathes of blanket bog dominate the landscape, contrasting markedly with the mountain of the south.

Attractions include Ballintuber Abbey, the Céide Fields (see p. 183), Foxford Woollen Mills, Moore Hall, Pontoon and the Turlough Round Tower. Annual festivals include the International Four Days Walks, the Blues Festival and Heritage Day.

Roscommon

The inland county of Roscommon is 100km from the top of the Arigna valley in the north to Shannonbridge. The Shannon is the boundary in the east and the River Suck for much of the west; in fact most of the county is bounded by water to some degree: in the north lie the large loughs Key, Gara and Boderg, with the great Lough Ree in the east. The county's limestone foundation and numerous lakes make it an angler's paradise.

In the east and west, as if pampering to the stereotypical notion of Ireland, one-third of the county is under blanket bog, bewildering, scientifically important and hugely fascinating, but somewhat iffy to explore. Roscommon Town is the county administrative centre.

Clare

Bounded north and south by Galway Bay and the Shannon, County Clare has an area of 3,147 square kilometres. Its capital town is Ennis. There are plenty of beaches and although most are gravel or stone, some are Blue Flag. Inland the county's most widely renowned feature, The Burren National Park, forms a massive region of rocky chaos, underlain by limestone that contains an incredible 75% of Irish plant species.

Children-friendly Events & Entertainment

Roola Boola Children's Arts Festival ★★

October. Castlebar, Co Mayo, 📞 *094 902 3733; www.linenhall.com.*

This is the antithesis of theme park entertainment: a funky arts festival for young people, with a busy schedule of shows, events and workshops for ages 2–16 and their families (plus a chance to get messy with paints). Roola Boola presents shows by some of the finest children's theatre companies in the world together with a whole range of quality, hands-on arts practitioners. Includes a spectacular lakeside finale with fireworks.

Roundstone ★★

July. Roundstone, Connemara, 📞 *095 21863; www.roundstone.ie.*

The annual Connemara Pony Show features the world-famous Connemara ponies, and is a lovely occasion for children obsessed with ponies. Anyone

View over Galway Bay

The Aran Islands

The Aran Islands (Oileáin Árann) are a group of three islands located at the mouth of Galway Bay on the west coast of Ireland. Between them they make for one or more fascinating days of walking, exploring and birdwatching. Traffic jams are unheard of here, and narrow winding lanes invite exploration. Sail boarding, boating, deep-sea angling and rock fishing are all popular, as is the simple pleasure of wandering aimlessly around.

The largest island is Inishmore, also known as Aranmore (*Árainn (Mhór)* or *Inis Mór*), and its principal port and village is Kilronan (Cill Rónáin). The population of 900 is spread over 14 communities. The middle and second-largest is Inishmaan (*Inis Meáin/Inis Meadhóin*), and the smallest and most eastern is Inisheer (*Inis Thiar* or *Inis Oírr/Inis Oirthir*). Inis Oírr, with a population of 300, is an outcrop from The Burren, and is regarded by many as the most beautiful of the three, consisting of bare limestone pavement with one of the loveliest beaches on the western seaboard.

Aran Direct (29 Forster Street, Galway; Victoria Place, Eyre Square, Galway; Rossaveal Harbour, Connemara: 📞 *091 566 535, 091 506 786, 091 564 769*; *www.arandirect.com*) sails to all islands, and during Jun–Aug offer island hopping tours. **Ferry times** to Inis Mór 10.30am, 1pm (Apr–Oct) and 6.30pm, returning 8am, noon (Apr–Oct) and 5pm; to Inis Meáin/Inis Oirr 10.30am and 6.30pm, returning from Inis Oirr 9.15am and 4.45pm, and Inis Meáin, 9.25am and 4.55pm. **Shuttle buses** depart Galway one hour ahead of sailing time, and meet the ferries for the return journey. **Fares** (return) adults €25, seniors €20,

less than thrilled with our four-legged friends might want to join in the Roundstone Tour de Bog, a family fun bicycle ride from Roundstone to Ballykineelly across the Bog Road and back to Roundstone. There are medals for all sorts of categories, from the most colourful dress or best hat, to the most colourful legs or craziest-looking bike.

St Colmans Garden Fete ★

July. Achill Island, 📞 *098 47353; www.achilltourism.com.*

Located between Keel and Pollagh on Achill Island, this garden fete is a weekend of family fun with numerous activities, games, music, stalls and a monster raffle.

Scoil Acla ★★★

July–August. Achill Island, 📞 *098 47353; www.scoilacla.com.*

This annual summer school on Achill Island has been promoting traditional Irish music, arts and culture for almost 20 years. Scoil Acla provides tuition for all ages and abilities in a range of children €15 (under–6s, free), family (2+2) €65, (2+3) €80, (2+4) €95. **Credit** all cards accepted.

Oileáin Árann Díreach (Aran Island Ferries, 127 Eyre Square Centre, Galway, Co Galway. ☎ *091 568 903; www.aranislandferries.com*) operates services to all three islands. **Ferry times** times vary: check website for schedules. **Fares** return fares: adults €25, seniors €20, children €13 (under–4s, free; family rates available: call for prices). **Return bus fares** adults €6, seniors €5, children €4. Island minibus tour (1 hour): €10 per person. **Credit** all major credit cards accepted. Sailings are from Ros A' Mhíl; Coach connection from Galway City one hour before sailing.

Cliffs of Moher Cruises (Liscannor, Doolin, Co Clare. ☎ *065 707 5949. www.mohercruises.com*) departs daily (Apr–Oct) from Doolin to Inis Oírr (Inisheer), the closest of the Aran Islands to the Clare coast. Times vary according to the tide table – check website for monthly updates. **Fare** adults €25, seniors €20, children €10 (under-5s, free), family (2+2) €60. **Credit** all major credit cards accepted.

Aer Arann Islands (Aerfort Chonamara, Caisleán, Indreabhán, Co Galway. ☎ *091 593 034; www.aerarannislands.ie*) makes regular 10-minute flights to the Aran Islands, departing mainland (winter) 8.30am, 9am, 10am, 10.30am and 3pm, (summer) plus 11.30am, 4pm, 5pm, 5.30pm; return flights (winter) 8.45am, 9.15am, 10.15am, 10.45am and 3.15pm, (summer) plus 11.45am, 4.15pm, 5.15pm and 5.45pm. **Fares** adults €45, children (under-12s) €25. **Credit** all major credit cards accepted.

traditional musical instruments, including the harp, uileann pipes, fiddle, concert flute, banjo, concertina, tin whistle and accordion.

Fee €90 payable when pupils register.

FUN FACT ▸ ## Crash Landing ◂

On the morning of the 15th June 1919, John Alcock and Arthur Whitten-Brown crash-landed their aircraft in a remote bog, a short distance south of Clifden in Co Galway, having left St John's, Newfoundland, 16 hours 27 minutes earlier. In so doing they became the first humans to fly non-stop across the Atlantic Ocean. The aircraft was a Vickers Vimy bi-plane powered by two Roll-Royce Eagle V111 engines of 350 horsepower each. The average speed was 150mph.

In the same area is the transmitter station site from which Marconi effected the first trans-Atlantic radio communication.

WHAT TO SEE & DO

Children's Top 10 Attractions

❶ Check out an island house at the Connemara Heritage and History Centre. See p. 181.

❷ See how our ancestors lived 5,500 years ago at the Céide Fields. See p. 183.

❸ Go in search of brown bears in the underground caves of The Burren. See p. 179.

❹ Marvel at the stupendous cliffs of Moher in Co Clare. See p. 178.

❺ Visit the dolphins on the Shannon Estuary. See p. 179.

❻ Get touchy-feely with a spider crab in Salthill. See p. 181.

❼ Dress up in medieval costume at Athenry Heritage Centre. See p. 180.

❽ Visit a Norman castle at Dunguaire. See p. 183.

❾ Discover the story of Clare at Clare Museum. See p. 178.

❿ Visit a living village at Bunratty Folk Park. See below.

Children-friendly Attractions

Co Clare

Aillwee Cave ★ ★ ★ ALL AGES

Ballyvaughan, The Burren, Co Clare, 📞 *065 707 7036; www.aillweecave. ie. Along the R480, S of Ballyvaughan.*

These caves used to be inhabited by the European brown bear, although it is doubtful that the bears would have appreciated the beautiful natural formations, frozen waterfall and chasms. There's a 30-minute tour but be aware that at some point they usually turn out all the lights, plunging everyone into darkness. In addition, be sure to mind your head in one or two low places and note that the caves aren't suitable for buggies or wheelchairs, and if it's been raining a lot, you can expect a moderate spraying of water underground.

Back above ground you'll find an excellent tearoom/Potato Bar Restaurant serving a variety of freshly made wraps and panini, and baked potatoes. Outdoors, there are a couple of walking trails, one through woodland and the other over the limestone terraces.

A little lower down the hillside is a new falconry centre, with regular flying displays, and a chance to see magnificent birds of prey up close.

Nearby, the farm shop is the perfect place to buy farmhouse cheese, made here. You can watch the cheesemaking but it's a slow business!

Open daily from 10am (last week of Nov and all of Dec by appointment). Adm adults €12, seniors €9, children €5.50, family (2+2) €29, (2+4) €35; (cheese tour) €2. Credit all cards accepted. Amenities gift shop.

Bunratty Castle and Folk Park ★ ★ ALL AGES

Bunratty, Co Clare, 📞 *061 711 200; www.shannonheritage.com. Located just off the N18 Limerick/ Ennis Road.*

This is a chance to see what life may have been like in a medieval fortress, as well as to explore the adjoining folk park. The castle displays mainly 15th- and 16th-century furnishings (the finest collection of medieval furniture in Ireland), works of art and tapestries. The Folk Park portrays the Irish way of life as it was in the 19th century, and features more than 30 buildings in a 'living village' setting, including eight farmhouses, two water-mills, a blacksmith's forge, and displays of 19th-century agricultural equipment. The restored village street is complete with pub, post office, school, doctor's surgery, pawn shop and hotel.

There's also a children's play area, which includes a maze.

Open Jan–Mar and Nov–Dec 9.30am–5.30pm, Apr–Oct 9am–5.30pm (Jun–Aug 9am–6pm). *Adm* prices vary throughout the year. *Credit* V, MC. *Amenities* gift shop, tearoom, pub, country kitchen.

The Burren Centre ★★
AGES 5 AND UP

Kilfenora, Co Clare, ☎ *065 708 8030;* *www.theburrencentre.ie. In the centre of the village.*

A visit to Kilfenora's Burren Centre is vital if you want to understand the Burren and its complex land forms. The centre gives a walk through time that will take you back to a period when the British Isles lay beneath a warm tropical sea. Here, you can follow the story of the formation of the Burren's amazing landscape where humans hunted bear and wolves roamed the forests, and find out more about the dolmens and burial chambers.

Open daily Mar–May and Sep–Oct 10am–5pm, Jun–Aug 9.30am–6pm. *Adm* adults €6, seniors €5, children (under-16s) €4. *Credit* V, MC. *Amenities* craft shop, tearoom, St Fachtan's 12th-century cathedral and a churchyard adjacent, which contains fine examples of medieval high crosses. (admission, free).

Bunratty Castle

Clare Museum ★ AGES 5 AND UP

Arthur's Row, Ennis, Co Clare, ☎065 682 3382; www.clarelibrary.ie. Clare Museum is located in the centre of Ennis, at Arthur's Row, off O'Connell Square, adjacent to the Temple Gate Hotel.

The story of Co Clare goes back 8,000 years and the museum tells it using the themes of earth, power, faith, water and energy. To appeal to a wide range of visitors there are traditional displays, colourful information panels, audio-visual and computer interactive presentations, models, replicas and some specially commissioned art pieces. There are also numerous Clare artefacts from the National Museum of Ireland, the de Valera Museum collection, and collected locally.

Open *Oct–May Tue–Sat 9.30am–5pm, Jun–Sep Mon–Sat 9.30am–5pm, Sun 9.30am–1pm (last admission 1 hour before closing).* **Adm** *free.* **Amenities** *parking, toilets, disabled access.*

Cliffs of Moher ★ ★ ALL AGES

Liscannor, Co Clare, ☎ 065 708 6140; www.cliffsofmoher.ie. 5km N of Liscannor and 8km S of Doolin.

In a country awash with breathtaking views, the Cliffs of Moher add a new dimension. At their highest point, the cliffs are 214 metres high and they range for 8km over the Atlantic Ocean on the western seaboard of County Clare. From the cliffs you can see the Aran Islands, Galway Bay, The Twelve Pins and the Maum Turk Mountains in Connemara, and Loop Head to the south.

The cliffs are home to one of the major colonies of cliff-nesting seabirds in Ireland, and the area was designated as a Refuge for Fauna in 1988 and a Special Protection Area for Birds (SPA) in 1989. Sadly commercialisation has brought a semi-subterranean visitor centre, exhibitions, shops and the construction of pathways, viewing platforms, seating areas and slab walling to protect against dropping over the cliff edge. The centre does however provide insights into the significance and development of cliffs such as these, the way the elemental forces play across the land, and the lengths that humans went to in order to eke a living from the harsh landscape. Reasonable lunches in the Puffins Nest Café and outside are six units occupied by craft workers.

Cliffs of Moher Cruises

Liscannor, Doolin, Co Clare, ☎ 065 707 5949; www.mohercruises.com sail along the base of the Moher cliffs (Apr–Oct, weather permitting). Departure times are based on tide and subject to change due to weather, but typically noon, 3.30pm and 4.30pm. Call the day prior to sailing to confirm times. **Fare** adults €20, seniors €20, children €10 (under-5s, free), family (2+2) €50.

The Burren

The Burren (Irish: Boireann, meaning 'great rock') is a unique karst-landscape region measuring 250 square kilometres, bounded by the Atlantic to the west and Galway Bay to the north. Strictly speaking 'Burren' is a sufficient title; the definite article has only been added to the name in the last few decades, as it has always been called *Boireann* in Irish and Burren in English. Whatever you call it, Burren is a stunning landscape of great, grey rolling hills formed millions of years ago as sedimentary rocks on the bottom of an ancient sea. The full story of Burren is explained in The Burren Centre in Kilfenora (see p. 177).

Burren is rich in historical and archaeological sites. There are many megalithic tombs in the area, portal dolmens, a Celtic high cross in the village of Kilfenora, and a number of ring forts, among them the exceptionally well-preserved Caherconnell stone fort, which is about 1,500 years old, and very much in its original state. (**Open** daily Mar–Oct. Adm (self-guided tour) adults €5, children €4, seniors €4, family (2+2) €14. **065 708 9999;** *www.burrenforts.ie*). The audio-visual presentation makes much more of the fort than can be gleaned from simply walking round it, so take the headsets. There is a convenient café and gift shop in the visitor centre.

The rolling Burren hills are composed of large tracts of limestone pavement with crisscrossing cracks known as grikes, leaving isolated rocks called clints. With the sun on them it looks like it has been snowing, but it's the sheer size and expanse that strikes the visitor first. Closer up it becomes clear that the unusual environment supports Arctic, Mediterranean and Alpine plants side-by-side, with for example the blue flower of the Spring Gentian, an Alpine plant, found in some of the crevices.

Among the dolmens worth seeking out is the Poulnabrone Dolmen, near Carron. This is a portal tomb about 5,500 years old, and one of the best known in Ireland. When all the tourists, apart from yourself, have gone, it's a most tranquil place to watch the sun go down. A car park is nearby.

Open *Jan–Feb and Nov–Dec 9.30am–5pm, Mar–Apr and Oct 9am–6pm, May–Sep 8.30am–7pm (Jun–Aug 8.30pm).* **Adm** *car parking €8, (Atlantic Edge) adults €4, seniors €3.50, children (4–16) €2.50 (under-4s free), family (2+4) €11.95.* **Credit** *all major cards accepted.* **Amenities** *toilets, wheel- and pushchair access, baby-changing facilities.*

The Shannon Dolphins ★★
ALL AGES

Kilruch, Co Clare, **065 905 1327;** *www.discoverdolphins.ie. Kilrush is in the S of Co Clare, overlooking the Shannon Estuary, SW of Ennis.*

A chance to get to see dolphins up close, something everyone will enjoy, unless prone to seasickness.

Poulnabrone Dolmen

The Shannon estuary is Ireland's first marine Special Area of Conservation (SAC) and home to the country's only resident group of bottlenose dolphins. You can sail from Kilrush Marina to observe the dolphins in their natural habitat. There are reliable records from 1849 of dolphins in the Shannon Estuary, and local children around Kilrush well remember watching and listening from Cappa Pier to what they used to know as sea pigs.

Times: *largely subject to demand, up to four trips daily in July and August.* **Fares** *(2 hour trip) adults €20, children (under-16s) €10. Pre-booking advised during July and August.*

Co Galway

Athenry Castle ★ ★ ALL AGES

Athenry, Co Galway, ☎ *091 844 797; www.heritageireland.ie. In the centre of Athenry.*

Athenry is one of the most notable medieval walled towns surviving in Ireland, owing its existence to Meiler de Bermingham who built his castle here c.1250. His great three-storey tower was surrounded by defensive walls, and entered at first-floor level through an unusual, decorated doorway. Recently re-roofed, the castle interior contains an audio-visual room and exhibition. A visit to the town also gives children a chance to visit the Athenry Heritage Centre, where they can dress up in period costume (see below).

Open *daily May–Oct 10am–5pm (May–Sep 10am–6pm).* **Adm** *adults €2.90, seniors €2.10, children €1.30, family €7.40.* **Credit** *V, MC.* **Amenities** *parking nearby, toilets, exhibition. There is access to the ground floor of the castle for people with disabilities.*

Athenry Heritage Centre ★ ★
AGES 4 AND UP

The Square, Athenry, Co Galway, ☎ *091 844 661; www.athenry heritagecentre.com. In the town centre.*

This is an ingenious use of an old church, and gives young children a chance to dress up in medieval costume and become a make-believe soldier or archer; there is even an archery range, supervised by trained staff. The centre also organises tours of this medieval town, the best pre-served of its kind in Ireland, exploring the walls and towers, a Norman castle (see p. 180) and a Dominican priory.

Open daily May–Sep 11am–4pm. **Adm** €5.

Atlantaquaria: The National Aquarium of Ireland ★★
ALL AGES

Toft Park, Salthill, Galway, ☏091 585 100; www.nationalaquarium.ie. On the promenade front in Salthill.

It's intriguing to see what the many fish that populate the British Isles waters look like before they turn up on the din-ner plate – though these ones after a spell in the aquarium are generally released into the bay and new inmates brought in to take their place.

There are two floors with themes from estuary to mill ponds, a ray pool and some touchy-feely opportunities. Although nothing is overly threatening, the conger eel looks a bit grumpy. You can hold starfish and secretive hermit crabs, and search under the rocks and weeds for spider crabs, blennies and even sea scorpions. Feeding time is always popular.

Children aged 7–10 may enjoy 'Be a Marine Scientist for a Day' – during which they carry out experiments in an interactive laboratory, use digital micro-scopes, and go out onto **Salthill Beach** to do beach exploration. (Cost: €40, includes lunch, tour of aquarium, T-shirt, snack and certificate.)

Open all year Mon–Fri 9am–5pm, Sat–Sun 9am–6pm (closed Mon–Tue during Nov–Feb). **Adm** adults €9, seniors €6.50, children €5.50, family (2+2) €26, (1+2) €18. **Credit** V, MC. **Amenities** part of a complex includ-ing toilets, bistro and restaurant.

Connemara Heritage and History Centre ★★★ FIND
ALL AGES

Lettershea, Clifden, Co Galway, ☏ 095 21246; www.connemara heritage.com. 10 minutes east of Clifden on the N59.

Dan O'Hara tells a poignant story, but one that everyone can appreciate. In 1845, he and his wife and seven children were evicted from their cottage because Dan refused to pay the new win-dow tax. They sailed for America, but only three of them survived the journey, and Dan was reduced to selling matches on the streets of New York. His cottage and homestead today has been restored, and offers a unique insight into the life and times of Connemara in the 19th century.

A crannog (an island dwelling) and a ring fort illustrate living conditions not only in Ireland but in many other parts of the British Isles, too, around 1,500 years ago. Try sitting in the straw of the fort house on a cold and blustery day for just a few

Connemara National Park

minutes if you want a taste of how bitter conditions were.

There are tractor tours and tales aplenty from proprietor Martin Walsh, the fifth (and sadly last) generation to farm the hills hereabouts. And when all the touring is done, take time out for lunch or a snack in the kitchen restaurant (see p. 186). Should you want a longer stay, the site has splendid farmhouse accommodation (see p. 184).

Open *daily 10am–6pm Apr–Oct.* **Adm** *(to Heritage site)* €2. **Credit** *all major credit cards accepted.* **Amenities** *audio-visual presentation, visitor centre, gift shop.*

Connemara National Park
★ ★ ★ AGES 3 AND OVER

Visitor Centre, Letterfrack, Co Galway, ☎ *095 41045.*

Although small as national parks go, Connemara nonetheless

holds great appeal for families that enjoy the ruggedness of untamed countryside, mountains, bog, heath and grassland. The visitor centre houses displays on the history, geology, flora and fauna of the park, and is the departure point for a number of walking trails, suitable for all but the smallest children.

The peak season, during July and August, brings organised children's activities with art, painting competitions, fun and games revolving around nature as a central theme.

Open *daily Mar–Oct 10am–5.30pm.* **Adm** *adults* €2.90, *seniors* €2.10, *children* €1.50, *family* €7.40. **Credit** *V, MC.* **Amenities** *access for the disabled to visitor centre, toilets, indoor and outdoor picnic areas, self-guided trails, guided tours (Jul–Aug, 2–3 hours duration).*

Dunguaire Castle ★★
AGES 3 AND UP

Kinvara, Co Galway, ☎ 061 360 788; www.shannonheritage.com. Along the N18, S from Galway.

This fine castle is every child's idea of a castle, set on a rocky outcrop surrounded by water – isolated and cut off. In fact, it's not a castle in a military sense, but rather a Tower House, a fortified residence built as a 'fashionable Irish house' for a gentleman.

It was built during a time of relative peace in Ireland, but its fortifications and internal structure are fascinating, and the interior design and fittings you see today are intended to give a clear and fair representation of the lifestyle in such a building from around 1520 to modern times.

There are medieval banquets – a four-course meal with wine, music, song and storytelling – during April to October at 5.30pm and 8.45pm; reservations necessary.

Open daily Apr–Sep 9.30am–5pm. Adm adults €5.50, seniors €3.15, children €3.15, family €13.25. Credit V, MC. Amenities parking nearby.

Co Mayo

Céide Fields ★★ **AGES 12 AND UP**

Ballycastle, Co Mayo, ☎ 096 43325; www.museumsofmayo.com/ceide. htm. 8km W of Ballycastle on R314.

The Céide Fields of Co Mayo are fascinating, at 5,500 or more years old the oldest known field systems in the world. They are arguably the most extensive Stone Age monument known

and certainly a unique Neolithic landscape of world importance, which has changed perceptions of our Stone Age ancestors.

The remains of stone field walls, houses and megalithic tombs are preserved beneath a blanket of peat over several square kilometres. These tell a story of the everyday lives of a farming people, their organised society, their highly developed spiritual beliefs, and their struggle against a changing environment beyond their control.

In addition, the wild flora of the bog is of international importance, and is bounded by some of the most spectacular rock formations and cliffs in Ireland. The Visitor Centre houses displays and exhibitions, and a small tearoom serves light lunches.

Open daily Feb–Oct 10am–6pm. Adm adults €3.70, seniors €2.60, children €1.30, family €8.70. Heritage card. Credit V, MC. Amenities toilets; guided tours.

FAMILY-FRIENDLY ACCOMMODATION

Co Clare

MODERATE

Rusheen Lodge Guest House
★★★ **FIND**

Ballyvaughan, Co Clare, ☎ 065 707 7092; www.rusheenlodge.com. On the N67 (Lisdoonvarna road), 0.25km from Ballyvaughan village.

Rusheen Lodge is an elegant 4-star guesthouse (AA 5-diamond and RAC 5-diamond) in one of the most beautiful parts of the west of Ireland, perfectly suited to families and having a variety of rooms and suites. This is a past winner of the 'Guesthouse of the Year' Award, given by the Good Food Guide, an accolade not bestowed lightly. The Lodge provides elegant en suite bedrooms, suites, dining room and residents' lounge (so parents can relax once the children are in bed), plus a wet room for anglers. Three ground floor rooms are suitable for wheelchair access.

Ballyvaughan, in the northwest corner of the Burren and on the southern shores of Galway Bay, is one of the most beautiful and atmospheric harbour villages on the western seaboard. Its restaurants serve locally caught seafood and the five pubs provide regular sessions of traditional music.

Rooms 9 *(including three family rooms and one suite).* **Rates** *(including breakfast) double/twin €40–50 pps Feb–Apr and Oct–Nov, €50 May–Sep. Child sharing parents' bedroom 50% discount, under-4s free. 10% discount three nights or more (excluding bank holidays and weekends); third person sharing room €32.* **Credit** *V, MC.* **Amenities** *guest lounge, parking, cots (free), highchairs available, WiFi Internet (free) throughout, some wheelchair access.* **In room** *9-channel TV, tea/coffee-making facilities.*

Co Mayo

MODERATE–EXPENSIVE

Hotel Westport ★★

Newport Road, Westport, Co. Mayo, ☏ *098 25122;* **www.hotelwestport.ie.** *In the heart of Westport on private parklands just a five-minute stroll to the town centre.*

Westport has been voted Ireland's tidiest town, and the hotel adds to the sense of pride by winning awards for its accommodation, offering the chance of a little self-indulgence, without the sinking feeling that you're breaking the bank.

The award-winning Ocean Spirit Spa and Leisure, winner of a White Flag for environmental and hygiene standards, offers a 20-metre pool, Jacuzzi, gym, sauna and steam room, lounger and toddler pools. Treatments on offer range from traditional Turkish massages to a hibiscus petal peel. The Islands Restaurant offers Clewbay seafood hors d'oeuvres, and dishes such as supreme of salmon, or pan-fried breast of pheasant.

Rooms *129.* **Rates** *double/twin, inclusive of breakfast and dinner, from €79 pps; family holidays (2+2 under-10s) (3 nights B&B, 2 nights dinner) €499; reduced rates for children.* **Credit** *all major cards accepted.* **Amenities** *guest lounge, bar, restaurant, spa and leisure centre.* **In room** *TV, iron and iron/board.*

Co Galway

INEXPENSIVE–MODERATE

Dan O'Hara's Farmhouse Accommodation ★★

Lettershea, Clifden, Connemara, Co Galway, ☏ *095 21808;* **www. connemaraheritage.com.** *10 minutes east of Clifden on the N59.*

Despite the name, this is anything but a conventional 'farmhouse', its bright and modern rooms being part of the Dan O'Hara Experience at the Connemara

Heritage and History Centre. With a café and restaurant on site, and a historical setting outside, this homely establishment just to the east of Clifden is a neat oasis of tradition, heritage, culture and a fair bit of *craic* (fun).

Rooms *9, including 2 family rooms.* **Rates** *double B&B €35 pps (Jul–Aug €38 pps); child sharing parents' room €20.* **Credit** *all major credit cards accepted.* **Amenities** *guest sitting room, complimentary access to Heritage Centre.* **In room** *TV, tea/coffee-making facilities.*

Clifden Station House ★ ★ ★

Clifden, Connemara, Co Galway, ☎ *095 21699 (central reservations* ☎ *1850 377 000);* www.clifden stationhouse.com. *Just outside Clifden centre, on the Galway road.*

The 4-star Clifden Station House is much more than a hotel. It also features a courtyard, where the railway once ended, houses, shops, restaurants, self-catering apartments and full leisure facilities, including an 18-metre indoor heated swimming pool, children's playroom and Jacuzzi. A nice touch is that when adults check in at the hotel, the staff also ask the children for their names, important in making them also feel welcome.

During July and August, the hotel runs a Railway Children's Club (Mon–Fri, 3–9pm, provided a minimum of five children have registered) which includes games, splash time in the pool, dinner in the restaurant, children's videos and competitions; every child receives a T-shirt and

certificate. For the under-4s, there's a supervised playroom session (Mon–Fri, 10am–noon) with 10 games, stories, toys and organised fun. Throughout December and into January, the hotel also has an ice skating rink in the courtyard of the hotel.

Rooms *76, plus 2 suites and 18 self-catering apartments.* **Rates** *package rates (2 nights B&B, 1 dinner) €149–209; children 0–2 years free, 3–12 years €25 per child per night B&B when sharing with 2 adults (limited to 2 children per room). Call for prices of apartments.* **Credit** *all major cards accepted.* **Amenities** *some rooms adapted for disabled visitors and wheelchair access, laundry service, baby-sitting service, railway museum, Railway Children's Club.* **In room** *TV, tea/coffee-making facilities, iron. For all rooms there is a choice of either a double and single bed arrangement, or double with sofa bed.*

Flannery's Hotel ★ ★

Dublin Road, Galway, ☎ *091 755 111;* www.bestwestern.ie. *Along the N6 Dublin road, SE of Galway.*

Lying just outside Galway, Flannery's family run hotel is an excellent base from which to explore Co Galway and Co Clare. There's traditional Irish and country entertainment virtually every evening, and although it lacks leisure facilities on site, it is only 2.5km into Galway, where there are plenty. There's an excellent breakfast menu and the Galwegian Restaurant and Frankie's Bar to cater for dinner and lunch respectively – with a Kiddies

Menu. Food is traditional Irish with a nod in the direction of the Spice Islands.

Rooms 134. **Rates** double/twin €69–150, children (0–11) sharing parents' room, free (12–15, 50% discount). Breakfasts (continental €6.50, full Irish €9.50), Kiddies Menu(€6.50). **Credit** all major credit cards accepted. **Amenities** cots (free), baby-sitting service on request at time of booking, free guest WiFi Internet connections. **In room** TV, tea/coffee-facilities.

Radisson SAS Hotel and Spa Galway ★★★

Lough Atalia Road, Galway, ☎ 091 538 300; www.radissonsas.com. Overlooking Lough Atalia, a few minutes from the city centre.

The spaciousness and the accommodating staff at this popular Radisson hotel are ideal for parents encumbered with luggage, buggies and young children. Facilities include Restaurant Marinas, the Atrium Bar and Lounge, plus the new Veranda Lounge.

Catering exclusively for the little ones, whether babes in arms, terrible twos or teenagers, Rad Kids provides a range of services from baby bottle warmers, microwaves to heat baby food, and baby and toddler cots, to a specially designed toy library that includes puzzles, toys and board-games.

While the older children can tuck into pork ribs with barbecue dip (from the special Rad Kids menu) before returning to the Playstation (from the Rad

Kids toy library), their younger sibling can be demolishing a baby bowl of bangers and mash and looking forward to more Lego construction work.

A spa includes a pool, sauna, steam room, Jacuzzi and outdoor hot-tub.

Rooms 217. **Rates** double/twin from €130, family from €140, but rates vary throughout the year. **Credit** all major credit cards accepted. **Amenities** child minding service, additional 21 one- and two-bedroomed luxury serviced apartments with private entrance within the hotel complex. **In room** sat TV, high-speed and WiFi Internet access and dial-up connections with ISDN or analogue modem, coffee and tea maker, a mini bar, safe, iron and ironing board. Disabled rooms on request.

CAFÉS & FAMILY-FRIENDLY DINING

Co Galway

Dan O'Hara's Kitchen ★
TRADITIONAL IRISH

Lettershea, Clifden, Connemara, Co Galway, ☎ 095 21808; www.connemaraheritage.com. 10 minutes east of Clifden on the N59.

Serving traditional Irish grub, including Irish stew, beef, gammon, fish and chips, steak, plus sandwiches and daily specials, this is a no frills, no fuss kind of place that will suit touring families on a budget.

Open all year, daily, 8am–9pm. **Main courses** €9.50–18 (children's menu, €5–6). **Credit** all major credit cards accepted. **Amenities** toilets; parking.

GBC ★ ★ FIND MODERN IRISH

Williamsgate Street, Galway, ☎ 091 563 087; www.gbcgalway.com. In the centre of Galway, just off Eyre Square.

This excellent little bistro/carvery does a roaring trade, and it's not surprising. The food is excellent, and the service quick and cheerful. Tuna pasta salads, seafood chowder, lamb, turkey and ham, chicken, steak, spring rolls, haddock, panini, baguettes, toasted sandwiches and wraps are typical of the dishes on offer. The downstairs coffee shop is ideal for a quick bite or cuppa, while the upstairs restaurant is for a longer sit down.

Open daily, (restaurant) noon–10pm, for lunch noon–4pm, à la carte menu from 4pm; (coffee shop) 8am–10pm.

The Dan O'Hara Experience

Main courses €7.50–14. Credit V, MC; Amenities toilets; baby-changing facilities, children's menu, highchairs available.

Off the Square ★ ★
MODERN IRISH

Main Street, Clifden, Co Galway, ☎ 095 22281; www.offthesquare restaurant.com. In the centre of Clifden.

The hand of a man with Michelin restaurant experience is evident in the superb food in this central restaurant. Specialising in modern Irish cuisine, the menus, both lunch and dinner, use local produce including smoked haddock and mussel chowder, lobster, sea bream, clams, paella, loin of wild venison, braised Connemara lamb shank, organic Clare Island salmon, plus breakfast menu, and a wide range of sandwiches and child-friendly dishes. Families find this an especially popular place, open more or less all day.

Open all year, daily, lunch 12.30–3.30pm, dinner 5–10pm (Fri–Sat 10.30pm). Main courses (lunch) €6.90–8.50, (dinner) €13.90–23. Credit all major cards accepted. Amenities highchairs available.

O'Dowds Seafood Bar and Restaurant and Roundstone Café ★ ★ FIND TRADITIONAL IRISH

Roundstone, Co Galway, ☎ 095 35809; www.odowdsretaurant.com. In the main street in Roundstone.

This very typical bar/restaurant set in the attractive village of

Roundstone has long been popular with touring families, and has earned a reputation for excellent food in a friendly and informal atmosphere. Originally known as Kelly's Hotel it became O'Dowds in 1906. For most of its life, in common with many similar establishments in Ireland, it was a combined grocery shop, pub and hotel, but for a short time it became a funeral parlour during the making of the movie 'The Matchmaker' in 1996. The grocery shop is gone – although you can still see the hooks in the ceiling – and O'Dowds is now a pub and a seafood restaurant. Wood-panelled walls and open fires make it feel warm and friendly.

There are plenty of international dishes but O'Dowds specialises in fresh, locally caught seafood, including hot, buttered lobster, clams, salmon, oysters and an unusual spicy fish curry. There's also lamb and beef stew and sirloin steak as well as a selection of chicken and vegetarian dishes. Children's portions are available for most dishes.

Immediately adjoining O'Dowds, and with the same owners, is the Roundstone Café, which serves everything from breakfasts to pizzas, soups, sandwiches, rolls, stews, teas and coffee. Internet access is also available.

Open daily, (O'Dowds) Apr–Sept noon–10pm, Mar–Oct noon–3pm and 6–9.30pm; (Roundstone Café) all year, 10am–3pm (Jul–Aug, 10am–10pm). *Main courses* €13.50–24.95 (lobster €42.50, but prices vary). *Credit* V, MC. *Amenities* highchairs available.

Co Mayo

INEXPENSIVE

Mary's Cottage Kitchen ★
FIND **COUNTRY COTTAGE FOOD**

Main Street, Ballycastle, Co Mayo, ☎ 096 43361. At the western end of the main street through Ballycastle.

Anyone driving the coast road from Ballina to Bangor will find Mary Munnelly's cottage kitchen perfectly placed for a quick lunch. It serves homemade cakes and pies, along with lasagne, quiche, salads, freshly made soup, panini, and toasted sandwiches. It's a lovely rustic old place, and popular with locals who use it as a takeaway. Mary seems to make everything herself, and does so with an age-old confidence: 'Just like mother used to make.'

Open all year, daily, 10am–5pm (Sat, 10am–4pm). *Main courses* €9.80–13.50. *Amenities* toilets.

9 The North-west: Donegal, Leitrim & Sligo

There's an immensely satisfying remoteness about the whole of north-west Ireland, a place off the beaten tourist trail offering unadulterated Irishness.

One of the historic nine counties of the Province of Ulster, and the fourth largest county in Ireland, Donegal ranks among the country's best kept secrets, a land of gusty headlands, sandy beaches and dramatic seascapes, fish-laden rivers and loughs set against misty purple-blue mountains.

The landscapes are as tempestuous as the Atlantic that fashioned them, forming a string of convoluted peninsulas that protrude into the sea and contrast starkly with the muted colours of upland heath and moor. The sweep of Donegal Bay, the cliffs of Slieve League and the coast up to Bloody Foreland, are all breathtaking scenery. Explore them by waterbus (see p. 201).

The austere scenery sometimes feels remarkably bleak, but it is unforgettable, and when you reach the beaches, especially the more remote ones, you forgive the twisting, bumpy roads. Many of the more remote beaches, such as Sheephaven (see Chapter 1), are as good as Blue Flag winners, but just aren't big enough or visited enough to merit their own rating. But be aware, a number aren't suitable for swimming because of strong tides and dangerous currents.

Sligo, like Donegal is another county of amazing beauty, in lakes, forests, mountains and rivers, beaches and waterfalls. This is very much a place for families who enjoy nature and wildlife, but is also one of the most important archeological destinations in Ireland, with an astonishing number of dolmens, stone circles, burial mounds and ring forts to wonder at and puzzle over.

Leitrim, almost split in two by the River Shannon and Lough Allen, is the smallest county in Ireland, often neglected by visitors in spite of exquisite walking country (for all but the very young) through northern mountains and glens, lakes and rivers.

Visit Costello chapel, the smallest in Europe, the Glencar waterfall, or Parkes Castle. In addition, the Shannon Erne Waterway, Europe's longest inland navigable waterway, runs through the county, which also boasts Ireland's earliest salmon river, the Drowes at Tullaghan. There are lively riverside towns and cruise bases, with friendly pubs and impromptu music sessions – places to enjoy folk traditions.

ESSENTIALS

Getting There

By Air Donegal has its own airport at Carrickfinn, Kincasslagh (☏ 074 954 8284 and 074 095 48232; www.donegalairport.ie) served by Aer Arann (☏ 0818 210210; www.aerarann.com) with twice daily flights from Dublin (50 minutes) and three times weekly to Glasgow Prestwick (50 minutes).

The website is worth checking for special offers.

Passengers travelling with Aer Arann to Prestwick will receive a 50% discount on the standard fare to/from anywhere in Scotland and to/from Prestwick to any ScotRail or Glasgow Underground Station.

AVIS Rent-A-Car offers special car hire rates available to passengers on Aer Arann flights, on presentation of Aer Arann tickets (Avis Donegal Airport: 074 954 8232; Avis Central Reservations: 1 890 40 50 60; www.avis.ie).

Donegal International Airport is on the west coast of Donegal, 15 minutes drive from Dungloe and Gweedore, and 45 minutes from Letterkenny.

The **City of Derry Airport** (www.cityofderryairport.com) is also a convenient airport for the greater part of northern Donegal. Derry Airport is located 11km northeast of Londonderry on the main A2 Londonderry to Coleraine road.

Leitrim does not have an airport, but Sligo does (**Sligo Airport**, Strandhill, Sligo. 071 916 8280; www.sligoairport.com). As with Donegal, flights are operated by Aer Arann, and include twice daily flights from Dublin, and four flights a week from Manchester.

Car hire, also AVIS (see above), is available at Sligo Airport.

By Bus Bus Éireann (see p. 24) run services from Dublin and other towns to Letterkenny and Donegal Town in Co. Donegal, and to Sligo.

By Rail Rail services to the north-west of Ireland are restricted. Donegal has no rail service, but there are several trains daily between Dublin Connolly and Sligo, which pass through Leitrim, stopping at Carrick-on-Shannon (www.irishrail.ie).

VISITOR INFORMATION

Donegal

Donegal Town 074 972 1148.

Letterkenny Tourist Office 074 912 1160; www.ireland northwest.ie.

There are seasonal tourist offices in:

Buncrana 074 936 2600

Bundoran 071 984 1350

Dungloe 074 952 1297

Leitrim

Leitrim Tourist Office The Old Barrel Store, Carrick on Shannon. 071 962 2045; www.leitrimtourism.com.

Sligo

Sligo Tourist Office Temple Street, Sligo Town. 071 916 1201; www.sligotourism.ie or www.discoversligo.com.

NORTH-WEST IRELAND

Attractions ●
Doagh Island Visitor Centre **1**
Glenevin Waterfall Park **2**
Clonmany Family Festival **3**
Leisureland **4**
Sheephaven Bay **5**
Ards Forest Park **6**
Glenveagh National Park **7**
Dunlewey Centre/Ionad Cois Locha **8**
Jungle King Play Centre **9**
Father McDyer's Folk Village **10**
Donegal Bay Waterbus Tour **11**
Donegal Castle **12**
Donegal Railway Heritage Centre **12**
Deane's Equestrian Centre **13**
Donegal Adventure Centre **14**
Donegal Bay Seafari **15**
Sligo Folk Park **16**
Eagles Flying/Irish Raptor Research Centre **17**
Swan Island Animal Farm **18**
Moon River Cruises **19**
Glencar Waterfall **20**
Dolly's Cottage **21**
Parkes Castle **22**
Leisure Center **23**
Carrowmore Megalithic Cemetery **24**
Gillighan's World **25**

Accommodation ■
Glen House **1**
Shandon Hotel **2**
Sea View Hotel **3**
An Grianán Hotel **4**
Radisson SAS Letterkenny **5**
Nesbitt Arms **6**
Radisson SAS Sligo **7**

Dining ◆
Waterfront Restaurant **1**
Yellow Pepper **2**
Nesbitt Arms **3**
Davis's Restaurant at the
    Yeat's Tavern **4**
Cryans Riverside Inn **5**
Dom Breslin **6**

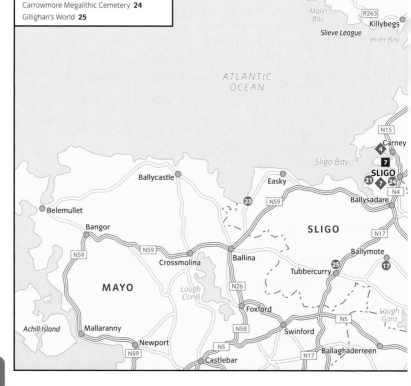

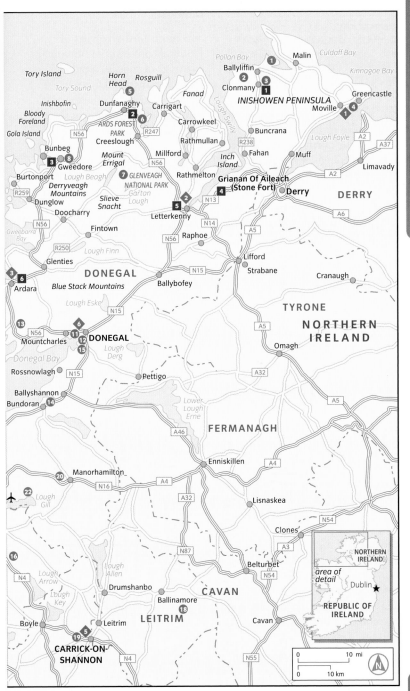

ORIENTATION

Donegal is 227km (142 miles) NW of Dublin, Sligo is 208km (130 miles) and Carrick-on-Shannon is 157km (98 miles). From Belfast, Donegal is 190km (118 miles) to the W, Sligo 198km (124 miles) SW and Carrick-on-Shannon 221km (138 miles) SW

Sligo Town is the largest settlement in the north-west, and, perhaps surprisingly, well equipped to deal with tourists. It has a good range of hotels and eating places, as well as a modern shopping mall with high street brands tucked away among its myriad narrow streets.

Donegal is home to Ireland's largest 'Gaeltacht' (Gaelic speaking area), where traditional music is widespread and traditions very strong. Legends live in the north-west: tales of dead queens, hermits and poets, a place of mountain top tombs and defensive castles.

Getting Around

By far the easiest and most convenient way of exploring north-west Ireland is by car or bicycle. A bevy of bus companies provide services around the individual villages, but primarily to meet the needs of local people, not visitors. Timetable information is available through the tourist information centres, and judicious planning can result in memorable bus tours to friendly villages.

Discover the Counties

Donegal

The most northerly parts of Donegal confront the Atlantic in a barrage of rugged, weather-beaten headlands. Donegal (*Dhún na nGall* – a reference to Viking invaders) is one of three counties in the province of Ulster that do not form part of Northern Ireland. The name comes from the Irish, meaning 'the Fort of the Foreigners', and the county was named after Donegal Town, the former administrative centre.

Donegal's isolation from the rest of the Irish Republic has bred people and customs markedly distinct from the rest of the country. The Irish language, one of the oldest languages in Europe, is spoken in several parts, from Fanad Head in the north, reached by homely villages and roads so narrow you can almost touch the walls, to Slieve League in the south west, the third highest sea cliffs in Europe, 601 metres above the Atlantic.

To understand Irish culture, a visit to the Irish-speaking Gaeltacht is vital, places such as Falcarragh (*An Fál Carrach*), Gortahork (*Gort a'Choirce*) and Gweedore (**www.gaothdobhair. com**) (*Gaoth Dobhair*), where you can enjoy the simple pleasures of life, fishing, bathing, folk music and a bit of '*craic*' (fun) in a singing pub or lounge.

But there are also modern leisure centres, sailing, adventure parks, horse riding, mountain climbing, walking, and cycling.

Lifford is the county town but the largest is the fast-growing is Letterkenny. Accommodation throughout the area is excellent, and offers some of Ireland's best holiday value.

Leitrim

Leitrim, the name from *Liath Druim*, meaning 'grey ridge', is known as a laid back, relaxed county with a gentle landscape of undulating hills and wide-sky plains, dotted with lakes, the largest of which are Lough Allen and Lough Melvin. Lough Allen is said to harbour a monster, 'with several bumps and an enormous head'. There's a reward for anyone who proves the beast exists.

Cruising on the Shannon is popular, or you can visit the beautiful Glencar Waterfall (see p. 207) just outside Manorhamilton. It's by no means big, but is delightful.

Parkes Castle (see p. 207) on Lough Gill, is the ancestral manor of the O'Rourke family and there's angling, golfing, walking, horse riding, and cycling.

The River Shannon and Lough Allen divide Leitrim into North and South Leitrim and Carrick-on-Shannon is the main

town, a lively and attractive settlement on the river, the smallest county town in the country.

Sligo

The name *Sligeach* means 'an area abounding in shells', a reference to the seafood still plentiful along the coast, mainly oysters, cockles, mussels and limpets.

The shadow of poet **W.B. Yeats** lingers everywhere. Yeats spent much of his childhood in the area, and the landscapes, particularly the Isle of Innisfree in Lough Gill, were the inspiration for much of his poetry.

Sligo is lush and green, dominated by limestone ridges such as the towering Benbulben and a dramatic headland above Sligo harbour, Rosses Point, is flanked by golden beaches that seem to go on for ever.

Standing at the mouth of the Garavogue River, the colourful Sligo Town is the largest in the north-west with a pedigree reaching back to the Vikings. It's a compact community, with plenty of restaurants and cafés.

The whole area is superb for hill walking, horse riding, fishing, diving, surfing, swimming, sailing and has one of the richest concentrations of prehistoric and more recent monuments in Western Europe – more than 5,000 in all.

FUN FACT ▶ **Irish Wisdom** ◀

A country's knowledge is contained in its language, mythology and mountains.

Child-friendly Events & Entertainment

An Tostal ★★★

May–June. Drumshanbo, Co Leitrim,
📞 *071 964 1069; www.antostal*
festival.ie.

The An Tostal was inaugurated in 1953 to depict the varied aspects of Irish life and culture throughout the country and Drumshanbo is now the only centre where it has survived in its original format. It's a bewildering festival of Irish music, song and dance, with children's entertainment, street parades, treasure hunts, competitions, and even a dog show.

Clonmany Family Festival ★★

August. Altan Rua, Clonmany,
Clonmany Parish, Inishowen, Co
Donegal, 📞 *074 937 6477; www.*
clonmany.com.

Clonmany parish is renowned for its lovely beaches and glens, but its annual Festival promises music, high jinks, fun and games with some of the top Irish artists, plus a variety of supporting events that are particularly Irish, including vintage car and tractor rallies, agricultural show, singing competition, car treasure hunt, disco, raft race, ceilidh dancing, tug-o-war, children's sports, car boot sales: delightful mayhem, really.

Strandhill Guitar Festival ★★

September. Strandhill, Co Sligo,
📞 *071 916 8339; www.warriors*
festival.com.

At this festival, as you might guess, you'll find the spirit of impromptu Irish music at its best. Strandhill comes alive with music during the festival with live gigs around the village showcasing the best of Sligo and Ireland's guitar players in a wide range of music styles including jazz, rock, blues and classical. Try standing there without tapping your feet. Visiting guitarists are welcome to join in a number of jamming sessions and there are often weekend workshops for adults and children.

WHAT TO SEE & DO

Children's Top 10 Attractions

❶ Abseiling and much more at Donegal Adventure Centre, the perfect place for burning off excess energy. See p. 200.

❷ Messing about in a farmyard at Dunlewey Centre, Ionad Cois Locha, and enjoying a boat trip, lakeside walks, go-karting, and craft demonstrations. See p. 202.

FUN FACT ⟩⟩ **Irish Wisdom** ⟨

A man begins cutting his wisdom teeth the first time he bites off more than he can chew.

❸ Looking for red deer at Glenveagh National Park with its 16,000 hectares of mountains, lakes, glens and woodlands populated by red deer. See p. 202.

❹ Watching birds of prey in flight at the Irish Raptor Research Centre, home to about 270 birds and animals. See p. 205.

❺ Fairy spotting at Gillighan's World, an adventure centre for the young. See p. 206.

❻ Seeing a traditional Irish cottage at Sligo Folk Park. See p. 206.

❼ Getting seriously wet at Waterpoint. See p. 207.

❽ Cruising leisurely along the Moon River. See p. 207.

❾ Visit a ring fort at Ards Forest Park. See below.

❿ Travel on the Donegal narrow gauge railway. See p. 201.

Child-friendly Attractions

Co Donegal

Ards Forest Park ★★ ALL AGES

Sheephaven Bay, Creeslough, ☎ 074 912 1139. 5km north of Creeslough on the N56 to Dunfanaghy.

Ideal for an ambling family adventure, Ards Forest Park features deciduous and coniferous woodlands, salt dunes and seashore, salt marsh and saltwater lakes, plus rock faces. It's the most varied and most northerly of Ireland's numerous forest parks, and home to very diverse plant and wildlife.

Alongside nature walks, picnic and play areas are features of historical and archaeological interest including the remains of four ring forts, a number of megalithic tombs, and the Mass Rock where religious services were held in defiance of the Penal Laws.

Numerous viewpoints along the trails offer colourful cameos of the surrounding countryside, in particular the golden sweep of Sheephaven Bay (see p. 204).

Open Apr–Sep 10am–9pm, Oct–Mar 10am–4.30pm. Adm free. Amenities children's play area.

Deane's Equestrian Centre and Open Farm ★ AGES 5 AND UP

Darney, Bruckless, ☎ 074 973 7160.

It's all about horses: here in rugged southwest Donegal the well-established Deane's Equestrian Centre caters for everyone from complete beginners to experienced competition riders. There's a large indoor arena, two outdoor arenas, the show jumping grounds, cross-country course and a network of forest tracks offering a variety of riding.

Open 10am–4pm, Tue–Sun, (Equestrian Centre) all year, (horse riding) by appointment, (farm) Easter–Aug. Charges (lessons) adults €21 per hour, children €18 per hour; (trek) adults €30 per hour, children €25 per hour. Credit V, MC.

Doagh Island Visitor Centre ★★ ALL AGES

Doagh Island, Inishowen, ☎ 086 8464 749 or ☎ 074 937 8078. Well signed from the Ballyliffin–Carndonagh road.

Good for the family's soul, you might say: a poignant if

Meet the North-west islands

Perfect for self-indulgent family escapism, the coastal islands of Donegal are a real thrill, especially given the excitement of the short sea crossing. If you can find time it's worth extending your stay on them.

Arranmore

The 18 square kilometres of **Arranmore Island** (*Árainn Mhór*) are wild and rugged with stunning cliffs, dramatic sea caves and golden sandy beaches. Inhabited by less than 1,000 people, the island is a cradle of traditional music – with an annual August festival – and local crafts, including the famous Aran knitwear. Shore angling is excellent and the island's freshwater lakes are stocked with brown and rainbow trout. Birdlife, too, invariably puts on a seasonal display, including migrating rarities from time to time.

Ferries (25–30 minute crossing) run from Burtonport to Arranmore all year, and you can even take your car. Tickets can be bought on board the boat or at the booking office on the pier during the summer months. Arranmore Ferry ☎ *074 952 0532; www.arranmoreferry.com.*

Tory Island

Measuring just 6km by 2km, **Tory Island** (*Oile Thoraigh*) is the most remote of Ireland's inhabited islands and lies just northwest of Horn Head. It's accessible by ferry from Magheraroarty or Bunbeg on the mainland.

This Irish-speaking island, a preserve of the native Irish traditions, songs, dances and way of life, has been inhabited since the earliest times and is rich in archaeological and monastic sites including a round tower that once protected monks from Viking raids, the ruins of St. Colmcile's 6th-century monastery, and the intriguing Tau Cross that suggests links to the Coptic Christians of Egypt.

It's popular with birdwatchers wanting to study the multiple sea birds, and there's also scuba diving, waymarked walking trails, cycling, sea angling, rock climbing, dolphin and whale watching.

Donegal Coastal Cruises (Strand Road, Middletown, Derrybeg). ☎ *074 953 1320/1340: Magheroarty Pier Office:* ☎ *074 913 5061; www.tory islandferry.com. The cruiser operates daily from April to October and five days per week all year around. Bicycles carried free of charge.*

The licensed boat Toraigh na dTonn operates from Tory Island, daily from April to the end of October. ☎ *074 913 5920; www.toryhotel.com. Sailings depart Tory Island 10am and 6pm, and depart Magheraroarty 11am and 7pm. Fares: return €15, single €10.*

Gola Island

Gola Island (*Oile Gabhla*) is a 200-hectare island just 1km off the Gweedore coastline. Uninhabited since the 1960s, it's becoming popular for the beautiful scenery and a relaxed lifestyle. The tranquil setting makes it an ideal location for artists, birdwatchers and walkers, but Gola is also ideal for rock climbing and camping.

Seod Ghabhla, a foot passenger ferry departs hourly from Magheragallen Pier throughout the day, and from Bunbeg Pier in the mornings (8-minute crossing). 087 247 4146. *Fares: adults €10, child €5, under-5s free.*

Innishmurray Island

Innishmurray, just off the Sligo coast contains the remains of an early Irish monastic settlement founded by St Molaise. According to the writings of de Cuellar, one of the survivors of the shipwreck of the Spanish Armada in 1588, monks were still present on the island at that time. No one is certain when or why they left, but the last of the islanders moved to the mainland in 1957.

Today the ruins of 19th-century houses pepper the island, along with altars, 'cursing stones', beehive cells and a women's church and burial ground. Innishmurray is also a wildlife sanctuary of national importance for both breeding and wintering birds, and large populations of arctic and common tern, shag, herring, common, great and lesser black-backed gull, eider, black guillemot, barnacle goose, storm petrel and fulmar.

Many licensed charter boats and operators run day trips to and from Innishmurray. The best time to visit is April to October. Northwest Tourism, Aras Reddan, Temple Street, Sligo. 071 916 1201; *www.irelandnorthwest.ie.*

Inishfree Island

Inishfree is where you find real Irish culture and traditions in a unique and spiritual atmosphere, and take a step back in time for storytelling in front of the hearth, plenty of music and craic. **Inishfree Island** (*Oile Inis Fraoich*) used to be home to 36 families in a tightly-knit, self-reliant community. Subsequently deserted, the island has been re-inhabited and the island's new residents offer courses on themes such as music, dancing, arts, crafts, poetry, nature and heritage.

With no television, traffic or distractions, Inishfree may not suit everyone. But outdoor pursuits, and the simple pleasures of gathering and cooking periwinkles, make Inishfree a perfect escape – just for a while.

somewhat inanimate exposé of a sad period in Irish history, the Doagh Island Visitor Centre tells the story of famine, fear and eviction. The famine village tells the story of life in the area from the Famine back in the 1840s, through the 1900s to the present day. This is an 'outdoor' museum that is largely under cover, a unique place, where old customs, traditions and history are preserved and set against some thought-provoking modern comment.

Different from any other tourist attraction, the Famine Village depicts Ireland as it was, uncommercialised, interdenominational, and interspersed with humorous anecdotes of Irish life.

There are resident singers, musicians and dancers from June to August, a time when the lovely beaches of Tullagh Strand and Pollan Bay add to the pleasure of visiting this remote settlement.

From mid-November to Christmas the island becomes Santa's Island and walking around you can see reindeer, elves at work, and have photos taken with Santa in his workshop.

Open daily Easter-Sep 10am–5.30pm. **Adm** €6 – price of admission includes tea and a guided tour. Admission to Santa's Island is strictly ticket only and must be booked in advance. Check website for details of when tickets go on sale. **Credit** V, MC. **Amenities** wheelchair accessible throughout; wheelchairs available.

Donegal Adventure Centre & Surf School ★ ★ AGES 8–18

Bayview Avenue, Bundoran Co Donegal, ☎ *071 984 2418; www.donegaladventurecentre.net.*

Donegal Adventure Centre and Surf School is a key outdoor and activity centre between the Darty Mountains and Tullan Beach, perfectly placed to get the best out of the hinterland of Donegal, and offering a good choice of activities including surf lessons for all levels and ages, climbing, abseiling, high ropes, kayaking,

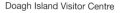
Doagh Island Visitor Centre

archery, skateboarding, canoeing, cliff jumping and body boarding. Family groups can book an activity session, day or weekend, and there are separate activities for 8–12s, and 12–18s. Accommodation is in 46 beds in en suite rooms sleeping 2–4 people, available on a self-catering, B&B or dinner/B&B basis.

Open all year round. **Charges** prices vary according to activity; call for information. **Credit** V, MC.

Donegal Bay Seafari ★★
AGES 8 AND UP

Donegal Pier, 📞 087 777 5755; www. donegalbayseafari.com.

From its base in Donegal Town and Killybegs a 12-seater all-weather RIB (rigid inflatable boat) takes you on a high-speed close-up tour of the beauty spots along the coastline of Donegal Bay. The regular trip, something of a rollercoaster on water, lasts an hour (outings are dependent on weather conditions).

Charges €25 per person for one hour; children must be over 8.

Donegal Bay Waterbus Tour ★★★ AGES 3 AND UP

Harbour Office, Donegal Pier, 📞 074 972 3666; www.donegalbaywaterbus.com.

Offering 60-minute tours of Donegal Bay, the waterbus, which is a not-for-private-profit business, is a delight for children, who will be regaled with tales about the legendary characters and history of Donegal. It's a wonderful opportunity to observe wildlife such as seabirds, seals and dolphins, but also the battle-scarred ruins of the Abbey – once the home of the legendary chieftain Red Hugh O'Donnell, and his saintly wife Nuala – where the first history of Ireland was penned by the scholars called the Four Masters.

Open sailing times are usually morning and afternoon or evening, but are dependant on weather and tides. Tickets can be obtained from the ticket office on the pier. **Fares:** adults €15, children €5. **Credit** V, MC. **Amenities** air conditioned, wheelchair friendly, tea/coffee, lounge bar.

Donegal Castle ★★ ALL AGES

Tyrconnell Street, 📞 074 972 2405; www.heritageireland.ie; In the centre of Donegal Town.

Donegal Castle, just off the town centre, was built by the O'Donnell chieftain in the 15th century on the banks of the River Eske, and then rebuilt in the Jacobean style in the 16th century after Hugh O'Donnell burnt it to the ground rather than let the castle fall into enemy hands. Information panels chronicle the history of the castle and guided tours are available.

Open Mar–Oct, Mon–Sat 10am–6pm; Nov–Mar, Fri–Sun 9.30am–4.30pm (last admission 45 minutes before closing). **Adm** adults €3.70, seniors €2.60, children €1.30, family €8.70. Heritage card. **Amenities** limited access for disabled visitors.

Donegal Railway Heritage Centre ★★ ALL AGES

The Old Station House, Tyrconnell Street, Donegal Town, 📞 074 9722655; www.countydonegal railway.com

Here you can discover what it was like to travel on the narrow gauge steam railways of Donegal. Stretching from Derry and Strabane to Glenties and Ballyshannon, the railway provided the essential transport for farmers and fishermen, businessmen and builders – anyone, in fact, who needed to get about.

The railway also provided jobs for hundreds of people and its very buildings contributed to the local scene with families settled and children raised in the station houses and crossing keepers' cottages.

Open *10am–5pm Oct–May Mon–Fri, Jun–Sep Mon–Sat and most Sundays.* **Adm** *adults €4, children €2, under-5s free, family (2+2) €10.*

Dunlewey Centre, Ionad Cois Locha ★ ★ ★ AGES UNDER 14

📞 *074 953 1699; www.dunleweycentre.com. 10km from Gweedore, 40km from Letterkenny and 80km from Donegal Town.*

Found below Mount Errigal, Donegal's highest mountain, and on the shores of Dunlewey Lough, the Dunlewey Centre (*Ionad Cois Locha*) has abundant attractions for children including pedal boats (treated like waterborne dodgems), go-karting, a farmyard, play area, boat trips into the Poison Glen, lakeside walks, and weaving demonstrations – delightful semi-organised chaos. There's also a restaurant (great Irish stew) and tearoom.

Open *Mar–Nov Mon–Sat 10.30am–6pm, Sun 11am–6pm.* **Credit** *no credit cards.* **Amenities** *gift shop.*

Father McDyer's Folk Village Museum ★ ALL AGES

Glencolmcille, 📞 *074 9730017; www.glenfolkvillage.com.*

Perfectly placed for viewing the spectacular scenery of the glen, and the golden beach of nearby Glenbay, the Folk Village Museum invites you to experience life as it was in the 18th to 20th centuries. A gathering of thatched cottages replicate those of the era. Here you can see how the Irish people lived and cooked, the tools they used, and how they generated light and heat. The integral tearoom offers scones, Guinness cake, apple tart, fresh home-made soup, and more.

Open *Easter to end Sep Mon–Sat 10am–6pm, Sun noon–6pm.* **Adm** *adults €3.50, children €2, family (2+4) €10.*

Glenveagh National Park ★ ★ ★ ALL AGES

Church Hill, Letterkenny, 📞 *074 913 7090; www.npws.ie. 24km NW of Letterkenny.*

The 16,000 hectares of wild and extravagantly beautiful countryside, populated by red deer, are the place for landscapes of uncompromising mountains, woodlands, lakes and glens. It's great walking country with both demanding ascents of craggy peaks and easy riverside strolls. And the golden eagle, long a resident of this remote, glacial glen, may be spotted above the mountain ridges.

Set in the middle of the Donegal highlands, the centrepiece of Glenveagh is its

Glenveagh National Park

Victorian castle, a four-storey rectangular keep built between 1870 and 1873 with ramparts, turrets and a round tower. Set above Lough Veagh and encircled by high peat-blanketed mountains, the 11-hectare gardens are in start contrast to the wild and rugged landscape.

Gardens and park are open all year. Access to the castle interior is by tour only. Morning and afternoon teas are served in the castle tearooms. Guided walks are held weekly in June, July and August, and there is a six-hour guided hill walk every month March to October.

The castle is 4km from the Visitor Centre and you can walk the road beside the lough. But there's also a shuttle bus running up the side of the lough every 15 minutes at peak times.

Open the National Park is open all year, with visitor facilities operating from Feb–Nov daily 10am–6.30pm, **Adm** (castle tour): adults €3, seniors €2, children €1.50, family €6.60; (shuttle bus) adults €2, concessions €1; (gardens) free. Heritage card.

Amenities exhibitions, toilets, self-guided trails.

Glenevin Waterfall Park ★★
ALL AGES

Straid, Clonmany, Inishowen. Along R238 north from Buncrana.

The village of Clonmany is small and welcoming, and each year the scene of a Family Festival (see p. 196). It is also the key to a couple of mini gems for families who like to get away from it all.

Nestling in the Urris Hills, the Glenevin Waterfall Park (through Clonmany, heading for Tullagh Strand) is a delightful community project. A walk begins from beside Glen House (accommodation – see p. 208), and follows an easy, wheelchair and buggy accessible path up a gently inclining valley lined with birch and gorse. A picnic area is an agreeable spot to rest and potter about, and the path continues to the waterfall.

Past Glen House you can branch off to **Tullagh Strand**, a wide golden sand and pebble

Glenevin Waterfall Park

beach washed by the waters of Pollan Bay. The bucket-and-spaders will love this, surfers may too, and (July and August aside) there'll be scarcely a soul in sight.

Jungle King Play Centre ★★
AGES UNDER 12

Oldtown, Letterkenny, ☎ 074 917 7731; www.jungleking.ie.

Jungle King is a purpose-built jungle theme indoor play centre where your children's imagination can run riot on the snake slides, tube slides, activity towers, and ball pool. There's a separate area for babies with soft padded animals and a ball pool. Under-4s can play in a two-level climbing frame and 5–12 year olds in a larger frame that includes a three-lane Astra slide, spiral slide, rope bridges, and a football court.

Open *daily all year 10am–7pm.* **Adm** *€7 for 90 minutes.*

Sheephaven Bay ★★★
ALL AGES

Northwest Donegal. 32km N of Letterkenny.

Promoting itself as a destination for fishing and walking, there are few formal attractions here but the area around Sheephaven Bay offers extensive golden Blue Flag beaches, numerous walks around Horn Head and Rosguill, Ards Forest Park (see p. 197), Doe Castle, and extravagantly beautiful countryside. The nearby Shandon Hotel (see p. 209) offers an incredible range of facilities for children of all ages.

Day tickets are required for fishing, mainly salmon, sea trout and brown trout, available from the Spar supermarket in Creeslough or Arnold's Hotel in Dunfanaghy.

Co Sligo

Carrowmore Megalithic Cemetery ★★ **ALL AGES**

Carrowmore, ☎ 071 916 1534; www.heritageireland.ie.

This is one of the biggest and most important megalithic sites in Europe, with more than 60 tombs, older than the pyramids of Egypt. A restored cottage houses a small but highly informed exhibition about the site, which is overlooked by Meabh's Cairn, claimed to be the gravesite of the legendary Queen Meabh of Connaught.

Open *Easter–Oct daily 10am–6pm.* **Adm** *adults €2, children €1, family €6. Heritage card.*

Achill Island

Ireland's largest island offers spectacular cliff walks (not for young children) and a total of five Blue Flag sandy beaches. The island is separated from the mainland Currane Peninsula by a narrow strait, crossed by a road bridge. It's a great place for outdoor activities and watersports of all types (see *www.achilltourism.com*).

It may be true, it may not, but in 1969, three local men were at Scaheens Lough on Achill Island when they say they saw a strange animal 3 metres long, and standing 1 metre high, with short brown hair, a long tail and sharp teeth. They described it as a cross between a greyhound and a sheep.

Could this be Ireland's own 'Loch Ness Monster'?

Achill Island

Dolly's Cottage ★ AGES 3 AND UP

Strandhill, 📞 *071 916 7564.*

This charming 200-year-old stone-built, thatched cottage has two rooms and a loft with original walls, roof, roof beams, fireplace and pouch bed, and gives a fascinating insight into how people lived in generations past. The cottage is named after Dolly Higgins, the last person to live here. When Dolly died in 1970

the cottage was bought by the Strandhill Guild of the Irish Countrywomen's Association with a view to preserving it for future generations.

Open daily Jun–Aug 2–6pm, Sat–Sun only in June.

Eagles Flying/Irish Raptor Research Centre ★ ★ ★
ALL AGES

Portinch, Ballymote. 📞 *071 918 9310;*
www.eaglesflying.com.

Ireland's largest raptor facility, the Irish Raptor Research Centre is a scientifically managed sanctuary for birds of prey, and home to about 270 birds and animals. Originally set up for research, increasing interest saw the attraction *Eagles Flying* open in summer 2003, so that visitors could watch the daily training with some of the birds. The shows are fun, and with commentaries from the handlers, also highly informative.

A pet zoo for young children includes goats, lambs, donkeys, horses, guinea pigs, rabbits, ferrets and pot-bellied pigs.

Open Apr–Nov 10.30am–12.30pm 2.30–4.30pm. *Adm* adults €8, children (3–16) €5, (under-3s) free, family (2+2) €24.

Gillighan's World ★ ★ ★
AGES UNDER 12

Lavagh, Nr. Tubbercurry, ☏ *071 913 0286.*

An adventure centre for young children, Gillighan's World, at the foot of Knocknashee (the Hill of the Fairies), begins with a stone tunnel entrance into botanical gardens, enlivened by 'faerie habitants' in miniature model villages and enchanted glades that make even the smallest child feel tall. Streams and secluded seating areas are designed to create a magical atmosphere, while a visit to the faerie fort offers panoramic views. There's a wildlife pond and aquatic cove, plus informal guided tour round the Pets Village. Quizzes and competitions are offered for the young, and special events at Easter and Christmas. There is also a gift shop and tearoom.

Open daily Easter to Sep Mon–Fri, noon–6pm, Sat and Sun 2–7pm. *Adm* adults €8, children €6.

Sligo Folk Park ★ ★ ★   ALL AGES

Millview House, Riverstown, ☏ *071 916 5001; www.sligofolkpark.com.*

Here the cultural history and heritage of Sligo at the end of the 19th century comes to life in a re-created village streetscape complete with a cottage, a working blacksmith's forge, farm implements, hen house, duck pond, creamery, grocer, traditional pub and a classroom complete with an intriguing lesson of the period. The park is in the grounds of Millview House, and there's a short nature trail along the Unshin River.

Open May–Oct daily Mon–Sat 10am–6pm (last entry 4.30pm), Sun 12.30–6pm (last entry 5pm), Nov–Apr by appointment. *Adm* adults €6, children €4, family (2+3) €20. **Amenities** on-site coffee shop, open Mon–Sat 10am–5pm, Sun noon–6pm.

FUN FACT ›› **Abbey's Silver Bell** ‹‹

Legend has it that at the time of the 1641 Rebellion, the faithful people of Sligo Town saved the Abbey's silver bell, by throwing it into Lough Gill, where it still lies. It is said that only those free from sin can hear it ring.

Waterpoint Leisure Centre ★
ALL AGES

Enniscrone, Sligo, 📞 (096) 36999; www.waterpoint.ie

Part of a regeneration scheme for the area, an all-weather leisure facility including a 65-metre water slide, an interactive children's fun pool, main pool, adult health suite with gym, sauna, eucalyptus steam room and Jacuzzi.

Open *Sat and Sun 10am–8pm, Mon–Fri 3–10pm.* **Adm** *Pool and gym: adults €9, children (4–15) €6, (3 and under) €3. Playground: €1.*

Co Leitrim

Glencar Waterfall ★ **ALL AGES**

Manorhamilton, Co Leitrim.

It's a short walk to the Glencar Waterfall's 15-metre drop, not high compared with some but magnificent after rain. The nearby Glencar Lough is quiet and secluded, and stocked with salmon and trout.

Open access.

Moon River Cruises ★★
ALL AGES

Main Street, Carrick-on-Shannon, 📞 071 962 1777; www.moon-river. net.

Moon River offers scheduled 90-minute trips on the Shannon, a perfect way to get to know the river. All trips depart quayside, Carrick-on-Shannon.

Charge *€12 per person.*

Parkes Castle ★★ **ALL AGES**

Five Mile Bourne, 📞 071 916 4149; www.heritageireland.ie.

Parkes Castle is a restored early 17th-century plantation castle, attractively perched on the shores of Lough Gill and formerly the home of Robert Parke. The grounds contain evidence of an earlier 16th-century tower house owned by the chieftain Brian O'Rourke, ruler of the kingdom of Breffni, who was subsequently executed at Tyburn, London in 1591 for treason – his crime was to shelter a Spaniard from the wrecked Armada.

Much of the structure is still in good condition and many rooms have been refurbished using traditional crafts and local material. Boat trips are available around the lough during the summer months on the Rose of Inishfree waterbus.

Open *mid-Mar–end Oct daily 10am–6pm (last admission 45 minutes before closing).* **Adm** *adults €3, children €2, family €8.*

Swan Island Animal Farm
AGES UNDER 12

Keeldrin, Corrawallen, 📞 049 433 3065.

Centred around Davy's 200-year-old Irish Cottage Restaurant, the Swan Island Animal Farm is home to more than 50 species of animals in a peaceful setting; an excellent chance for young children to get up close to hairy things.

Open *all year daily 10am–late.* **Adm** *adults €4.50, children €4.*

Blue Flag Beaches

Donegal and Sligo are justly renowned for their Blue Flag beaches, miles of golden sand, sea breezes and acres of sky. **Donegal**: Bundoran, Carrickfinn, Culdaff-Inishowen, Fintra-Killybegs, Lisfannon-Buncrana, Murvagh, Marbel Hill, Narin, Portsalon, Rossnowlagh, Shroove-Inishowen; **Sligo**: Mullaghmore Beach, Rosses Point.

Not all beaches are suitable for swimming because of strong currents and tides. Few of them are near catering facilities, and so visitors to the remote beaches need to take their own refreshments.

The Blue Flag for beaches is valid only during the bathing season, which runs from June until the end of August, but it does mean that beaches are cleaned on a regular basis; daily in the peak season, and have sufficient lifeguards or lifesaving equipment to ensure a response in an emergency.

FAMILY-FRIENDLY ACCOMMODATION

It would be difficult in the north-west of Ireland to find anywhere that wasn't family friendly, and even the imposing 4-star hotels put on special events for children throughout the year, usually school holidays.

Co Donegal

MODERATE-EXPENSIVE

An Grianán Hotel ★★★

Speenogue, Burt, Co Donegal, ✆ 074 93 68900; www.angriananhotel.com. On the N13 almost midway between Derry and Letterkenny.

This modern hotel complex was built behind the original façade of the old church in Burt. Today it's a good stopover for anyone touring Donegal or looking to stay in the area outside town centres. An open fire welcomes you as you enter and as well as

all the amenities you would expect in a 4-star hotel, the suites and executive rooms are fitted with Jacuzzi baths, hi-fi and reclining chairs.

The restaurant, found in the old church (open Tue–Sun 7–9.45pm), has a reputation for sourcing local produce including duck, salmon, lamb and chicken.

Rooms 43. *Rates* double/twin €135–180, family plus €30 per child (almost two-thirds of the hotels rooms are family rooms). *Credit* all major credit cards accepted. *Amenities* some rooms suitable for disabled guests. *In room* tea/ coffee-making facilities, flat screen TVs, safe, Internet access.

MODERATE

Glen House ★★ FIND

Straid, Clonmany, Co Donegal, ✆ 074 937 6745; www.glenhouse.ie. Continue through Clonmany, heading for Tullagh Strand.

This is a real find, a small out-of-the-way place with an appealing feel to the rooms, and well worth travelling to. It nestles in the valley between Rachtion Mor and the Atlantic ocean on the Inishowen Peninsula, and is immediately adjacent to the beautiful Glenevin Waterfall (see p. 203) and Tullagh Strand. The restaurant serves lunches and dinners at very reasonable prices, making the most of local produce including sea bass, monkfish, Irish lamb and chicken.

Rooms 8. **Rates** *double €40–50 pps; ask about special packages that combine two nights B&B and dinner from €99–119.* **Credit** *V, MC.* **Amenities** *wheelchair accessible to ground floor only.* **In room** *TV, tea-making facilities.*

MODERATE

Nesbitt Arms Hotel ★★

Main Street, Ardara, Co Donegal, ☏ *074 954 1104; www.nesbitt arms.com. In the centre of Ardara, NW of Donegal Town.*

Originally built in 1838, and refurbished in 2004, the family-run 3-star Nesbitt Arms is ideal for touring Donegal, being based in the centre of the Heritage Town of Ardara, famed for tweeds, hand-knitted garments and unspoilt sandy beaches. Close to Maghera Waterfall and Caves, Loughros Point, many archaeological sites, and Sheskinmore Wildlife Reserve.

Rooms *50 (3 adapted for wheelchair users).* **Rates** *€45–65 pps; special offers at weekends; reduction for children.* **Credit** *V, MC.* **Amenities** *baby-sitter service, lounge bar/bistro and restaurant, children's meals.* **In room** *TV, tea/coffee-making facilities.*

INEXPENSIVE–MODERATE

Sea View Hotel/Ostan Radharc Na Mara ★★

Gweedore, Co. Donegal. ☏ *074 9531 159; www.visitgweedore.com.*

Located in the Gaeltacht, guests at the Sea View Hotel can use all the leisure facilities in the adjacent luxury Ostan Gweedore Hotel, including a 17-metre swimming pool, Jacuzzi and health club. Excellent food from an à la carte menu includes seasonal seafood dishes, with salmon, trout, lobster and oysters a speciality.

Rooms *20.* **Rates** *B&B from €50–70 pps, family room €140; midweek family breaks (Mon–Thurs) 1 night's B&B + 1 dinner for 2 adults and up to 3 children (under 12), and use of leisure facilities; all inclusive deal €200; reductions for children; children's meals.* **Credit** *V, MC.* **Amenities** *highchairs available.* **In room** *TV.*

MODERATE–EXPENSIVE

Shandon Hotel ★★★ FIND
GREEN

Marblehill Strand, Port-na-Blagh, Co Donegal, ☏ *074 913 6137; www. shandonhotel.com. Overlooking Marble Hill Strand on a minor loop road.*

Overlooking the beautiful Blue Flag Marble Hill Strand on Sheephaven Bay (see p. 204), every room here has a view. Run by the same family for 50 years and open February to November, the hotel is wholly dedicated to providing everything for families; a host of family rooms (including separate mini bedrooms for the children) and a playhouse supervised by trained child minders with arts, crafts, toys, slides (for ages 3–7s), and pool, table tennis and soccer table for over-8s).

A leisure centre with a 17.5-metre exercise pool, children's pool, sauna, steam room and whirlpool spa sits at one end of the hotel, while at the other is a 929 square metre stand alone spa and wellness centre (to which children aren't admitted) offering a full range of hydro and therapy treatments.

Outdoors there's a grass tennis court and floodlit all-weather court, plus 9-hole pitch and putt course. The beach is only a short walk away.

The hotel is ideally placed for exploring the Ards Forest Park (see p. 197), Glenveagh National Park (see p. 202) and Dunlewy Lakeside Centre (see p. 202), as well as enjoying coastal cruises or visiting nearby Tory Island (see p. 198).

Rooms 24 standard, 28 family, 18 superior and 4 junior suites. *Rates* (inclusive of breakfast and dinner) superior: from €209 pps for 2-night weekend break; family €189 pps for 2-night weekend break; suite €249 pps for 2-night weekend break. Many other pricing combinations available. *Credit* all major cards accepted. *Amenities* baby-sitter service, baby listening, trained child minders, cots (free), restaurant, bar, coin-operated guest laundry, freezer, microwave, pay-as-you-go Internet. *In room* sat TV, tea-making facilities.

Radisson SAS Hotel, Letterkenny ★★★

Paddy Harte Road, Letterkenny, Co. Donegal, ☎ 074 919 4444, toll free from UK ☎ 0800 3333 3333; www.radissonsas.com. On the town loop road.

Children are most welcome at this luxury 4-star property; in fact up to two children under 17 years stay free in their parents' room.

The Health Club and Leisure Centre includes a 17-metre pool plus a sauna, steam room, gym with a separate weights and cardiovascular room. Children under 16 are welcome here, but must be supervised by an adult.

The health centre also offers treatments from head, neck and shoulder massage to acupuncture, detoxes, traditional Chinese medicine, and more.

To offset all that activity, the restaurant serves an excellent selection of well-prepared mainstream Irish cuisine (also available in child-sized portions), but no separate children's menu.

Rooms 114. *Rates* double/twin, B&B from €180, family €180 (children under 17, free) (breakfast €15, not included). *Credit* all major credit cards accepted. *Amenities* baby-sitter service, children's meals, cots (free), foyer Internet connection, laundry and dry cleaning. *In room* sat TV, high speed Internet; tea-making facilities, safe, mini bar, pay movies.

Co Mayo

Park Inn ★★★

Mulranny, Westport, Co Mayo. ☎ 098 36000; www.parkinnmulranny.ie. Close to Achill Island, W of Newport.

Originally a railway hotel, built by Midland Great Western Railways, the Park Inn targets the weddings and conference market, but is also good for travelling families given the proximity of Achill Island and the Belmullet Peninsula.

The hotel is set in 17 hectares of woodland, close to a Blue Flag beach, and all rooms offer views either of the bay or woodland. There's a fully equipped leisure centre with pool, sauna, Jacuzzi and outdoor Canadian Hot Tub, and accommodation includes two-bedroomed apartment suites, including the retro-styled John Lennon suite in which the Beatle stayed in the 1960s.

The Waterfront Bar and Bistro, with views of Clew Bay, and the Nephin Restaurant serve Irish food using local produce.

Rooms 41 plus 20 two-bedroomed apartments. **Rates** (B&B) €75–105, but ask for seasonal deals. **Credit** all major credit cards accepted. **Amenities** games room, Internet. **In room** tea/coffee-making facilities, flat screen cable TV, Internet modem access port along with individual voice mail, baby-sitting service by arrangement.

Co Sligo

MODERATE

The Beach Hotel and Leisure Club ★★

The Harbour, Mullaghmore, Co Sligo, 071 916 6103; www.beachhotel mullaghmore.com. Head for Mullaghmore from the N15; the hotel is at the end of the road.

Above the harbour of an attractive fishing village, the 2-star Beach Hotel is close to a fine Blue Flag beach and has a leisure club with 15-metre indoor pool,

Jacuzzi, steam room, sun shower, sauna and hi-tech gym.

The restaurant dishes up excellent food such as Mullaghmore mussels, crab salad and wild boar or rabbit, with the menu (€30) varying daily according to availability of produce.

Rooms 28 plus five self-catering apartments. **Rates** double/twin €45–65 pps (children sharing with parents 0–2 years, free; 3–11 years €20, B&B per night; 12–15 years €25 B&B per night). Over 60s' 10% discount Sun–Thu (except Jul–Aug). **Credit** V, MC, Amex. **Amenities** baby-sitting service on request, entertainment. **In room** TV, tea/coffee-making facilities.

EXPENSIVE

Radisson SAS Hotel and Spa, Sligo ★★★

Rosses Point Road, Ballincar, Co Sligo, 071 914 0008; www.sligo. radissonsas.com. Turn along the Rosses Point road just to the north of Sligo Town. 3km from town centre.

Set along a peninsula leading out to Rosses Point (sandy beach, rugged coastline, stunning views and the annual West of Ireland Golf Championships), the Radisson in Sligo is away from the bustle and traffic of Ireland's fastest growing city.

The Classiebawn Restaurant does a busy trade in locally sourced dishes on a modern Irish theme, and meals are also available in the Benwiskin Bar. The Sólás Spa and Wellness Centre offers holistic treatments and the Leisure Club (shorter hours for children) features a gym, 18-metre pool, children's pool, steam room, sauna, Jacuzzi and outdoor Canadian hot tub.

Rooms 132. **Rates** (including breakfast) double/twin €130, family from €140. Check website for special deals and summer treats. **Credit** all major credit cards accepted. **Amenities** baby-sitter service, children's meals, cots (free), laundry. **In room** standard rooms feature cable and pay television, voicemail, free broadband, in-room safe, coffee/tea-making facilities, mini bar.

CAFÉS & FAMILY-FRIENDLY DINING

Co Donegal

INEXPENSIVE–MODERATE

Dom Breslin's Bar and Restaurant ★★ VALUE
TRADITIONAL IRISH

Pier 1, Quay Street, Donegal Town, ☎ 074 97 22719. Adjoining the tourist information office.

This splendid restaurant (the bar is in a separate area) offers a children's menu (€5.25–6.25) a lunchtime carvery, steak and kidney pies big and full enough to share, poultry, game, open sandwiches, seafood and truly fresh fish with chips.

Open daily all year 11am–10pm (9.30pm in winter). **Main courses** €14.50–25. **Credit** V, MC, Amex, Switch. **Amenities** highchairs.

INEXPENSIVE–MODERATE

Waterfront Restaurant ★★
FIND TRADITIONAL IRISH

James' Street, Moville, Co Donegal, ☎ 074 938 2123; www.waterfront moville.com. Close to the harbour, overlooking Lough Foyle.

This restaurant is an excellent discovery. Located on the shorefront of Moville, with splendid views over Lough Foyle, the Waterfront is a modern establishment spread over three floors. The basement provides a pool table and fruit machines. The central floor houses the main bar and on the top floor is the restaurant with views of the shoreline and across Lough Foyle. It's very friendly to children, who are provided with drawing pads.

Lunchtime dishes include options such as Chicken Maryland, steak, curry, lasagne, pasta and baked potatoes, with à la carte options such as Colmcilles smoked haddock, monkish, rib-eye steaks, mussels, and lamb shank. Afternoon tea is €1.50.

Open daily (lunch) noon–4pm, (à la carte) 5–9.45pm (Sun 5–10pm). **Main courses** €10–14, children's menu €4.95. **Credit** all major credit cards accepted. **Amenities** highchairs available, free parking nearby.

MODERATE

Nesbitt Arms Hotel ★
TRADITIONAL IRISH

Main Street, Ardara, Co Donegal, ☎ 074 954 1103; www.nesbitt arms.com. 37km NW of Donegal.

The welcoming Weavers Bistro, decorated in traditional wood with wooden floors, is happy to see children. There is a wide menu serving everything from mixed grills and deep fried scampi and haddock to Thai Green Chicken Curry with Rice. The children's menu offers the usual standards (€4–5).

Open daily, noon–10pm. *Main courses* €9.50–16.50, set dinner menu €25, Sunday lunch €17.50. *Credit* V, MC. *Amenities* highchairs available.

MODERATE

Yellow Pepper Restaurant
★ ★ MODERN IRISH

36 Lower Main Street, Letterkenny, Co Donegal, 074 912 4133; *www. yellowpepperrestaurant.com.*

A restored shirt factory dating from 1896 now hosts The Yellow Pepper, a family run restaurant, with original floor and stone walls. With children running around everywhere, it's not a place for a quiet meal but the locals give it the thumbs up.

Dishes include pasta, stir fries, salads, stroganoff, lamb shank and breaded pork in a Malaga sauce, chicken satay, tiger chilli prawns, and an excellent children's menu (€4–8.50) with mini sirloin steak, chicken breast, and the usual run-of-the-mill favourites.

Open daily all year noon–10pm. *Main courses* €12.50–20.50. *Credit* V, MC. *Amenities* highchairs available.

Co Sligo

INEXPENSIVE

Pepper Alley ★ ★ SNACKS

Rockwood Parade, Sligo Town, Co Sligo, 071 917 0720.

This splendid eatery overlooking the river is hugely popular with local mums and dads being buggy-friendly, squawky-child tolerant, and serving a good selection of snacks, sandwiches, panini, baps, wraps and baguettes, as well as an ice cream menu.

Open all year Mon–Sat 8.30am–5pm, Sun 10am–4pm. *Main courses* €8–12. *Credit* V, MC. *Amenities* highchairs available.

INEXPENSIVE–MODERATE

Bistro Bianconi ★ ★ ★ FIND
VALUE SNACKS PIZZA, PASTA & PANINI

44 O'Connell Street, Sligo Town, 071 914 1744; *www.bistro bianconi.ie. In the centre of town.*

This informal licensed restaurant right in the heart of Sligo Town, offers a huge and bewildering array of pasta, panini and pizza salads; eat in or takeaway. Not surprisingly it's heaving with children.

In the evenings there are also the likes of meatballs, steak, and seafood. The service is fast and friendly, and although there's no separate menu for children, you can get smaller versions of the regular dishes.

Open for lunch (noon–2.30pm) and evening meals (5.30–11pm) (closed Sun). *Main courses* (lunch) €10.95–13.95, (dinner) €18.95–31.95. *Credit* all major credit cards accepted. *Amenities* highchairs available.

MODERATE

Coach Lane @ Donaghy's
★ ★ ★ FIND MODERN EUROPEAN

1–2 Lord Edward Street, Sligo Town, 071 916 2417; *www.coachlane. com. In the centre of town, near the bus station.*

You may well have to make a reservation to get into this superb two-floor restaurant above Donaghy's where you're welcome to stay with children until 9pm. Serving the very best of local produce you can expect superb seafood chowder, beef, lamb, and free range duck as well as pastas and chicken. There is no children's menu, but you can get half portions of virtually every dish – and the desserts are wonderful.

Open *daily, bar food from 3pm, à la carte in the restaurant from 5.30pm (last orders 10.30pm).* **Main course**: *€17–24.50.* **Credit** *all major credit cards.* **Amenities** *highchairs available, private room for up to eight (pre-booking essential).*

Davis's Restaurant @ the Yeats Tavern ★★
TRADITIONAL IRISH AND SEAFOOD

Drumcliffe Bridge, Drumcliffe, Co Sligo, ☏ 071 916 3117; www.yeats tavernrestaurant.com. On the main Donegal road (N15), just 8km from Sligo Town.

One of Sligo's oldest drinking and eating establishments, Davis's Restaurant offers consistently good pub grub and service, with emphasis on local ingredients – chicken, beef and lamb, plus outstanding seafood, complemented by a fine cellar of wines. There is also an outstanding selection of

vegetarian dishes, sandwiches, pasta, rice and noodle dishes, and daily lunch specials. It's child-friendly and the children's menu – anything with chips or pasta – includes steak €2.50–9.90.

Open *daily, noon–9.30pm (9pm on Sun.* **Main courses** *€12.90–19.90.* **Credit** *V, MC.* **Amenities** *children's menu, highchairs available.*

Co Leitrim

MODERATE

Cryans Riverside Inn ★★
TRADITIONAL PUB GRUB

Bridge Street, Carrick-on-Shannon, Co Leitrim, ☏ 071 962 0409, Close to the marina.

This bar and restaurant is traditional and very conducive to relaxation. The speciality is traditional home-cooked food, particularly steaks, seafood, mixed grills and daily specials, served in both bar and restaurant.

The inn is well known for its Irish music and it's not uncommon to find an impromptu session in full swing. Organised sessions with top musicians are arranged on most nights in summer and every weekend in winter.

Open *(breakfast) 8–9.30am, (lunch) noon–3.30pm, (à la carte and dinner) until 9.30pm.* **Main courses** *€15–24.50.* **Credit** *V, MC.* **Amenities** *highchairs available.*

10 Northern Ireland

NORTHERN IRELAND

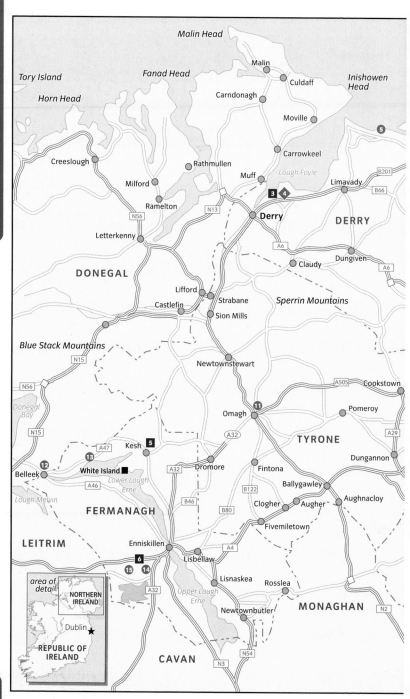

Malin Head

Malin

Culdaff

Fanad Head

Inishowen
Head

Tory Island

Carndonagh

Horn Head

Moville

Creeslough

Carrowkeel

Rathmullen

Lough Foyle

B201

Milford

Muff

Limavady

B66

Ramelton

N13

3 ◆**4**

Derry

DERRY

N56

Letterkenny

A6

Claudy

Dungiven

A6

DONEGAL

Lifford

Castlefin

Strabane

Sperrin Mountains

Sion Mills

Blue Stack Mountains

Newtownstewart

N15

N56

*Donegal
Bay*

A505

Cookstown

Omagh

11

Pomeroy

N15

A32

TYRONE

A29

Kesh

5

Dungannon

13

A47

Dromore

Fintona

12

White Island ■

A32

Ballygawley

Belleek

A46

*Lower Lough
Erne*

B122

Aughnacloy

Lough Melvin

B46

Clogher

Augher

FERMANAGH

B80

Fivemiletown

LEITRIM

Enniskillen

6

Lisbellaw

A4

15 **14**

Lisnaskea

Rosslea

*Upper Lough
Erne*

A32

Newtownbutler

MONAGHAN

N2

area of
detail

**NORTHERN
IRELAND**

Dublin ★

**REPUBLIC OF
IRELAND**

CAVAN

N54

N3

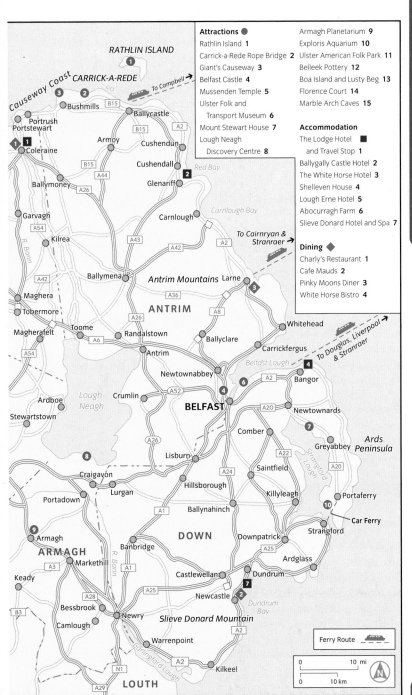

Attractions ●

Rathlin Island **1**
Carrick-a-Rede Rope Bridge **2**
Giant's Causeway **3**
Belfast Castle **4**
Mussenden Temple **5**
Ulster Folk and
    Transport Museum **6**
Mount Stewart House **7**
Lough Neagh
    Discovery Centre **8**
Armagh Planetarium **9**
Exploris Aquarium **10**
Ulster American Folk Park **11**
Belleek Pottery **12**
Boa Island and Lusty Beg **13**
Florence Court **14**
Marble Arch Caves **15**

Accommodation
The Lodge Hotel ■
    and Travel Stop **1**
Ballygally Castle Hotel **2**
The White Horse Hotel **3**
Shelleven House **4**
Lough Erne Hotel **5**
Abocurragh Farm **6**
Slieve Donard Hotel and Spa **7**

Dining ◆
Charly's Restaurant **1**
Cafe Mauds **2**
Pinky Moons Diner **3**
White Horse Bistro **4**

RATHLIN ISLAND
Causeway Coast CARRICK-A-REDE
To Campbell
Bushmills
Portrush
Portstewart
Coleraine
Armoy
Ballycastle
Cushendun
Cushendall
Glenariff
Red Bay
Ballymoney
Carnlough
Carnlough Bay
Garvagh
Kilrea
To Cairnryan &
Stranraer
Ballymena
Antrim Mountains Larne
Maghera
ANTRIM
Tobermore
Magherafelt
Toome
Randalstown
Whitehead
To Douglas, Liverpool
& Stranraer
Antrim
Ballyclare
Carrickfergus
Belfast Lough
Newtownabbey
Bangor
Ardboe
Crumlin
BELFAST
Newtownards
Stewartstown
Lough
Neagh
Comber
Ards
Peninsula
Greyabbey
Lisburn
Craigavon
Saintfield
Killyleagh
Portaferry
Portadown
Lurgan
Hillsborough
Car Ferry
Ballynahinch
Strangford
Armagh
DOWN
Downpatrick
ARMAGH
Banbridge
Markethill
Ardglass
Keady
Castlewellan
Dundrum
Bessbrook
Newcastle
Newry
Slieve Donard Mountain
Dundrum
Bay
Camlough
Warrenpoint
Kilkeel
LOUTH

Ferry Route

0   10 mi
0   10 km

It may seem ironic, given the area's decades of unrest, but Northern Ireland is where you can find some of the most peaceful and achingly beautiful countryside in the whole of Ireland. There are superb beaches, parks, forests, islands, easy walks, plus plenty of entertainment. It's all lifted by the newly blossoming economy and confidence in the future.

Northern Ireland radiates from Belfast, an extraordinary city, knowingly coping with the legacy of years of strife, and doing so with typically inspiring Irish resilience and panache.

Northern Ireland includes six counties in addition to the city of Belfast: Antrim, Armagh, Down, Londonderry and Tyrone all have a toehold on the largest inland lake in the British Isles, Lough Neagh, and although the other county – Fermanagh in the southwest – doesn't, it does have plenty of lakes of its own.

The bucket-and-spade brigade will find some of the best beaches in Europe here, the natural formations along the coastline producing long stretches of golden sand and dunes. And all the coastal scenery is superb, not least in Antrim where the coast and Glens Area of Outstanding Natural Beauty offer just that, and the Giant's Causeway is a worthy and hugely popular World Heritage Site.

A shortish ferry ride from Ballycastle, Rathlin Island is a wonderful diversion for children, the only inhabited offshore island in Northern Ireland, a rare and wild place with all the dramatic landscapes you might associate with a geological hotchpotch of basalt and limestone, and a delight for birdwatchers. But it's hard to pick one area over another; the whole of Northern Ireland is rare, wild, rugged, beautiful and delightful.

As with the whole of Ireland, children are very much part of the family, with the difference that in Northern Ireland wheelchair users and parents with a buggy will find that many places have thought about you, and few attractions are inaccessible.

ESSENTIALS

Getting There

By Air Many daily flights link Belfast's two airports with the four London airports – Heathrow, Gatwick, Luton and Stansted – plus there are daily scheduled flights from most British regional airports and those of the Republic of Ireland. Full details of airlines are on p. 22.

George Best Belfast City Airport is just 5km from the city centre. A regular City Airlink bus service operates into the city centre every 20 minutes and a rail link every 20 minutes (6.20am–8.40pm), Mon–Fri.

Belfast International Airport at Aldergrove is 30 minutes drive via the M2 motorway. An airbus service operates between the airport and Belfast city centre every 10 minutes

(7am–6.45pm), Mon–Fri. Check timetable for services outside these times.

By Sea Northern Ireland is easily accessed by sea crossing from Scotland and England, with new routes continuing to develop. Travel by high-speed catamaran or traditional ferry with impressive journey times from just 90 minutes. Full details of ferry operators are on p. 24.

By Rail The frequent cross-border Enterprise service to Belfast Central Station from Dublin is deservedly popular. Seats can be reserved in the 'First Plus', first class carriage, ☏ *028 9089 9409*. The Enterprise service runs 8 times daily (5 on Sundays); the journey time is approximately 2 hours (Northern Ireland Railways ☏ *028 9066 6630*; *www. translink.co.uk*).

Central Station is also the main departure point, along with **Great Victoria Street Station**, for the regular trains from Belfast to the suburbs and Londonderry, the ferry port of Larne, and the main seaside resorts of Bangor and Portrush.

The bus/rail **Freedom of Northern Ireland Ticket** is excellent value if you're planning an extended stay: (£14 a day (child £7); £34 for 3 days in an 8-day period (child £17); £50 (child £25) for 7 days unlimited travel).

By Bus Metro Bus is Belfast's bus service. For information call the Translink Call Centre (☏ *028 90 66 66 30* (7am–8pm); *www. translink.co.uk*).

Cross-Border Ulsterbus (☏ *028 9066 6630*; *www.translink.co.uk*) express services from Dublin and some northerly towns in the Republic of Ireland arrive daily at the Belfast Europa Bus Centre. There are also Ulsterbus express services from major British cities via Stranraer.

By Car Visitors arriving by ferry into Dublin Port (preferable to Dún Laoghaire, which is on the south side of the city) will find that it's less than 2 hours driving to Belfast, more than half of which is on motorway, with road building continuing northwards (2007). Be ready on leaving the dock area to take the M1, which soon passes through a toll tunnel (payment in euros).

VISITOR INFORMATION

Northern Ireland Tourist Office, St Anne's Court, 59 North Street, Belfast BT1 1NB. ☏ *028 9023 1221*; *www.discover northernireland.com*.

Belfast

Belfast Welcome Centre, 47 Donegall Place, Belfast BT1 5AD ☏ *028 9024 6609; www.goto belfast.com*.

Co Antrim

Antrim 16 High Street, Antrim ☏ *028 9442 8331*; *www.antrim. gov.uk*.

Ballycastle Sheskburn House, 7 Mary Street, Ballycastle. ℡ *028 2076 2024; www.moyle-council. org*.

Ballymena 76 Church Street, Ballymena. ℡ *028 2563 8494; www.ballymena.gov.uk*.

Carrickfergus 11 Antrim Street, Carrickfergus. ℡ *028 9335 8049; www.carrickfergus.org*.

Giant's Causeway 44 Causeway Road, Bushmills. ℡ *028 2073 1855*.

Larne Narrow Gauge Road, Larne. ℡ *028 2826 0088; www. larne.gov.uk*.

Portrush The Dunluce Centre, Sandhill Drive, Portrush. ℡ *028 7082 3333; www.colerainebc. gov.uk*.

Co Armagh

Armagh 40 English Street, Armagh. ℡ *028 3752 1800; www. armagh.gov.uk*.

Co Down

Bangor 34 Quay Street, Bangor. ℡ *028 9127 0069; www.northdown tourism.com*.

Downpatrick The St Patrick Centre, 53a Market Street, Downpatrick. ℡ *028 4461 2233; www.discovernorthernireland.com*

Hillsborough The Courthouse, The Square, Hillsborough. ℡ *028 9268 9717; www.lisburn.gov.uk*.

Newcastle 10–14 Central Promenade, Newcastle. ℡ *028 4372 2222*.

Newry Town Hall, Bank Parade, Newry. ℡ *028 3026 8877; www. seenewryandmourne.com*.

Newtownards 31 Regent Street, Newtownards. ℡ *028 9182 6846; www.kingdomsofdown.com*.

Portaferry The Stables, Castle Street, Portaferry. ℡ *028 4272 9882; www.ards-council.gov.uk*

Co Fermanagh

Enniskillen, Wellington Road, Enniskillen. ℡ *028 6632 3110; www.fermanagh.gov.uk*.

Co Londonderry

Coleraine Railway Road, Coleraine. ℡ *028 7034 4723; www.coleraine.gov.uk*.

Derry 44 Foyle Street, Londonderry. ℡ *028 7126 7284; www.derryvisitor.com*.

Limavady Council Offices, 7 Connell Street, Limavady. ℡ *028 7776 0307; www.limavady.gov.uk*.

Magherafelt The Bridewell, 6 Church Street, Magherafelt. ℡ *028 7963 1510; www. magherafelt.gov.uk*

Co Tyrone

Cookstown The Burnavon, Burn Road, Cookstown. ℡ *028 8676 6727; www.cookstown. gov.uk*.

Omagh 1 Market Street, Omagh. ℡ *028 8224 7831; www.omagh. gov.uk*.

Strabane Abercorn Square, Strabane. ☏ *028 7188 3735; www. strabanedc.com*.

ORIENTATION

Belfast (from the Gaelic Béal Feirste or 'mouth of the sandbank') is the main centre, in the eastern part, sandwiched between Co Antrim and Co Down. It's best explored on foot. Leafy Queen's Quarter around Queen's University is the place for bars, boutiques and bistros, plus each autumn the Belfast Festival with theatre, dance, music, literature, comedy and visual arts. The Cathedral Quarter takes its name from **St Anne's Cathedral**. With the University of Ulster (specialising in Arts) close by, it's home to visual and performing artists.

The Titanic Quarter commemorates the legend and the history of shipbuilding here whereas the Falls Road is where the Irish language still flourishes. And the **Golden Mile** round Great Victoria Street is a commercial hub with restaurants, cafés and pubs.

Beyond the city, the **Causeway Coastal Route** running from Belfast Lough to Londonderry at the southern edge of Lough Foyle is a holiday in itself.

Inland, every county has its mountainous scenery, from the beautiful Sperrins of Derry and Tyrone to the fabled Mountains

of Mourne in Down. Undulating farmland predominates, but there's no escaping the superb coastline with the lure of numerous golden sandy beaches.

Getting Around

It's perfectly possible to work your way around Northern Ireland by public transport, reaching every county from Belfast in a couple of hours. **Translink** is the main provider, the brand name of a wonderfully integrated operation that combines the **Ulsterbus, Northern Ireland Railways** and Belfast's **Metro** bus.

However, for the most flexible arrangement and to get the most out of Northern Ireland, where roads are generally excellent (compared to the rest of Ireland), the best way is by car.

Public Transport Timetables and information on all forms of public transport are available from local bus and rail stations and from the Translink Call Centre (open Mon–Sun, 7am–8pm. ☏ *028 9066 6630*, or ☏ *028 9038 7505* for **Textphone** for callers who are deaf or hard of hearing. *www.translink.co.uk*). **Translink's** excellent booklet *Travelling with Translink* explains the many and varied ways you can travel around using public transport.

If you're keen to use public transport, check the website for special offers.

BELFAST

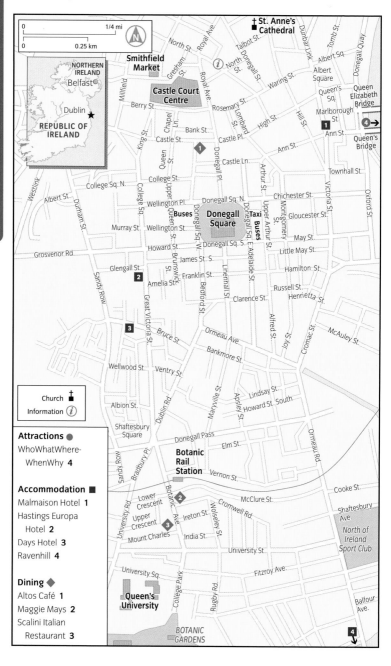

0   1/4 mi

0   0.25 km

NORTHERN
IRELAND
Belfast

Dublin ★

REPUBLIC OF
IRELAND

† St. Anne's
Cathedral

Smithfield
Market

Castle Court
Centre

Donegall
Square

Buses

Taxi
Buses

Botanic
Rail
Station

Queen's
University

BOTANIC
GARDENS

North of
Ireland
Sport Club

Church †
Information ⓘ

Attractions ●
WhoWhatWhere-
   WhenWhy **4**

Accommodation ■
Malmaison Hotel **1**
Hastings Europa
   Hotel **2**
Days Hotel **3**
Ravenhill **4**

Dining ◆
Altos Café **1**
Maggie Mays **2**
Scalini Italian
   Restaurant **3**

Freedom Of Northern Ireland Pass ⟪

A 'Freedom of Northern Ireland' travel pass (available from main bus and rail stations) offers unlimited travel on scheduled bus and rail services throughout Northern Ireland (1-day £14, 3-day £34 (out of 8 consecutive days), 7-day £50). Ulsterbus serves all the main towns and villages in Northern Ireland from 21 main passenger service facilities.

Using a taxi is an economical option for short journeys. Taxis are generally metered but if not be sure to agree a fare before setting off. In common with taxi drivers everywhere, those in Northern Ireland are founts of knowledge, not always credible, but that's part of the fun.

Visitors planning on passing west from Co Londonderry to Donegal can use the **Lough Foyle Ferry Service** between Magilligan and Greencastle. This operates a continuous shuttle service during peak periods, weather permitting. The service operates daily, Apr–Sep, 7.20am–9.50pm (Sat and Sun, 9am); Oct–Mar until 7.50pm. Fare: (car) single £7, return £11; (pedestrians) single £2, return £3; (seniors and children) single £0.70, return £1. ℂ *074 938 1901.*

Child-friendly Events & Entertainment

Appalachian and Bluegrass Music Festival ★★

August–September. Ulster American Folk Park, Omagh, Co Tyrone, ℂ *028 8224 3292; www.folkpark.com.*

This annual festival is the largest of its kind in Europe and features performances by musicians and dancers from all over the world in the fabulous setting of this outdoor museum. Booking is required for evening concerts.

Apple Blossom Festival ★★

April. Co Armagh, ℂ *029 3752 1800; www.armagh.gov.uk.*

Celebrate the beautiful Apple Blossom season in the orchard country. Events include outdoor music concerts, guided tours and a speciality food market.

Belfast Children's Festival ★★
AGES UNDER 12

Young at Art, Stranmillis College, Belfast, ℂ *028 9023 0660; www. belfastchildrensfestival.com*

An annual international festival for children up to 12 years and their accompanying adults, this is renowned for its unique blend of quirky events and innovative programming, with more than 100 performances, workshops and exhibitions throughout Belfast city centre, and a worldwide programme that draws artists from Korea, India, UK, Denmark, Japan, Africa and Ireland.

Lady of the Lake Festival ★★

July. Irvinestown, Co Fermanagh, ℂ *028 6862 1656; www.fermanagh lakelands.com.*

TIP >>

Activity Guides

Download activity guides from www.discovernorthernireland.com **and** www.landwaterair.co.uk for details of outdoor activities and events.

This splendid festival always includes a wide range of wacky children's entertainment, fancy dress and a fishing competition.

Lord Mayor's Show ★★★

May. Belfast, ☎ 028 9024 6609; www.gotobelfast.com.

Exactly what it says on the tin; this is the Lord Mayor's annual knees-up, a colourful carnival through the centre of Belfast with music and floats.

Oul' Lammas Fair ★★★

August. Ballycastle, Co Antrim, ☎ 028 2076 2024; www.causeway coastandglens.com.

Ireland's oldest traditional market fair offers horse trading, and street entertainment such as clowns, fire eaters and even people turning up with their banjo or flute for an impromptu performance. There are also attractive market stalls.

St Patrick's Day Celebrations ★

March. Co Armagh, ☎ 028 3752 1800; www.armaghanddown.com.

A week-long festival of free-range entertainment for families to dip in and out of, depending on the ages of your children, it includes dance and drama, live music, language classes, walking tours, a spectacular Carnival parade, and outdoor music concert.

More of the same, with a parade through the city centre, and lots of lively music.

March. Belfast, ☎ 028 9024 6609; www.gotobelfast.com.

FAST FACTS: BELFAST

Hospitals The Royal Victoria Hospital, Grosvenor Road, Belfast, ☎ *028 902 40503* and the **Mater Hospital**, Crumlin Road, Belfast, ☎ *028 907 41211*, are both found near the centre of the city.

Belfast Internet Cafes Belfast Welcome Centre, 47 Donegall Place, Belfast BT1 5AD. ☎ *028 902 46609*. Open Jun–Sep Mon–Sat 9am–7pm, Sun 12–5pm, Oct–May Mon–Sat 9am–5.30pm
    Linenhall Library, 17 Donegall Square North, Belfast BT1 5GB (public entrance on Fountain Street) ☎ *028 9032 1707*. Open Mon–Fri 9.30am–5.30pm, Sat 9.30am–4pm.

WHAT TO SEE & DO

Children's Top 10 Attractions

❶ **Take a swinging trip** across a rope bridge at Carrick-a-Rede and explore a fisherman's island. See p. 226.

❷ Get the authentic seal of approval at Exploris Aquarium. See p. 230.

❸ Travel back in time and see old forms of transport and ways of life at the Ulster Transport Museum. See p. 231.

❹ Walk where giants once walked at the Causeway. See p. 227.

❺ Make a planetary date with the stars in Armagh. See p. 229.

❻ Get close to nature on Rathlin Island; don't forget your binoculars. See p. 228.

❼ Take a ride on a steam train. See p. 226.

❽ Answer all your questions at Whowhatwherewhenwhy. See p. 226.

❾ Have quirky fun at Belfast's Children Festival. See p. 223.

❿ Take an underground boat ride and explore the Marble Arch caves among the hills of Fermanagh. See p. 233.

Child-friendly Attractions

Belfast

Belfast Castle and Cave Hill Country Park ★ ★ AGES 3 AND UP (Castle) AGES UNDER 14 (Adventure Playground)

📞 *028 9077 6925; www.belfast castle.co.uk. Off Antrim Road, 6.5km north of the city centre.*

Belfast Castle

For more than 120 years Belfast Castle has been a landmark on the slopes of the Cave Hill. Its story is told in the Visitor Centre on the second floor and the cellars have been transformed into Victorian narrow, paved streets and shop fronts with gaslights, etc. There's also an excellent restaurant (see p. 239).

In the grounds is Cave Hill Country Park, offering views and walking trails, named after the Neolithic caves found there. McArt's Fort, on the summit of Cave Hill, is an ancient earthwork, all that remains of a defence built against the Vikings, and in 1795 used by Wolfe Tone and fellow United Irishmen to plan the 1798 rebellion.

An extensive and well-designed playground caters for 3–14 year olds with slides, swings, and an aerial runway for the older ones.

Open castle all year, daily, 9am–10pm (Sun 9–5.30pm), park dawn to dusk. **Adm** free. **Amenities** antiques shop; refreshments.

Steam Trains Ireland ★★
ALL AGES

47 Donegall Place, Belfast. ☎ 028 9024 6609; www.steamtrains ireland.com.

Steam Trains Ireland operates mainline public steam trains throughout Northern Ireland, including seasonal specials, using lovingly restored steam locomotives and preserved carriages.

Tickets from Belfast Welcome Centre, 47 Donegall Place, Belfast.

Whowhatwherewhenwhy – W5 ★★★

Odyssey, 2 Queen's Quay, Belfast, ☎ 028 9046 7700; www.w5online.co.uk.

W5's 140 interactive exhibits are spread over five action-packed exhibition areas. Activities include creating cloud rings, making and racing your own cars and boats, beating the lie detector, playing music on a laser harp, and making your very own animated film. There's a special section for the under-8s where they can, for example, build a house. W5 also offers live science shows, holiday workshops and regular special events and guest speakers.

Open Mon–Sat 10am–6pm, Sun 12 noon–6pm (last admission 5pm). **Adm** adult £6.50, children (3–15) £4.50 (under-3s free), family tickets: 1+3 £17, 2+2 £19, 2+3 £22.50, 2+4 £26.50, 2+5 £30.50.

Co Antrim

Carrick-a-Rede Rope Bridge ★★★ AGES 8 AND UP

119a Whitepark Road, Ballintoy, Co Antrim BT64 6LS, ☎ 028 2076 9839; www.nationaltrust.org.uk.

For more than 350 years fishermen have erected a rope bridge here to access the rich harvests of migrating salmon. This spectacular 20-metre bridge, linking the mainland with Carrick Island 30 metres above the sea, is something everyone should think about crossing. However, it's not for children who won't hold on – or vertigo sufferers – because the bridge is open-sided and sways. Furthermore, it's more than 1km from the car park and involves quite a few stony steps.

However, if you go you will see kittiwake, guillemot and fulmar (you can hire binoculars)

FUN FACT ➤ **The Antrim Coaster** ◀

The Bus Service 252 plies the Antrim Coast from Belfast to Coleraine, and is an excellent way of exploring the coast at a leisurely pace; hop on, hop off as you wish – see Ulsterbus, p. 219 for details. From Coleraine, take the train to Londonderry, and enjoy one of the most beautiful rail journeys in Ireland.

clinging precariously to the cliff face, framed by lush grassland, sea pinks and white sea campion, and views back to the stunning coastline and beyond to Kintyre in Scotland. Children aged 8–14 can follow the new Children's Discovery Trail.

This is one of Northern Ireland's best-loved attractions, and with good reason – which means you are unlikely to enjoy it alone.

Open *10am–6pm daily Mar–Oct (Jun–Aug 7pm), weather permitting.* **Adm** *adults £3, children £1.50, family £7.50. Gift Aid admission + 10% (voluntary donation).* **Credit** *V, MC.* **Amenities** *toilets (baby-changing facilities), café, buggies not allowed.*

Carrick-a-Rede Rope Bridge

Giant's Causeway ★ ★ ★
ALL AGES

44a Causeway Road, Bushmills, Co Antrim BT57 8SU, 📞 *028 2073 1582;* **www.nationaltrust.org.uk.**

Northern Ireland's only UNESCO World Heritage Site is well worth the journey. It never fails to impress, including as it does a calculated 38,000 polygonal basalt columns, formed 60 million years ago by the cooling of molten lava produced by the volcanic hiccough that produced the Antrim plateau.

The walk down to the causeway from the information centre is easy, but there is also a **shuttle bus** from the rear of the information centre (adult single £1, return £2; child single £0.50, return £1).

Those interested in birds will delight in the choughs and gannets plus innumerable LBJs (Little Brown Jobs) along the cliff faces.

But be warned: there are often strong winds blowing in from the sea, and, if you get too close, you'll get a serious soaking from the waves. Moreover, basalt can be slippery when wet. Wear sensible shoes, and take warm clothing and a waterproof, even in summer.

Open *daily, except 25 and 26 Dec.* **Adm** *free, but parking (not National Trust) costs £5 per car.* **Amenities**

Giant's Causeway

information centre, including theatre, National Trust centre, shop and teashop, toilets.

Rathlin Island ★★★ ALL AGES

Ballycastle, Co Antrim, www.antrim. net. Via ferry from Ballycastle.

Rathlin Island, inhabited for 8,000 years and today just a 45-minute ferry ride across the Sea of Moyle from the pretty seaside resort of Ballycastle, is steeped in history, folklore and legend. It's a good place to relax but the main interest is the flora and fauna of this internationally important site.

The island is 6 miles long and 1 mile wide, L-shaped, almost treeless, and dotted with numerous lochans (small lochs) that reflect the sky with amazing intensity. Much of the coastline is over 70 metres high and as well as chough, guillemot, kittiwake, fulmar and gannet, it's a good place to see puffin, especially between April and August. Private cars aren't permitted, and so the roads are good for walking

 DID YOU KNOW? >> **Causeway Coastal Route** <<

The Causeway Coastal Route runs from Belfast Lough to Londonderry along the shores of Lough Foyle, over 160km of stunning coastal scenery taking in the Antrim Coast and Glens Area of Outstanding Natural Beauty. It's one of the best ways of getting a taster of the Northern Irish countryside. However, though easy, it's a convoluted road and so might not work for children prone to car-sickness. You can mitigate that with regular stops, maybe to one of the nine Antrim Glens. You will also pass through a host of interesting villages where you can make halts for lunch or afternoon tea.

FUN FACT » ## The legend of the Giant's Causeway «

A long time ago there lived in Ireland a gentle giant, Finn MacCool, at 52 feet 6 inches a relatively small giant. Not far away, across the sea in what is today southern Scotland there lived another giant Ben-an-Donner; the two regularly hollered at one another across the water, spoiling for a trial of strength. On this they finally agreed, and kindly Finn MacCool built the causeway so that Ben-an-Donner, who lived on the island of Staffa, could walk across to Ireland dryshod. But when Finn MacCool saw the Scottish giant approaching he realised just how much bigger he was than himself, and ran indoors to hide. His wife, recognising that Ben-an-Donner was truly a giant, disguised her husband as a baby. When Ben-an-Donner finally arrived she cautioned him not to wake the sleeping 'bairn'. But when Ben-an-Donner peered inside and saw the sleeping 'baby', he fled for his life. If the child was so huge, he had no wish to meet its father. As he raced back to Scotland, he destroyed the causeway as he went so that the bairn's father couldn't follow.

or cycling, but you can also get around using the Puffin Bus (📞 *028 2076 3451*), or by hiring a bike and following the Sustrans National Cycle Network Route 93 to a number of lighthouses (📞 *028 2076 3954*).

During the summer months the island holds festivals and events including yacht races and a Robert the Bruce Festival.

Ferry pre-booking essential. Calmac Ferries Ltd. 📞 *028 2076 9299; www. calmac.co.uk. Ballycastle: Apr–Sept, daily, 10am, noon, 4.30pm 6.30pm; Oct, daily, 10.30am, 4pm (Fri, 4.30pm); Rathlin: Apr–Sep, daily, 8.30am, 11am, 3.30pm, 5.30pm; Oct, daily, 9am, 3pm.* **Fares** *adult day return £10, children (5–16) £5 (under 5, free); family (2+2) £26.50.* **Credit** *V, MC.* **Amenities** *accommodation (Manor House (NT, 12 rooms)* 📞 *028 2076 3964. Double en suite £60, double/twin £55, family £60); gift shop; cafés; restaurants; birdwatching (RSPB* 📞 *028 2076 3948); aqua sports (📞 028 7082 3563); guided walking tours (📞 028 7032 7960).*

Co Armagh

Armagh Planetarium ★★★
ALL AGES

College Hill, Armagh, Co Armagh BT61 9DB, 📞 *028 3752 3689; www. armaghplanet.com. The planetarium can be found on the Portadown road, opposite the Royal School.*

Under the guise of a modern astronomical research institute, the Armagh Planetarium offers a chance to travel back in time to remote stars and galaxies, to see the view from distant planets and their moons, and to discover the universe via stunning 360° video shows, and an outdoor 'solar system' made up of large metal balls in a park.

There are regular telescope nights when you can visit to use Ireland's largest telescope to view the night sky, or take part in interactive workshops on rocket building, meteors and space robots.

Lakes, Lakes, Lakes

There are more than 1,600 lakes in Northern Ireland ranging in size from little more than small ponds to Lough Neagh, the largest freshwater lake in the British Isles.

Open Jan–Jul Tue–Fri 1–5pm (show at 3pm), Sat–Sun 11.30am–5pm (public shows on the hour from 12 noon. First show at noon is intended for the under-5s. Other shows Sat and Sun from 1pm, ages 6 and over only. Summer months, daily, 11.30am to 5pm with shows on the hour from noon. All shows are different and pre-booking is essential. *Credit* V, MC. *Adm* adults £6, children £5, family (2+3) £18. *Amenities* disabled access, café.

Lough Neagh Discovery Centre ★★ ALL AGES

Oxford Island National Nature Reserve, Craigavon, Co Armagh BT66 6NJ, ☎ *028 3832 2205; www. oxfordisland.com. At the southern end of Lough Neagh, Junction 10 on the M1.*

Reputedly filling the void created when the legendary giant Finn MacCool scooped up a handful of earth to throw at England (and missed, so creating the Isle of Man), Lough Neagh is the largest inland sea in the British Isles. Oxford Island, where the centre is based, is actually a peninsula, with reedbeds, woodland, wild flower meadows and wildlife ponds making a superb nature reserve with herons, Canada geese and occasionally osprey visiting.

There are walking and cycling trails of varying length, though there are no cycle hire facilities on site.

Open daily (except 25 Dec), 9am–5pm (Mon–Fri), 10am–5pm (Sat, Sun), centre closes 6pm Easter until Sep. Café: daily, 10am–4.30pm. *Adm* free. *Amenities* café, toilets, disabled access to most hides.

Co Down

Exploris Aquarium ★★
AGES 5 AND UP

Castle Street, Portaferry, Co Down, ☎ *028 4272 8062; www.exploris. org.uk.*

Exploris, sited on the shores of Strangford Lough, is a marine nature reserve and site of special scientific interest. It offers a chance to learn about seals, in particular injured or orphaned ones. Discovery pools allow touchy-feely experiences.

Open Centre: 10am–6pm daily (Sat 11am, Sun noon) Apr–Aug; 10am–5pm daily (Sat 11am, Sun 1pm) Sep–Mar. Café: 10.30am–5.30 daily in summer, 11am–4pm during winter. *Credit* V, MC. *Adm* adults £7, children (4–16) £4 (under-4s, free), family (2+4) £20, (1+4) £18; 60+ £4. *Amenities* café, disabled access (wheelchairs available at reception), baby-changing facilities.

Mount Stewart House, Garden and Temple of the Winds ★★ ALL AGES

Portaferry Road, Newtownards, Co Down BT22 2AD, ☎ *028 4278 8387; www.nationaltrust.org.uk. On A20,*

8km from Newtownards on the Portaferry road.

On the shores of Strangford Lough, Mount Stewart is the home of the Londonderry family. The beautiful setting and internationally admired gardens are intriguing and there are activities for children during school holidays throughout the year.

Open (house) daily noon–6pm (1–6pm May–Jun) Mar–Oct, (Sat–Sun only Mar–Apr, except Easter, and Oct, closed Tue in May and Sep); (gardens) 10am–6pm (8pm May–Sep) daily Apr–Oct; Temple of the Winds: 2–5pm Sun and bank/public holidays only, Apr–Oct. **Credit** all major cards accepted. **Adm** adults £6, children £3, family £15 (gardens only: adults £5, children £2.50, family £12.50). Gift Aid admission + 10% (voluntary donation). **Amenities** shop, baby-changing facilities, loan of hip-carrying infant seats, family activity packs, children's quiz/trail, restaurant (licensed) with children's menu, picnic area.

Ulster Folk and Transport Museum ★★★ VALUE ALL AGES

Cultra, Holywood, Co Down BT18 0EU, ☎ 028 9042 8428; www.uftm.org.uk or www.magni.org.

This enterprising and exciting folk museum depicts life in the imaginary town of Ballycultra in the early 1900s (houses largely transported from actual locations), while the transport museum boasts a wonderful array of rail and road transport over the years. The whole site covers 70 hectares, with many attractions and activities in the open air, and you'll need a full day to do it justice.

Open 10am–5pm Mon–Fri (Sat 6pm, Sun 11am-6pm) Mar–Jun; 10am–6pm Mon–Sat (Sun 11am) Jul–Sep; 10am–4pm Mon–Fri (Sat 5pm, Sun 11am–5pm) Oct–Feb. **Adm** (folk museum) adults £5.50, children (5–18) £3.50 (under-5s, free), family (2+3) £15.50, (1+3) £11, seniors £3.50; (transport museum charges as Folk Museum); (combined ticket for both museums) adults £7, children (5–18) £4 (under-5s, free), family (2+3) £19, (1+3) £13, seniors £4. Credit all cards. **Amenities** disabled access but not to whole site, wheelchairs available, tearoom in Culra Manor, museum shop.

Co Fermanagh

Belleek Pottery ★★ ALL AGES

Belleek, Co Fermanagh. ☎ 028 6865 9300; www.belleek.ie. Along the N3, east from Ballyshannon, where it meets the A47.

Kids are fascinated by the craftsmanship that goes into the delicate lattice work and individual

---

DID YOU KNOW? >> **The Mountains of Mourne** «

Arguably the best known mountain group in Ireland, the Mourne Mountains, just south of the busy, family friendly town of Newcastle on Dundrum Bay, rise to the cone-like summit of Slieve Donard. The area around the Mournes is already an Area of Outstanding Natural Beauty, and may in time become Ireland's first national park. The mountains provide excellent walking and cycling for all ages, though some of the ascents can be quite demanding (**www.mournemountains.com**).

petals of the pottery produced here.

In the main reception area hangs a large white bell, well over 100 years old, first used to call the staff back to work after tea and dinner breaks and today summoning visitors to begin a guided trip. This takes around 30 minutes and offers a chance to chat with the craftspeople. There's also a museum telling the story of the pottery from the early earthenware days to the present fine translucent parian china, and a tearoom serving light lunches.

Open *daily Jan–Feb Mon–Fri (only), 9am–5.30pm, Mar–Jun 9am–6pm (Sat 10am–6pm, Sun 2-6pm), Jul–Oct Mon–Fri 9am–6pm, Sat 10am–6pm, Sun noon–6pm), Nov–Dec 9am–5.30pm (Sat 10am–5.30pm, closed Sun).* **Credit** *all cards.* **Adm** *(tour) adults £4, children/seniors £2 (under-4s, free).* **Amenities** *audio-visual presentation.*

Boa Island and Lusty Beg ★★ ALL AGES

Boa Island, Kesh, Co Fermanagh BT93 8AD, ☎ *028 6863 3300; www.lustybegisland.com. A few kilometres past Enniskillen, continue on the B82 along Lower Lough Erne.*

The route to Lusty Beg takes you past some truly beautiful lakes, rivers and streams, and eventually down a side lane where you 'Dial 0' from a phone to call an ancient ferry. It's only two minutes to get to the island and a different world.

The Island Lodge Restaurant and Courtyard motel are built round a small natural marina, where you can canoe, fish, and even swim if you are brave enough for the chilly Irish waters.

Among the trees are 11 log chalets and 10 more upmarket Scandinavian style lodges. Landscaping is kept to a minimum but facilities include an indoor pool, tennis court, a nature trail around the islands shoreline, football pitch, canoes and a games room for children.

Close by on Boa Island, is one of the most remarkable monuments in Ireland, the Janus Stones on Caldragh Cemetery, a 1,000-year-old, two-faced Celtic figure.

Open *The Lusty Beg ferry operates on demand.*

Florence Court ★★ ALL AGES

Enniskillen, Co Fermanagh BT92 1DB, ☎ *028 6634 8249; www.national trust.org.uk. 13km SW of Enniskillen via A4 Sligo road and A32 Swanlinbar road.*

Offering family fun days, concerts and country fairs, Florence Court, surrounded by a large area of parkland, garden and woodland, is a splendid example of an 18th-century Irish country house and demesne, in a spectacular setting among the mountains and forests of west Fermanagh. There are extensive walks in the grounds, a sawmill, holiday cottage and walled garden. 'Living History' tours offer an entertaining insight into life here in the 1920s.

Open *(grounds) daily Apr–Sep 10am–8pm, Oct–Mar 10am–4pm,* *(house) variable but generally Apr–May and Sep, Sat–Sun, 1–6pm, Jun 1–6pm (except Tue), Jul–Aug daily, noon–6pm.* **Adm** *(grounds) £3.50; (house tour) adults £5, children £2.20, family £12.20.* **Credit** *V, MC.* **Amenities** *children's playground and picnic area.*

Marble Arch Caves ★ ★ ★
AGES 8 AND UP

Marble Arch Caves European Geopark, Marlbank, Florencecourt, Co Fermanagh BT92 1EW, ☏ *028 6634 8855; www.marblearch caves.net. SW of Enniskillen, near Florence Court.*

You need to feel comfortable underground, be reasonably fit (there are 120 steps at one point), and confident that young children won't be too alarmed, but Marble Arch Caves are some of the best in Europe.

You explore a fascinating, natural underworld of rivers, waterfalls, winding passages and lofty chambers. Spectacular walkways allow easy access while strategically positioned lighting exposes the beauty and grandeur of the caves. Electrically powered boats glide through huge caverns carrying visitors along a subterranean river. Tours last for 75 minutes and comfortable walking shoes and warm sweater are recommended.

Open *daily Apr–Sep 10am–4.30pm (5pm Jul–Aug). The caves may close for safety reasons following heavy rain so phone before setting out during bad weather.* **Credit** *V, MC.* **Adm** *adults £8, children (under-18s) £5, seniors £5.25, family (2+3) £18.* **Amenities** *souvenir shop, restaurant, exhibition area, audio-visual theatre.*

A Janus Stone on Boa Island

Co Londonderry

Mussenden Temple and Downhill Demesne ★ ALL AGES

Mussenden Road, Castlerock, Co Londonderry BT51 4RP, ☏ *028 2073 1582; www.nationaltrust.org.uk. Just east of Downhills along the A2 (Causeway Coastal Route)*

Set on a wild and rugged headland with views over Ireland's north coast, Downhill Demesne was designed and built in the late 18th century by the eccentric Earl Bishop (Earl of Derby, Bishop of Derry). The site includes the ruins of a once-elegant mansion, a mausoleum, beautiful gardens, dovecote and walks and, originally built as a library, the renowned Mussenden Temple on the cliff edge. There are sea cliff walks offering lovely views of the coast – unsuitable for young children.

Open daily 10am–5pm Jun–Aug, rest of year, weekends and bank holidays. *Credit* no facilities. *Adm* adults £2, children £1.60, family (2+3) £5.50. Gift Aid admission + 10% (voluntary donation). *Amenities* toilets (baby-changing facilities).

Co Tyrone

Ulster American Folk Park ★★ ALL AGES

2 Mellon Road, Castletown, Omagh, Co Tyrone BT78 5QY, ☎ 028 8224 3292, *www.folkpark.com*. Along the A5, north of Omagh.

This historic outdoor museum tells the story of the millions who emigrated from Ulster to America in the 18th and 19th centuries. Costumed demonstrators go about their everyday tasks in authentically furnished Old and New World buildings, while the Ship and Dockside Gallery features a full-size reconstruction of an early 19th-century sailing ship of the type that carried thousands of emigrants. It's all outdoors, and in September the venue of the annual Appalachian and Bluegrass Music Festival (see p. 223).

Open Apr–Sep Mon–Sat 10.30am–4.30pm, Sun and public holidays 11am–5pm; (museum coffee shop) daily 10.30am–5pm. *Credit* V, MC. *Adm* adults £5, children (5–16) and seniors £3 (under-5s, free), family (2+3) £12. *Amenities* park operates a Child Protection Policy and has two Designated Officers to whom any issues relating to child protection can be referred.

FAMILY-FRIENDLY ACCOMMODATION

Belfast

MODERATE

Days Hotel ★★★

40 Hope Street, Belfast, ☎ 028 9024 2494, *www.dayshotelbelfast.co.uk*.

Opened in 2003, Days is Northern Ireland's largest hotel, with 250 modern en suite bedrooms including inter-connecting. There's a 150-seat restaurant, a hotel bar, and more than 300 car parking spaces. It's excellent value for money given its central location just off the Golden Mile.

Rooms 250. *Rates* double or twin room Mon–Thu £75, Fri–Sun £65. Children aged up to 12 stay free when sharing parent's room. Continental breakfast £4. *Credit* all major cards accepted. *Amenities* vending machines, on site parking, laundry service. *In room* sat TV and in-room movies, computer games, high speed (BT Openzone) modem connection, voicemail messaging system, tea/coffee-making facilities.

MODERATE

Hastings Europa Hotel ★★★★

Great Victoria Street, Belfast, ☎ 028 9027 1066; *www.hastingshotels. com*.

With more than 200 rooms, this cosmopolitan hotel is in the heart of Belfast's Golden Mile, ideally located for exploring the city, and within easy reach of the main shopping and entertainment areas. It's spacious and elegant, with Piano Bar and Restaurant.

Rooms 204. **Rates** B&B, Mon–Thu £60, Fri–Sun £50, single supplement £25; weekend break £80 per person sharing. **Credit** all major cards. **Amenities** baby-itter listening service, reduced rates for children. **In room** TV.

EXPENSIVE

Malmaison ★★★

34–38 Victoria Street, Belfast, ☏ 028 9022 0200; www.malmaison.com.

A touch of luxury without really breaking the bank, the Malmaison occupies a magnificent landmark building at the very centre of Belfast offering 62 individually designed rooms and two suites. The brasserie and bar serve mainly French food. There is no hotel parking, but a car park is close by.

Rooms 62. **Rates** Mon–Thu, room only, £140, Fri–Sun B&B £99. **Credit** all major cards. **Amenities** baby-sitter listening service, reduced rates for children. **In room** plasma screen TV, CD/DVD player, cable TV, free Internet access, 'naughty nibbles, seductive toiletries and vroom room service'.

MODERATE

Ravenhill Guest House ★★

690 Ravenhill Road, Belfast, ☏ 028 9020 7444; www ravenhillguest house.com. City centre location.

Considered to serve one of the best breakfasts in Ulster, Ravenhill is a restored Victorian home in south Belfast, just 3km from the city centre, offering a relaxed sitting room, and comfortable bedrooms. As much

food as possible is homemade, including a vegetarian breakfast, bread and preserves.

Rooms 6. **Rates** from £35 per person, reduced rates for children. **Amenities** baby listening service.

Co Antrim

EXPENSIVE

Ballygally Castle Hotel ★★

Coast Road, Ballygally, Co Antrim BT40 2QZ, ☏ 028 2858 1066; www. hastingshotels.com. Along the A2 Causeway Coastal Route, north of Larne.

This 4-star hotel, built around an ancient castle, is a fine stopover for families exploring the Antrim Glens, or simply pootling along the Antrim Coast road. Its great position faces out into the lovely Ballygally Bay with its soft, sandy beaches.

The hotel has an apparently friendly resident ghost, Lady Isobella Shaw, who wanders the hotel corridors at night but has her own 'Ghost Room'. It's in one of the towers in the oldest part of the 17th-century castle and intrepid visitors are welcome to visit.

The Garden Restaurant, framed by splendid gardens, overlooks the castle grounds and provides value-for-money lunches and dinner. Once food has been ordered, the colourful children's menu can be used to learn how to turn a table napkin into a duck, for word searches, and simple games to play.

Rooms 42 and 2 suites. **Rates** classic twin/double £145, family £165, suite £250, all inclusive of breakfast.

Ask about Leisure Break rates. **Credit** V, MC, Amex, DC. **Amenities** baby cot (free), children's menu, guest Internet in foyer (£1 per 10 mins). **In room** tea-making facilities, safe, WiFi Internet access, sat TV.

Co Down

EXPENSIVE

Slieve Donard Hotel and Spa ★★★

Downs Road, Newcastle, Co Down BT33 0AH, ☎ 028 4372 1066; **www. hastingshotels.com**. At the end of the A50 from Castlewellan, overlooking Dundrum Bay.

In 2.5 hectares of private grounds at the foot of the Mourne Mountains, the 4-star hotel was built as an 'end of the line' luxury holiday destination by the Belfast and County Down Railway (now long gone). It takes its name from the mountain directly opposite, at 852 metres the highest in Northern Ireland.

The Oak Restaurant offers a reasonably priced dinner menu (two sittings on Saturdays) and the spacious Lighthouse Lounge adjoining the Spa does light lunches of panini, wraps, sandwiches and soups.

There's a long list of spa treatments or the family can all use the gold-flecked mosaic swimming pool.

The hotel has its own access to the beach (public), which runs in a narrow strip along the edge of the Bay; for golfers there are a number of testing courses nearby and a direct service to them from the hotel.

Rooms 178. **Rates** double/twin £180, family £150, plus £30 per child (up to 2 per room; children under-4s free), inclusive of breakfast. Ask about Leisure Break rates. **Credit** V, MC, DC, Amex, Switch. **Amenities** baby listening and baby-sitting service, disabled access, laundry service, non-smoking rooms (smoking rooms on request). **In room** tea-making facilities, safe, WiFi Internet access, sat TV, music centre.

MODERATE

Shelleven House ★★

61 Princetown Road, Bangor, Co Down BT20 3TA, ☎ 028 9127 1777; **www.shellevenhouse.com**. Near the centre of town.

With a particular welcome for families, this 3-star guesthouse in a Victorian townhouse in a quiet conservation area of Bangor is delightfully homely and relaxing, with a touch of luxury.

The house is close to the marina, the promenade and the town centre, which makes it an ideal base from which to explore the north coast of Co Down, or to slip into town. Shelleven House is also convenient for the bus and rail stations from where there are direct links to Belfast City Airport and the Dublin Rail Service. There are several golf courses nearby, and the host is himself a keen golfer.

Rooms 11. **Rates** £30–35 per person sharing. **Credit** V, MC. **Amenities** à la carte menu, baby-sitter service, children's meals, reduced prices for children. **In room** TV, tea-making facilities.

Co Fermanagh

Abocurragh Farm Guest-house ★★ FIND

Letterbreen, Enniskillen, Co Fermanagh, BT74 9AG, ☎ 028 6634 8484; www.abocurragh.com. On the A4 Sligo Road, 13km from the county town of Enniskillen.

Abocurragh Guest House has spacious and attractive rooms with beautiful views. The owners combine running the guesthouse with managing a 49-hectare dairy farm, and younger visitors may be invited to help with the milking. Food is good: as well as the usual traditional Irish at breakfast there are interesting options such as cinnamon-flavoured porridge with honey and cream.

***Rooms** 3 (2 family and 1 double, all en suite). **Rates** £27.50 pps, children under 12 are half price if sharing parents room. **Credit** V, MC. **Amenities** evening meal. **In room** TV, tea/coffee facilities.*

Lough Erne Hotel ★

Main Street, Kesh, Co Fermanagh BT93 1TF, ☎ 028 6863 1275; www.loughernehotel.com. On the main street in the village of Kesh.

On the banks of the Kesh River, this small hotel makes a point of welcoming families and is in a really lovely setting. The Riverside lounge and Bridgewater Restaurant offer an excellent choice of food, there's a riverside terrace, garden, and also regular entertainment. Self-catering cottages and studio apartments are also available.

***Rooms** 16. **Rates** double/twin £35 pps, reduced rates for children, weekend and midweek breaks throughout the year. **Credit** V, MC, Amex. **Amenities** cot available, baby-sitting service, Internet access, laundry. **In room** TV.*

Co Londonderry

The Lodge Hotel and Travelstop ★★

Lodge Road, Coleraine, Co Londonderry BT52 1NF, ☎ 028 7034 4848; www.thelodgehotel.com. On the A26 (Belfast) road, just a few minutes from the town centre.

Offering a main hotel complex (16 rooms) and a quieter, adjacent annex (Travelstop – 40 rooms, slightly cheaper), the Lodge Hotel is perfect for families on the move. This is a welcoming, 'no frills' place, and popular for that reason alone. There's a bistro and restaurant with speedy and friendly service and generous portions, plus a supermarket next door for picnics and snacks.

Rooms are bright and spacious, simply furnished, clean and warm. With the Giants' Causeway (see p. 227) only 15 minutes drive away, the Carrick-a-Rede Rope Bridge (see p. 226) just a little farther, and the ferry to Rathlin Island (see p. 228) from Ballycastle about 30 minutes distant, this is an ideal base for exploring Londonderry and the Antrim coast.

Rooms 56. *Rates* (including breakfast) double £88 in Lodge Hotel and £78 in TravelStop; family (TravelStop only) £78, plus £8 for children aged 5–11, and £12 for 12–16s. Ask about prices for two-night breaks and weekend specials. *Credit* V, MC, Amex. *Amenities* baby cots (free), children's menu, disabled access (two rooms), laundry, WiFi Internet throughout hotel, room service. *In room* sat TV, tea-making facilities.

MODERATE

The White Horse Hotel ★★

68 Clooney Road, Derry, Co Londonderry BT47 3PA, ☎ *028 7186 0606; www.whitehorsehotel.biz. Along the A2, east of Londonderry.*

Just a few minutes from the centre of Londonderry, the White Horse offers peace and quiet but is the closest hotel to Derry Airport. There's a well-priced bistro and restaurant (see White Horse Bistro and Grill, p. 240) and although the hotel is basic it includes a health and fitness suite with shallow 20-metre swimming pool, spa pool, sauna and steam room, aerobic studio and gym.

Rooms 60. *Rates* (including breakfast and full use of Leisure Centre) double/twin from £70, family (2+2) from £75. Ask about special deals, such as the Pamper Package (includes 2 night stay with full Irish breakfast and one evening meal plus Pamper Package). *Credit* all major cards. *Amenities* baby-sitting service, Internet access, dry cleaning, laundry. *In room* sat TV, tea-making facilities, WiFi Internet.

CAFÉS & FAMILY-FRIENDLY DINING

Belfast

INEXPENSIVE

Maggie May's ★★
TRADITIONAL IRISH

50 Botanic Avenue, Belfast, ☎ *028 9032 2662.*

This is a Belfast-themed restaurant with local food and Belfast-themed murals. The Ulster fry, a hefty traditional breakfast, is a favourite, but the emphasis is on quality Irish grub, with plenty of vegetarian options. There's a basic children's menu.

Open Mon–Sat 8pm–10.30pm, Sun 10am–10.30pm. *Main courses* £6. *Credit* V, MC. *Amenities* baby-changing facilities, highchairs.

MODERATE

Altos Café Bar Restaurant ★★★
ITALIAN, IRISH, MED

Unit 6, Fountain Street, Belfast, ☎ *028 9032 3087.*

Healthy, snazzy food in the city centre, in a family run café-bar with flavours from Italy, Ireland and the Med. Drop in for coffee or a scone, bottle of wine, or probably the best burger in Belfast. There's al fresco dining, good beer, wheelchair and buggy access, and people travel miles just to see the art on the walls.

Open Mon–Wed 10am–5pm, Thurs 10am–8pm, Fri and Sat 10am–6pm. *Main courses* around £8, with various dishes around £7. *Credit* V, MC. *Amenities* children's menu.

MODERATE

The Cellar Restaurant, Belfast Castle ★★ MODERN IRISH

Off Antrim Road, 6.5km north of the city centre, ☎ *028 9077 6925; www.belfastcastle.co.uk.*

This is renowned for its excellent and wide-ranging menu, using fresh local produce to create innovative and modern dishes served in a funky but historic castle cellar.

There's morning coffee, and dishes like salmon, lamb shank, burgers, pasta, lasagne and steak.

Open (lunch) Mon–Sat 12.30pm–3pm, Sun 12.30–4pm; (early evening meal) Tue–Sat 5–6.30pm; (dinner) Tue–Sat 6.30–9pm; snacks and light refreshments available daily, 11am–5pm. Main courses (lunch) £5.95–12.95), (dinner) £9.50–16.50. Credit V, MV. Amenities parking, highchairs available.

MODERATE

Scalini Italian Restaurant ★★★ FIND ITALIAN

85 Botanic Avenue, Belfast, ☎ *028 9032 0303.*

A restaurant and pizzeria, this is one of the latest arrivals on the restaurant scene and a huge success. Children and family groups are especially welcome with colouring pages supplied to amuse the youngsters.

Open Mon–Fri 5pm–11.30pm, Sat 4pm–11.30pm and Sun 4pm–10.30pm. Main courses pizzas and pasta £7–9, meat and fish courses £10–17, desserts around £4. Credit V, MC. Amenities baby-changing facilities are available.

Co Antrim

INEXPENSIVE

Charly's Restaurant ★★
PAN EUROPEAN-CHINESE-AMERICAN

34 New Bridge Road, Coleraine, Co Londonderry, BT52 1TP, ☎ *028 7035 2020; www.charlysrestaurant.com. Along the A26 (Belfast) road, 2km out of Coleraine.*

Wacky, weird and wonderful, this popular diner serves a bewildering array of dishes, including Chinese. Neo-Tiffany lamps hang over each red-and-white striped table, offset by an eclectic collection of old bicycles, model aeroplanes and film memorabilia, hanging from the ceiling or pasted to the walls.

Full-on family friendly, with balloons and colouring pads and crayons for the young, along with cartoons on TV at weekends. A children's menu includes fried rice and sirloin steak as well as the staples.

Open Mon–Thu noon–2.15pm and 5–9pm, Fri and Sat noon–9.30pm, Sun noon–9pm. Main courses £5–8.50, children's menu £4.50. Credit V, MC. Amenities highchairs, baby-changing facilities, balloons and colouring pads for children.

MODERATE

Pinky Moons Diner ★★
RETRO AMERICAN

82–84 Main Street, Larne, Co Antrim BT40 1RE, ☎ *028 2827 4297. In the centre of Larne.*

You can't fail to be bowled over by the 1950s posters featuring James Dean, Johnny Cash and Elvis, multi-coloured plastic and chrome furniture, family cubicles, 'original' jukebox and uncrowded space.

And when it comes to food, they've thought of every conceivable combination: burgers, wraps, pasta, vegetarian, toasties, salads, and baked potatoes. There's an under-12s menu, and with 'Beat the Clock' dining on Mondays and Tuesdays between 4pm and 7pm, the time you order is the price you pay. Perfect for anyone arriving into Northern Ireland at Larne, or making their way along the Causeway Coastal Route.

Open *Mon–Tue 9am–8pm, Wed 9am–9.30pm, Thu–Sat 9am–10.30pm, Sun 10am–9.30pm.* **Main courses** *£6–10.* **Credit** *V, MC.* **Amenities** *highchairs, baby-changing facilities.*

Co Down

MODERATE

Café Mauds ★ ★ VALUE
ANGLO-ITALIAN FAST FOOD

106 Waterfoot, Newcastle, Co Down BT33 0AE, 📞 *028 4372 6184; www.mauds.co.uk.*

Beside the River Shimna and just a few strides from the promenade, Café Mauds offers an outdoor terrace overlooking the river on one side, and one of Café Mauds' renowned ice cream parlours on the other. Between the two, waffles, club sandwiches, quiche, savoury pancakes, burgers, salads and

panini make for an inexpensive quick lunch.

You'll find Café Mauds' outlets throughout Ireland, sometimes just selling delicious ice cream, but often also with cafés attached – and they are always good value.

Open *9am–9pm daily.* **Main courses** *£5–8.* **Credit** *V, MC.* **Amenities** *highchairs.*

Co Londonderry

INEXPENSIVE

White Horse Bistro and Grill
MAINSTREAM EUROPEAN

68 Clooney Road, Derry, Co Londonderry BT47 3PA, 📞 *028 7186 0606; www.whitehorsehotel.biz. Along the A2, east of Londonderry.*

Adjoining the White Horse Hotel on the edge of Londonderry, the Bistro and Grill is simply but attractively designed and serves a wide range of meals including salads, panini, wraps, omelettes, sandwiches and lasagne. There are family group alcoves and Sunday is Funday with an indoor bouncy castle.

Open *daily, Bistro and Grill Menu served 2.30–9.30pm, Special Tea Time menu served Mon–Fri 5–7pm. Carvery (two-course) noon–2.30pm, Mon–Sat, (three course Sun).* **Main courses** *£5–8.50; children's menu £3.40; Special Tea Time menu (two courses) £9.95]; two-course carvery £6.95], three-course carvery £11.95.* **Amenities** *baby-changing facilities, highchairs.*

Index

See also Accommodations and Restaurant indexes, below.

General

A

Abbey's silver bell (Sligo Town), 206
Accommodation, 30–32.
    See also Accommodation Index
    best, 7–8
    the east coast, 34–86
    the Midlands, 131–134
    Northern Ireland, 234–238
    the north-west, 208–212
    the south-east, 108–111
    the south-west, 158–162
    the west, 183–186
Achill Island, 205
Aer Arann Islands, 175
Aer Lingus, 23
Aillwee Cave (The Burren), 176
Air Canada, 24
Airfield House & Farm (Dundrum), 58
Air travel, 22–24, 28–29
Altamont Gardens (Tullow), 101
American Airlines, 23
An Oige (Irish Youth Hostel Association), 32
An Tostal (Drumshanbo), 196
Antrim
    accommodation, 235–236
    restaurants, 239–240
    sights and attractions, 226–229
    visitor information, 219–220
The Antrim Coaster, 226
Appalachian and Bluegrass Music Festival (Omagh), 223
Apple Blossom Festival (Armagh), 223
Aran Direct, 174–175
Aran Island Ferries (Oileáin Arann Díreach), 175
The Aran Islands (Oileáin Arann), 174–175
Ards Forest Park (Creeslough), 197
The Ark (Dublin), 50
Arklow Maritime Museum, 79
Armagh
    sights and attractions, 229–230
    visitor information, 220

Armagh Planetarium, 229–230
Arranmore Island, 198
Ashtown Riding Stables (Dublin), 58
Athenry Castle, 180
Athenry Heritage Centre, 180–181
Atlantaquaria: The National Aquarium of Ireland (Salthill), 181
ATMs (cash points), 16
Avondale House and Forest Park (Rathdrum), 79–80

B

Ballindoolin House and Gardens (Carbury), 128
Ballylanders Pattern Festival, 145
Banks, 33
Bannow and Rathangan Agricultural Show (Duncormick), 97
Barry Dalby (Kilcoole), 84
Beaches
    Achill Island, 205
    best, 5
    Blue Flag, 33
    Donegal and Sligo, 208
    Dublin, 57
    the east coast, 72
    the south-east, 105–107
    Tullagh Strand, 203–204
Bed and Breakfast Association of Northern Ireland, 31
Bed & breakfasts (B&Bs), 31
Belfast
    accommodation, 234–235
    hospitals, 224
    Internet access, 224
    orientation, 221
    restaurants, 238–239
    sights and attractions, 225–226
    visitor information, 219
Belfast Castle, 225–226
Belfast Children's Festival, 223
Belfast International Airport, 218–219
Belleek Pottery, 231–232
Beltaine, 78
Belvedere House Gardens and Park, 124–125

Biking, 29
    Killarney, 152
    the Midlands, 131
    The Táin Trail, 83
Birds and bird-watching
    Eagles Flying/Irish Raptor Research Centre (Portinch), 205
    Glenveagh National Park, 202
    Grove Garden and Tropical Bird Sanctuary (Kells), 77
    Wexford Wildfowl Reserve, 105
Birr Castle Demesne and Historic Science Centre, 127
Blarney Castle, 155
Blarney Stone, 155, 156
Blasket Island (Ionad an Bhlascaoid Mhóir) The Great Blasket Visitor Centre (Dún Chaoin), 148–149
Blennerville Windmill, 154
Bloomsday (Dublin), 47
Boa Island, 232
Boat tours and cruises
    Cliffs of Moher Cruises (Doolin), 178
    Donegal Bay Seafari, 201
    Donegal Bay Waterbus Tour, 201
    Moon River Cruises (Carrick-on-Shannon), 207
    Skellig Cruises, 154
    Whale of a Time (Cork), 158
Book of Kells (Dublin), 57
Books, recommended, 29–30
Bord na Mona Water Festival (Ballyleague), 122
The Bram Stoker Dracula Experience (Dublin), 50
Breastfeeding, 33
BritRail Pass + Ireland, 28
Browneshill Dolmen (Carlow Town), 101
Brú Ború Cultural Centre (Cashel), 98
Brú na Bóinne, 5, 75–76
Buckley's Tours (Killarney), 142
Bunmahon, 106
Bunmahon Beach, 106